FROM A RED ZONE

FROM A RED ZONE

Critical Perspectives on Race, Politics, and Culture

Patricia Penn Hilden

The Red Sea Press Inc.

Publishers & Distributors of Third World Books

P.O. Box 1982
Trenton, NJ 08607

P.O. Box 48
Asmara, ERITREA

The Red Sea Press Inc.
Publishers & Distributors of Third World Books

P.O. Box 1982
Trenton, NJ 08607

P.O. Box 48
Asmara, ERITREA

Book design: Sam Saverance
Cover design: Ashraful Haque
Cover Photo by Edward H. Latham, Courtesy of University of Washington Libraries, Special Collections Division, NA 1021

Library of Congress Cataloging-in-Publication Data

Hilden, Patricia.
 From a red zone: critical perspectives on race, politics, and culture/Patricia Penn Hilden.
    p. cm.
 Includes bibliographical references and index.
 ISBN 1-56902-244-5 (cloth) -- ISBN 1-56902-245-3 (pbk.)
  1. Indians of North America--Ethnic identity. 2. Indians of North America--Public opinion. 3. Indians of North America --Social conditions. 4. Ethnology--United States. 5. Indians in popular culture--United States. 6. Indigenous peoples in popular culture--United States. 7. Racism in anthropology--United States. 8. Museum exhibits--Moral and ethical aspects--United States. 9. Politics and culture--United States. 10. Public opinion--United States. 11. United States--Race relations. 12. United States--Social conditions. I. Title.
 E98.E83H55 2005
 305.897'073--dc22

2005024932

To

Timothy J. Reiss, ta'c hama

and

William S. Penn Jr., ta'c pist
July 7, 1916-May 27, 2004
Qe'ciyéwyew

TABLE OF CONTENTS

ACKNOWLEDGMENTS

A s with all collections of essays, these were born out of engage-ment with the ideas of dozens of scholars and from exchanges with dozens of friends. Timothy Reiss, in his work and in his life, exemplifies the many ways someone born into the zone of Western privilege can move beyond those privileges of maleness and white-ness to imagine a different world. All my conversations with Suzanna Reiss have been similarly lively and challenging, and I thank her, too. Shari M. Huhndorf, friend and collaborator, shapes so much of what follows that I often do not know where my ideas begin and hers leave off, though of course she bears no responsibility for my interpretations. All my thinking about museums and issues of representation has benefited from insights shared by present and former graduate students, including Francisco Casique, Dulcinea Lara, Lilia Soto, Robert Gonzalez, Rebecca Hurdis, Eric Avila, Yolanda Venegas, Jeffrey Ow, Robert Soza, Ananda Sattwa, Mimi Nguyen, Dilan Mahendran, and Delberto Ruiz.

Ngugi wa Thiong'o has been essential throughout this work, especially in helping me think about the ways museums create safe spaces of racial otherness where white people can come to "perform" that otherness, whether defined as African, Native American, Pacific Islander, African American, or other racialized categories. I thank him for his work and his friendship, and also for the courage, grace, and faith in humanity that he shares with Njeeri wa Ngugi. Her courage and love are unbounded and we, across the world, owe her a debt of gratitude.

Kassahun Checole's tireless work in opening the gates so militantly guarded by European and European American scholars has provided the world with a marvelous literature that might otherwise go unrecognized outside the communities that produce this work. I thank him for providing me this opportunity to reach the audiences he has created and informed for so many years. I also want to thank Angela Ajayi for her graceful overseeing of the whole project and Katie Chase for providing painstaking and careful copy editing.

And of course both the friendship and work of Kamau Brathwaite, celebrated in the final chapter of this work, are gifts I cherish. Arnold Krupat has also remained a generous and willing reader, critic, and friend, and I thank him, again, for all he has done. Of colleagues and friends there are many to thank for their willingness to exchange ideas and comments: José Davíd Saldívar, Simon Ortiz, Beth Piatote, Haruo Aoki (who deserves a special thanks for his patience and humor as I struggle to learn the language and stories of my ancestors), Stephen Small, Robin Kelley, Gordon Hutner, Richard Schechner, Arturo Aldama, Alfred Arteaga, and Julia Sudbury. I have benefited from endless discussions with indigenous people, first at New York University, where Shari Huhndorf, Carol Kalafatic, and I first began thinking about museums with Harriett Skye, Chris Eyre, Dean Curtis Bear Claw, and Frances Peters-Little, and more recently in the American Indian Graduate Student Association room at the University of California, still with Harriett Skye as well as new students/colleagues/friends: Danika Medak-Saltzman, Dory Nason, Majel Boxer, Mishuana Goeman, John Carlos Perea, Dewey St. Germaine, Joanne Rondilla, Vika Palaita, Michael Tuncap, and Jordan Gonzales. From Toeutu Fa'aleava, t'ac nípe, I have learned more than he realizes—about the production of indigenous knowledge, about commitment to community, about grace, about integrity. Luz Mena's work and comradeship have shaped much of the thinking here, as have many many conversations with Ellen Arnold, Janet McAdams, John Howard, Ellen Fernandez-Sacco, Lynne Horiuchi, Julio Ramos, the late Lee Francis, and Tiya Miles. The Red Feminist Collective helps all of us thrive as we begin to shift the "red" male center to something more inclusive. The support of all the women involved with this group, including many listed here, continues to make this kind of scholarly, politically engaged work possible.

Finally, I thank other members of my family, including most particularly my beloved father, William Penn, who died before he could see the whole book though he read and remarked on most of it. Others include my sister and brother-in-law, Anne and Bruce Hamilton, Matthew Reiss, and Abena Ankrah. All deserve my gratitude for their stalwart support, interest, and patience.

Last, I must thank the journals and collections in which versions of these essays first appeared. They include *American Literary History* (Chapter 1); *TDR: The Drama Review* (Chapter 2); *Social Identities* (Chapter 3); University of California Press (Chapter 4); Indiana University Press (Chapter 5); and Africa World Press (Chapter 6).

ZONED OUT: AN INTRODUCTION

The rote repetition of the past makes a desolation.
—Timothy J. Reiss[1]

SETTING THE SCENE

Writing a "Letter from Perth" for the London-based *Times Literary Supplement* (*TLS*) of February 22, 2002, Nicola Walker described a shift in white Australians' attitudes toward that country's Aboriginal population, deciding that "a large majority of white Australians genuinely desire to make amends." This sanguine view of white Australians' chagrin at the facts of their collective history is shared by other writers for this journal. Almost exactly one year later, Mark Abley added, "Australia's self-image has altered profoundly over the past few decades." Abley adduces the Australian public's embrace of "Phillip Noyce's 2002 film *Rabbit Proof Fence*" as evidence not only for a national shift from ignorance and neglect to shame, but also for an entirely new attitude that goes well beyond the straightforward regret noted by Walker. Indeed, citing Mark McKenna's recent *Looking for Blackfellas' Point: An Australian History of Place*, Abley argues that those elements commonly assigned in white stereotype to Aboriginal (and other indigenous) people are not exclusive to them: "A rootedness in the land, an awareness of place as sacred, can be felt by Australians of any colour" Abley contends (Abley 2003:6).

Furthermore, even the deleterious effects of racialization processes are being overcome: "If," Abley suggests, "many Australians of all colours are longing to 'celebrate their blackness,' then the country and its people deserve high praise" (7). Here Abley expresses some themes common throughout this collection: the wish that the positive elements of racial stereotypes could be shared by hegemonic whites, together with the erasure of systematic racism by a "universal" desire to "be black"—or red or yellow or brown, depending on the offended racialized group. Both these practices are explored in depth in the chapters that follow.

Of course stereotypes are not all positive, and Nicola Walker's piece shows how whites avoid accepting the less desirable traits assigned "others." For Walker, results of Australian attempts to compensate for the long history of Aboriginal abuse have been problematic. In her view, the "patronage" that resulted from well-intentioned efforts at "positive discrimination" created only "a greater inequality in the long term." This is such a seductive view: "we'd like to help, we'd like to repair decades of terrible damage we and our forebears have inflicted on you and your forebears, but if we try to do so in any genuine manner, we—rather than you, of course—know that all will just be made worse for you and your people." Given such attitudes it is not surprising that Walker's encounter with the indigenous scholar/activist Pat Mamanyun Torres produced a highly racialized and gendered *TLS* portrait. Of this young lecturer at the University of Curtin's new Center for Aboriginal Studies, Walker wrote: "Torres is a diminutive activist, articulate and passionate about her spiritual and social kinship connections to the Broome region, and keen to promote awareness among white Australians of past and present injustices. I admire her fighter's instinct," Walker confesses disingenuously. "Torres's enthusiasm for and participation in community self-help projects are also impressive, but sit oddly with her embrace of the theories of post-colonialism, in which there seems to me an unwillingness to concede that the ugliness in Aboriginal contemporary life— glue-sniffing, drugs, alcoholism, welfare dependency, violence against women—may also be rooted in a wider social phenomenon: the 'victim' mentality." Worse still, "It is hard for Aboriginals who are successful in white Australian terms [because] they are often accused by their 'brothers' of selling out" (Walker, 2002:15). The passive voice here hints again of Walker's inability to abandon stereotypes of "others," a problem common in the European and European American worlds.

Thus despite the fact that Torres did not cite any such "anti-success" attitudes among Aboriginal people, Walker felt free to apply beliefs widespread in non-indigenous communities. Read in the context of contemporary race debates in the United States, the attitudes underlying Walker's comments are familiar. Popular belief in the white community condemns African Americans (and, increasingly, Latinos, as that population grows and becomes more visible to the white community) for mocking their successful brothers and, less often, sisters. Dismissals of white responsibility for a myriad of similar "ugly" conditions (most of them identical to those cited as "typical" of aboriginal communities) permeates reporting of Native American reservation life.[2] Walker's condemnation of Torres's use of "postcolonial" scholarship (analytical practices that seek to dismantle the structures of power in which processes of racialization and gendering unfold) is similarly familiar. Accusations that scholars of color produce a constant litany of "poor us, poor us" victimology are common across the U.S. political landscape. Thus these scholars and activists aid and abet denial of the negative realities of everyday life within communities of color. As with Walker's Torres portrait, so with U.S. conservatives' picture of ethnic studies scholars, all preoccupied with spreading obfuscatory lamentations of white wrongs. Indeed many believe that while our communities waste away, we intellectuals persistently indulge ourselves in limning our rage against whites' depredations, both present and past.

For some few of us from the world Walker decries, those at least who bother with the *TLS*, Walker's words elicit only a great sigh of despairing recognition. The imperative intellectual shift outward from Europe, outlined a decade ago in Ngugi wa Thiong'o's eloquent manifesto, *Moving the Center: The Struggle for Cultural Freedoms* (1993), has evidently scarcely touched most writers for the *Times Literary Supplement*, despite some impressive map-making by European intellectuals willing to struggle against their privileged place in the world.[3] But then my own experience suggests that most white European and European American intellectuals do not understand what Ngugi meant in that book or, indeed, even what those of us who cite it might mean. A few years ago, at an international conference of feminists that aimed to bring feminists of color from all over the world into contact with white feminists (from the United States, Canada, England, France, Spain, and Israel if I recall correctly), I was asked to join a panel "summing up" three days of discussion. Like most feminists of color, I had been dismayed throughout the conference by our collective inability to get white feminists even to hear our voices, let alone consider shifting their work or their intellectual foci. In trying to find a way to speak to this in the five minutes allotted for our individual comments, I reached—once again—for Ngugi's work and his words. "We need to follow the lead of Ngugi wa Thiong'o," I said, "moving the center from Europe, and European America, to include centers across the globe." I quoted Ngugi on "the need to move the center from its assumed location in the West to a multiplicity of spheres in all the cultures of the world." This center-moving must take place in "two senses—between nations and within nations" (Ngugi 1993:xvi, xvii). These words so startled a white British geography lecturer that she cut me off as I began my next sentence. "I'm so tired of this center-periphery stuff," she declared loudly from across the room. "Let's not have any more of that!" And with that, oblivious both of the fact that she had rudely interrupted me and of the fact that her haste to reject what I had said—replacing Ngugi's more sophisticated concept with what she recognized, the once popular "center-periphery" dichotomy used to describe both imperial capitals and their colonial outposts or metropolitan capitals and rural outposts—revealed her stunning ignorance of Ngugi's work, she unknowingly provided striking evidence of the problem of the whole conference. "Quod erat demonstrandum," I wanted to shout, though I did not. She was an unquestioning participant in the world into which she was born, where everyone, wherever they live, is basically equal. What she did not see is that hers is the world where "we-ness" is white: "they-ness" is nonwhite. "Feminism," as practiced by these Euro and European American women, means letting "them" enter the wide world of WE. The center does not move, it just expands outward, sucking in everyone who wants to live a "healthy," "successful" life—though all their own community will probably disdain them for doing so, as will the white community that absorbs them, if we accept the kind of judgment expressed by Walker and others.[4]

The Euro-center is, after all, a powerful force, not only sucking in outsiders but also covering its occupants with a thick coating through which, it often seems, nothing whatever penetrates. As Nicola Walker's piece suggests, moreover, indigenous worlds seem to present a special case of impenetrability for white observers. Tenaciously, stereotype-ridden indigenous communities cling to the quaint themed worlds given them by generations of anthropologists and ethnographers. At one point Walker refers to the single thing she and virtually every other white person on the planet knows about Aboriginal people when, again arguing for assimilation and against white guilt or recompense, she insists that "it might help if everyone just admitted that sometimes 'Toyota Dreaming' is as powerful a cultural factor as the Dream Time" (15).[5]

FROM AN INUIT ZONE: *ATANARJUAT*

With indigenous people everywhere, a similar problem of immovable stereotypes, avidly consumed by white society, combined with a vast ignorance and indifference, afflicts all attempts to move the center from New York-Paris-London to centers of indigenous worlds. One last example, and this, too, is a recent one. By now, millions of people in Europe and the United States have seen *Atanarjuat* (or, in English, *The Fast Runner*), the first internationally distributed all-Inuit film ever made. Zacharias Kunuk, its director, chose a screenplay written by another Inuit, Paul Apak Angillirq.[6] All the characters are played by Inuit actors; audiences of non-Inuktitut speakers must depend upon subtitles to understand the dialogue. The whole film takes place in the Canadian Arctic and no references to the European or European American world ease non-Inuit viewers' experience of the film. Two conversations, one with my friend and sometime collaborator, Shari Huhndorf (who is herself Yup'ik) and one with Arnold Krupat, drove me to seek out movie reviews written by non-Natives who—both my friends told me—encountered a film that "took no hostages," giving non-Inuit viewers not a single respite, no glimpse of the Euro-known, no concessions to cultural ignorance, for the entire three hours of the film.

The first review I found appeared in a newspaper that is a legacy of Berkeley's 1960s, when radical ideas and politics found their way first into one of several free papers, distributed throughout the city, read in every coffeehouse or folk music venue. *The East Bay Express*'s reviewer, Bill Gallo, reacted to *Atanarjuat*'s challenges as did so many others, quickly moving the center, driven elsewhere for the three hours of the film, right back home. The review begins, "It has been eighty years since the adventurous son of a Michigan iron miner trained a silent-movie camera on the everyday life of an 'Eskimo' family in the Canadian Arctic and virtually invented documentary film making." And who was this paragon? Robert Flaherty, whose shockingly racist *Nanook of the North* has taught generations of white Americans and Europeans "all about" those quaint and fun-loving people who so interestingly and bravely struggle against the terrible environment none of "us" could bear. Gallo admits that "Flaherty staged some scenes and the white man's bias is evident in places—but no one has ever questioned the purity of the pioneer director's intention to show Nanook's confrontation with nature as it really was" (Gallo 2002). Well first, someone *has* questioned that "purity." Shari Huhndorf's *Going Native*, the first published critique by an indigenous scholar, is, in fact, only the most recent in a line of native and nonnative criticisms of Flaherty's motives, his movie, his work and its consequences, not the least of which is the positioning of all of the Arctic's indigenous peoples as timeless and unchanging, all carefully encased in relentless snow and ice and cold (Huhndorf 2001:chap.2; also Fienup-Riordan 1995:47-55; Christopher 1998: 81-89; Lidchi 1998:197-206). But ignorance of the scholarship surrounding both *Nanook* and the "ethnographic film making" Gallo also approves is, perhaps, less offensive than the reviewer's tactic of "whitening" or Europeanizing *Atanarjuat* by placing it squarely within a hyperwestern tradition of film making. The film thus becomes not a narrative film—albeit one that challenges many ideas of Western narrative—but rather just another "educational" experience, another chance for white audiences to play with Eskimos. Indeed, Gallo is thrilled by the "progress" in this enterprise *Atanarjuat* represents: "In the history of ethnographic film making since Flaherty, good sense and moral suasion have increasingly put cameras and microphones into the hands of 'exotic' films' subjects as often as the outsiders who want to tell their stories, and it's encouraging to behold the near-total control an Inuit cast and crew were able to exert over *The Fast Runner.*" *Whose* "good sense"? *Whose* "moral suasion"? "*Encouraging*" to whom? And against whom were they "able to exert" a "near-total control?" It's the white guys again, sitting at the center, letting the natives have a bit of autonomy, then viewing their own good works out there. Thus a film meant for another center—in the Arctic, amongst Inuit people—is easily slipped inside "our" center. In the end, nothing moves outward, only back inward.

A more interesting review of this provocative film, and one that does not patronize the film's maker, is by Jacqui Sadashige, published in the *American Historical Review* (2002). I read this review after discussing the film with a group of graduate students— Rebecca Hurdis, Dulcinea Lara, Joyce Lu, Danika Medak-Salzman, Dory Nason, and Ananda Sattwa —at the University of California. All these young scholars had seen the film in commercial theaters, and all reported a similar "universalizing" response among those sitting around them. Among the variety of comments they heard included one noting that the film was like "Bible stories," another that it was "Shakespearian," and still another lamenting that understanding the film must require knowing a lot about "Eskimo myths." So Prof. Sadashige's review, which does not seek to suck this film into a Western world, came as a relief. She not only condemns the widespread "exoticizing" of the film by both viewer and reviewer, but also adds a critique of the gender relations as they are depicted, in her view uncritically, in the film. In many ways a perceptive viewer, Sadishige similarly notes the importance of the indigenous time frame that slows the film to an unusually long three hours. Nevertheless, this reviewer is not free of misunderstanding. Indeed, because she locates the film solidly within the "ancient legend" framework employed by many other reviewers of the film, she expects the filmmakers to have legitimated "our" learned ability to comprehend "native" stories by identifying and describing the timeless myths, clearly noting that what "we" are seeing on the screen is, indeed, *mythical.*[7] Sadashige was disappointed. "Kunuk and company consequently naturalize everything they present. Thus, while the invasive presence of a documentari-an's gaze is absent, it is never clear whether the values and attitudes expressed by the characters are native, to what century they date, whether or not they are specific to this community, or whether they fit the demands of legend" (990). [I should note what all the gradu-ate students noted as well: that this filmmaker's gaze *is* noted, quite clearly, in the scene that unfolds after the close of the formal film, wherein the whole staff of the film—actors, camera people, direc-tor, and so on—appears running, laughing, carrying hot coffee and a blanket to the film's star who is shivering after a long naked run across ice.] These remarks lead into a critique of "representations of gender." "*Atanarjuat* maintains a strict gender hierarchy," the reviewer notes. "The film fails to question this balance of power, and in fact validates it through the governing trope of nostalgia." Her focus here is on the uses of nudity: when Atanarjuat runs across the ice naked, he represents "heroism and mythic athleti-cism." When females are nude, their nudity is "sexualized."

Both these readings, however sensitive, retain a Euro-focus that prevents Sadashige from understanding this film on its own terms. Shari Huhndorf and I spent some time discussing this film, and I recounted this review to her as we talked. In the end, we decided together that Sadashige, like all the other non-Natives whose reviews we read or heard, simply could not enter the indigenous world. She simply lacks the terms, those demanded of indigenous participants in those myriad ceremonies that mark indigenous life. Had she realized, as many of us had, that this film invited all participants—all viewers—into a healing ceremony, Sadashige might have experienced this film more fully, and on its own terms rather than her own. Ceremonies, and the stories that constitute them, that carry those ceremonies along to their conclusions, are not "legends" and hold no rigid structures that must be endlessly and painstakingly replicated in order to achieve "authenticity." The holy people who direct the ceremony—here, the sister and brother— choose those aspects of the stories, those ways of telling, those songs and dances, that accompany the particular events. Indeed, even the language chosen carries significance for the pur-poses of that singular ceremony that is at the same time connected to the indigenous past. All aspects—"values and attitudes," if you will—are "native" and expressive of now, just as they express past and indeed, future.[8] Moreover, gender is carried here not by the handful of central characters and their relationships (which are, in this case, distinctly masculine in their focus and orientation) but rather by the ceremony itself, carried out in perfect equality by a woman and a man working together.

At the end, when the healing is finally brought to its conclusion, it is the sister who pronounces the community's action against the evil. Against the background of her brother's ceremonial dance, the holy woman announces the sentence of expulsion from the community of the whole evil-bearing family of three brothers and one sister. It is a full healing, completed by "female" and "male" together. The world—contemporary or ancient, it doesn't matter—is again whole. It may be that Jacqui Sadashige, Bill Gallo, and others will find Zacharias Kunuk's next project less difficult to access. Clearly dated, with a clear and understandable documentary purpose, this historical film will focus on "the arrival of missionaries and fur traders in the nineteenth century." But for indigenous viewers all across the world, *Atanarjuat* is a very special gift from Kunuk to Inuit people, from Kunuk to all of us carrying the lenses we inherit when born into the Red Zone.

IN THE ZONE

These anecdotes suggest the myriad problems that this book aims to address. That they are personal stories, records of experience sited within a material and social reality, in no way minimizes their validity, whatever the claims of much "postmodern" scholarship. Recently, Paula Moya has elegantly argued that those who occupy the particular social spaces described here have "a special advantage with respect to possessing or acquiring knowledge about how fundamental aspects of our society (such as race, class, gender, and sexuality) operate to sustain matrices of power." She calls this advantage "epistemic privilege" (Moya 2002:38). It is from this privileged space, then, that I see that so voracious are the jaws of European culture, and so dominant the constituent elements that identify what is and what is not central to that culture, that inhabitants of that mental space can easily draw into their intellectual center any challenges to its hegemony. An Inuit film becomes the descendant of European American ethnography, of canonical Western literature, of the Bible. Calls to move the center join a boring old European debate about "centers and peripheries." Aboriginal people, their politics, their concerns, viewed through the eyes of a visiting white British woman or a white male book reviewer, merge imperceptibly into the discourses developed to inhibit or dismiss or "universalize" communities of color in Europe and the United States. Everywhere, it seems, despite generations of struggle, the Euro-world's giant suction machine defies the laws of physics and vacuums up everything into itself. What cannot be drawn inside and reidentified as recognizably "us" rather than "them" is sometimes left to drift along the edges, a colorful, "multicultural" decoration but as effective against the workings of the cultural machine as dust. A blissful ignorance of everything beyond the Euro-world reigns on.

This collection of essays is another effort to de-center U.S. culture, sometimes through painstaking rereadings of texts, sometimes by walking readers through museum exhibitions and interrogating one of the most pernicious and unquestioned narrative practices of white hegemony maintenance, sometimes by adding forgotten histories and stories that lurk behind many cultural phenomena, from ballot initiatives in California, to "gifted children" public school programs, to United States history textbooks produced and consumed across the nation. Some chapters—"'Til Indian Voices Wake Us...' and "How the Border Lies"—challenge another kind of silencing, this the consequences of overly narrow scholarship in African diaspora and Chicano studies. In one case, the extent of the trade in North American Indians, sold into Caribbean slavery by the English, suggests a broader understanding of the region. In "How the Border Lies," I am, in small part (though most contentiously) challenging the widespread 1998 celebration by many New Mexicans of Spanish and Mexican (and thus mixed Spanish, African, and indigenous) descent of the Cuartocentenario of the invasion of the Pueblos by a Spanish expedition led by Juan de Oñate. What is a bloody and terrible memory to the indigenous people of New Mexico and the Southwest has become a marvelous and heroic event to many Chicanos.

Fortified by some Chicano Studies scholarship that often rewrites Pueblo history into an unrecognizable (and angering) form, politicians and public figures of Mexican descent have used this 1998 commemoration to define another "in" and "out," another center that functions not to broaden but rather to exclude. In the case of the best-known of the "Ur texts" of this New Mexico scholarship, Ramón Gutiérrez's *When Jesus Came, the Corn Mothers Went Away* (1991), the arguments turn the whole story upside down, so that Pueblo women—girls and adults—become partly responsible for the conquest of their lands and their nations by, Gutiérrez claims, deploying their sexuality as a tool of control against conquistador and priest alike. The result, Gutiérrez argues, was a mixed-race society, though one, as he does not acknowledge, dominated by a Spanish government and Spanish church.[9]

The counter narratives here are written from two perspectives, two "zones." The first is what my friend Beth Piatote calls "the Red Zone" (a term she first heard used by an American Indian journalist talking to young indigenous students). From here the essays interrogate European and European American narrative practices not by claiming a special, essentialized space that only Native Americans occupy, but rather by adopting what some scholars have recently begun to call "post-positivist realist" definitions of such identity zones, as "historically and materially grounded perspective[s] from which we can work to disclose the complicated workings of ideology and oppression" (Moya 2002:18).[10] Furthermore, I see the Red Zone as a shifting field, as, in Robin D.G. Kelley's words, a "zone of engagement; not the product of bloodlines or some essence all Indians possess." In other words, thinking from the red zone is, again in Kelley's words, "a political stance, not a racial being" (Kelley 2003). And this political stance does not only concern those born into the Red Zone. Identifying as any kind of racialized person, any "person of color," does not, as I argue in several of these essays, automatically prevent misapprehension. Rather, lived experience and political choices, plus the willingness to *engage*—constantly and often painfully—with other racialized peoples, as well as with European Americans and one's own group —inflect all our understanding, both of the Euro-world and of all its excluded peoples.

The second, though no less vital, zone is that of feminism, albeit a very distinct feminism, one informed both by decades of struggle and by the gradual separation of women of color from other feminists. The recent founding of the Red Feminist Collective, a group of indigenous women scholars from the United States and Canada, has been part of a new articulation of "red feminism," a practice (described in a manifesto that is still in progress) shaped both by a radical critique of Western patriarchy and by a deep commitment to indigenous communities. This second zone, then, is a zone-within-a-zone, informed by continuing, and often radically different, oppressions suffered by women both within and without the indigenous world. That not all those in the Red Zone "get" the feminist perspective will not surprise many women readers. That not all those in the women of color feminist zone "get" the liberation projects underlying readings from either zone will similarly not surprise many. Here, "getting it" is not an inborn ability. Instead, it is a learned and practiced relationship to what is known, as Michel-Rolph Trouillot, citing another scholar, describes it (1995:148).

Essays such as these, written by a single individual or, in one case, by two individuals, working in isolation, published one by one in very disparate but all Euro-American venues, constitute a group of stories that represent only a single voice rather than the cacophony of voices that should accompany any activity of community storytelling. They offer no alternative voices; they contain no dissident remarks, no "that's not the way it happened," no "well, this happened too," all remarks and activities that would accompany such story-telling in any group—formal or informal—of American Indian people. In fact, despite centuries of European-style literacy,[11] a very different practice, familiar to most indigenous people in its many variations, remains prevalent in Indian communities.

That stories are also living, changing constantly in a fluid, breathing world, is eloquently demonstrated by Frances Manuel in her *Desert Indian Woman: Stories and Dreams*, a work produced in collaboration with Deborah Neff (2002). When Neff asked her to talk about Tohono O'odham "legends," Manuel replied:

> Long ago they would set us down and tell us the
> stories, the stories and all the things that are connected

> to them, the Ho'oki a:gida. And now they are all gone.
> I don't want the [full-length] legends in the book.
> They tell them over and over in different ways, and it
> changes—it's changing and it's going to change more in
> a modern way....Every one of us has different stories or
> different language and it comes out differently....
>
> That's the way I think about all those things that have
> been told. The legends have been told a simple way,
> then pretty soon somebody else tells and adds a little
> more to make the story more interesting, and more
> and more (141).

Manuel adds another story that illuminates the problem of a certain imposed Euro-modernity:

> Now this Hopi man spoke at a meeting, he spoke about
> the reservation. When he was ten years old, he could
> run in an open range for miles and miles, then later on,
> they sent him to school and it seems like he was just
> in a closed-in fence or house, and a person right there
> says, "Stand up, sit down, go that way, go this way, go
> to bed, get up." It's like that. And it ruined his thinking.
> He doesn't think anymore like an Indian. And he gave
> up and he thought, "Well, if I can't have what I had
> before, I might as well not think"; Because thinking of
> a white person gets mixed up with an Indian (161).

Manuel's judgment is rather different from that Nicola Walker might have made. She is not condemning success in the white world. Instead, she is noting a terrible loss. For all of us highly educated into the white person's thinking, our voices, together or separate, can never "think Indian" without getting at least slightly confused.

And yet, we do "think Indian" and can talk and act Indian as well as white. So when we speak, we are conscious that we are speaking as only one sound in what is really a multitude. And we know, too, that if we do not speak in the little space we manage to find in the overwhelming world of U.S. overculture, all the voices—of the past and of the future—will cease living in the air and the air will be as silent as that in a polluted modern city whence the birds have fled.

ISOLATION

This imperative to speak leads to a second difficulty for indigenous people. Across the academic world created by scholars of color over the past many decades, the voices least heard are those of American Indians. Of course the venues where white America's talking heads hold forth—the *New York Review of Books*, various other journals, television and radio "news and discussion" programs—pay only desultory attention to any people of color. But when occasionally—thanks to the tireless efforts of scholars of color—voices are heard in these spaces, when texts and writers are allotted a place inside the canons, Native Americans, with only rare exceptions, remain among the missing. An essay here, a film or novel there, each appears and disappears quickly leaving little dust needing to be vacuumed up into the overcultural center. Take a look. Even in my own department, where every scholar claims competency in "comparative ethnic studies," only a few outside the field of Native American Studies, however long their years in the comparative program, could cite more than a handful of Native American texts and, I would guess confidently, these would all be the same texts. Here, too, two new Native American graduate students, in a cohort consisting mainly of Chicana/os and Asian Americans, are—to their dismay—welcomed, patronizingly, by one of my colleagues: "Oh it's a good thing you two are here: no one knows anything about Native America so your job will be to educate all of us!" A year later, two Pacific Islander students are welcomed by another faculty member with constant references to their assumed love of football and the presumably ancillary necessity for them to eat more than the others. As none of these students—vulnerable to the power wielded by their professors—accepted such outrages without brave and vehement protest, so must we all speak, with however many *caveats* about breaching Native American practice, about "talking white."[12]

These essays have another role to play in addition to opening a little space in the intellectual air that has so long excluded Native America. They also contest much recent rhetorical practice in the broad fields of ethnic or cultural studies. Thus they are unashamedly grounded in practical readings of various texts and acts and quite deliberately written so that everyone who would like to read them can do so without a dictionary of "postmodern" terminology to hand, and indeed, without experiencing a headache. Each such reading comes, I hope, from what Paula Moya describes as "a historically and materially grounded perspective" and works "to disclose the complicated workings of ideology and oppression" (18). At the same time, I hope they offer an occasional smile, if only one of irony.

The book is organized into two parts, the first concerned with cultural practices, particularly those that contribute to the formation of those "practices of everyday life" limned by Michel de Certeau (1984), the second with history. Part I, consisting of the first three chapters, thus interrogates a variety of overcultural manifestations and practices as at the same time it tries to shake the Euro-center off its axis. It opens with a critical reading of several "Indian" oriented texts in three academic disciplines: cultural studies, history, and anthropology. The following two chapters question Eurocentric museum practices in two New York City venues, the George Gustav Heye Center of the National Museum of the American Indian[13] and the Museum for African Art. Part II is about history—both personal and collective. Here I am making a passionate claim that history, much under assault by a variety of postmodernists, matters. With Michel-Rolph Trouillot, I want to occupy my own space, informed by experience that is not forever rendered tangential, murky, or amorphous by scholars. As Trouillot declared recently, "being who I am and looking at the world from there, the mere proposition that one could, or should, escape history seems to me either foolish or deceitful. I find it hard to harness respect for those who genuinely believe that postmodernity, whatever it may be, allows us to claim no roots. I wonder why they have convictions, if indeed, they have any" (1995:xviii).

These essays most certainly have conviction. Moreover, they move in a roughly chronological fashion, taking up three events: the passage of Proposition: 187 in California in 1994, the 1998 commemoration in New Mexico of Spain's 16th century invasion, and the celebration of Kamau Brathwaite's life and work on the occasion of his 70th birthday in New York in 2000. Each uses history (albeit in complicated ways) to reflect, critically, upon them. In each chapter, the intention is to locate the historical center, and widen it to accommodate other centers with other languages and other voices, some of which have been long silenced, some of which are highly tendentious. Polemics, yes, but aimed so that "older stories and different histories are laboriously freed, rise to the surface, become available as counters," in the eloquent words of Timothy Reiss (Reiss 2002:442). So here they are, each an exemplar of a dissident practice; each a little counter-narrative; each a celebration of a different center, another world. Each means not only to help move the center, however slightly, toward other centers with their other languages, their other cultures, but also to help re-zone so that genuine cultural diversity and gender equality might come into existence.

PART I
RACE AND REPRESENTATION

CHAPTER 1

READINGS FROM THE RED ZONE: CULTURAL STUDIES, HISTORY, ANTHROPOLOGY

Like so many other things, the emergent field of cultural studies, born in England's red brick universities, underwent a curious depoliticization during its trip across the Atlantic. Originally a critical response to the socially anomic, Thatcherite world of "postindustrial" global capitalism, the cultural studies that reached U.S. shores quickly assumed the hyper-precious, decadently fashionable air of a Soho nightclub. For many U.S. intellectuals, archaeologies of popular culture simply replaced the Derridean musings of literary deconstruction, the selfindulgence of Lacanian (self-)analyses of repressed texts and countertexts.

For many post-1960s academics, their disciplines rendered moribund by shifting racial demographics and the consequent decolonization of minority minds,[1] cultural studies offered new vistas and potentially fresh, politically unsuspect methods. First off the blocks were anthropologists and their comrades, ethno-historians. Seizing on the new languages of cultural studies, both aimed to move their projects out of the prison house of Western traditions into the fresher air breathed for so long with so little interference from the European center by those marginal to it, the United States's racial and cultural "Others."

The works discussed here exemplify some of the resulting successes and failures. Their authors include one anthropologist, one literary scholar, and three historians. Each work reflects the influences of contemporary cultural criticism, though all suffer to some extent from the a-political blandness endemic in mainstream U.S. scholarship. All the works study "otherness," three admitting to excluding most of their subjects' voices from their texts, one attempting, bravely, to include a Native voice and even a Native epistemology. Taken together, the authors' new methods and old subjects challenge readers to ask whether the results are more "outsider" texts, locked inside the Euro-American intellectual center or something genuinely innovative. Or, as minority scholars might ask of each author, in starker terms, "Does X get it?"

This query vexes most intellectual encounters between "marginals" and "centrals," uses and thems. Recently, I gave a talk at a national conference of Native American studies scholars. My talk was, in essence, a review of the "new" National Museum of the American Indian, an attack on organizers' claims that this museum (the first venue of which opened in New York City in 1994) breaks new ground, gives "voice to the silent," lets the descendants of the makers of the Museum's collections create their own exhibition space, their own ways of showing some of the 1.5 million artifacts.[2] Taking my audience step by step through the George Gustav Heye Center,[3] I argued that these pretensions were hollow, that this "new museum" was not new at all but was, rather, exemplary of traditional practices long associated with "Indian museums."

The talk elicited many reactions, but one theme ran through all non-Natives' comments. "I liked that museum," said one with typical chagrin. "Why couldn't I see what you saw?" There are many responses, none of them, I think, entirely satisfactory. Do "we" get it because of our "subalternity"? Is life on the margins the requisite experience for understanding the practices of objectification rampant in the museum captivities of Native cultures? Is it, finally, as one friend is wont to conclude, "something in the blood?" I don't know. I don't know why "we" get it and others— smart, sincere, rigorously analytical in other matters—often don't. But I do know that "we" speak of these things from a different space, Gloria Anzaldúa's "space in-between, *from where* to think" (quoted in Mignolo 1995: xiii). Beth Piatote calls this Indian place "the Red Zone," from which we speak when we are speaking our collective hypersense of our "we-ness."[4] It is from that Zone that I spoke about "our" museum, from inside, seeing behind the museum's many disguises, all those forms and shapes and positions that have so long hidden the genocidal colonial project at the heart of U.S. museum narratives.

Several academic disciplines are implicated in this and similar projects of national obfuscation, though anthropology and history (including their hybrid, ethnohistory) have long provided the scouts. I should like to use these four works, all affected by the practices of cultural studies, to consider the possibilities of escape from the Euro-center into a more nuanced border world for those not resident since birth. First is James C. Faris's *Navajo and Photography* (1996), a work by a man well aware that his is the discipline that has offended most against indigenous Americans (so much so that his fellows are disdained by all but the most right wing tribal people as "anthros"[5]). The single clear exemplar of cultural studies, Leah Dilworth's *Imagining Indians in the Southwest* (1996), comes next, and I conclude with two histories, one a collection of careerspanning essays by the dean of America's ecohistorians, Wilbur Jacobs, the other a brave revisionist history of a small, local event, blown out of proportion because of its venue —Southern California —and its actors —cowboys and Indians. Because James Sandos and Larry Burgess have tried to give space to Indians to tell their own events in their own way, their modest work, *The Hunt for Willie Boy* (1994), offers a distinct contrast to the other works here as well as several salutary lessons to those from outside the Red Zone who would record life within.

FIRST, AN EXEMPLARY TALE

I know an anthropologist who has made a career studying Indians. Like his fellows, he dresses the part, favoring cowboy boots and denim, shirts and jeans divided by a great big silver belt buckle. [A Tejano friend: "You know what we say back in Texas. The bigger the belt buckle, the smaller the...brain."] He sits in his campus office, all dressed up for a round-up he's never seen except in movies. Like his colleagues, he strides manfully into Indian Country, summer after summer, returning, as Floyd Red Crow Westerman puts it, "like death and taxes to our land."[6]

His most recent subjects are some California indigenous people who live comfortably alongside the Anglos who own and run their little city. Although he sees their living as both "survival" and "accommodation," they are actually living science fiction's parallel lives. Thus when Anglos took their sacred spring and built over it a "water temple," those popular Depression-era pseudoclassical shrines to American civic ingenuity, local tribal people were unimpressed. Month after month, after dark, they continued their ceremonies at *their* spring, indifferent to arrogant marble columns and domes, to pump-fed fountains. Anglo monument: Indian water.

Their burial ground lies high on a hill at the edge of what are now the town's boundaries. An immigrant, rich from the gold— and killing—fields of 19th century California, bought the hill, built himself a mansion right on top. Gardeners dug and planted; flowers bloomed, grass grew. But whenever a tribal person died, the ceremonially blessed ashes were carried straight to the traditional resting place. The next morning, a tiny hump in the vast green lawn, unnoticed by Anglos, marked an Indian grave.[7]

I was delighted. "They are living the East European resistance movement's 'as if...'" I said. He looked blank so I explained, "They are living 'as if' Anglos had never appeared in their midst, greedy for gold, frenzied by the local sport of Indian killing." He still didn't get it, so I tried again. "You need a poet to tell these stories, they are stories intricate with nuance, with complicated ways of understanding and explanation, with many voices in different tones and registers. You need Simon Ortiz or Wendy Rose, or perhaps Kamau Brathwaite." Into his startled face I explained, "Brathwaite, poet/historian of Barbados."

I didn't realize it was hopeless, that he was imagining only another dull monograph—perhaps replete with the "poor me, poor me," apologies wherein the scholar (so disingenuously) confesses complicity with the colonial project, dismay at the appropriative act in which he or she is engaged, guilt at the history of the discipline. "Poets?" I could hear him thinking, "She may have a Cambridge PhD in history but she *isn't* one of us. And," I read in the little bubble rising over this Indian scholar's head, "who *is* this Brathwaite, anyway? Not even an Indian."

This anthropologist wears more than just industrial-strength earplugs, that could, with effort, be removed. Instead he lives secure in his world at the center of the universe. He could just as well stay at home and think up his judgments after a leisurely afternoon with *National Geographic*. But here at the beginning of the 21ˢᵗ century, the situation is complicated. Although this man has never asked himself whether or not he *should* tell these stories, *we* can ask. And I think the answer is a qualified yes. He's learned these stories now, been given them by the people. Now he should tell them, give them to others, especially to those Natives who form the vast red diaspora, ties to home cut by war, by forced removals, by government relocation in the 1940s and 1950s.[8] Buried in what anthropologists consider "scientific data" are elements from which others, tribal people, tribal poets, can make their very different stories. Or perhaps (I am not a racial essentialist) some other, non-Native scholars might seize upon his work, see through the sentiment and romance that freezes his subjects in a timeless, a-political "Indian" world, link these Native people's ways with those of other anti-colonial indigenous people around the world.

IN THE SOUTHWEST

Sometimes an anthropologist or, more likely, a cultural studies scholar steps in to rework such "data." Both James Faris and Leah Dilworth have done just that. Both excoriate the usual practices of anthropology and its contiguous disciplines (eth-nohistory, ethno art history) while exploring their subjects. At the same time, however, the authors' keen awareness of their "outsider" status, the chagrin both feel when reading their pred-ecessors' arrogant appropriations of an alien Indian world, raise our questions. Do these works move the center from the West to the worlds of the Rest? Have Faris and Dilworth, freed by the techniques and preoccupations of cultural studies, crossed into the borderlands?

James Faris's *Navajo and Photography* is a stimulating work, replete with insights drawn from contemporary cultural criticism as well as with the self-reflexivity beloved of conscience-stricken anthropologists. Issues of representation, analyses of cultural pro-duction and consumption, move him beyond Walter Benjamin, well beyond Susan Sontag, to Johannes Fabian, whose markers of modernism flow through this book. *Navajo and Photography* begins, however, with its other project, an attack on Faris's fellow Westerners:

> ...this is a critical volume. Photographs of a minority indigenous group were produced largely by a dominant, aggressive, and exploitative majority foreign culture with institutional trajectories and disciplines that emphasized vision and was oriented toward the consumption of images....My purpose is...polemical—to counter the hegemonic discourses currently commanding analysis of photography of Navajo and to suggest alternatives (xi).

This is the aspect of Faris's book that is of interest in any assessment of insider/outsider, center/periphery problems. At the same time, the work offers a thoroughgoing history of the ways in which the Navajo nation has provided a seemingly endless stream of images (captured, Faris argues, in a small number of constantly repeated tropes) for camera-wielding Westerners. All the well-known Indian photographers put in an appearance, introduced chronologically following two theoretical essays, "The Gaze of Western Humanism" and "The Registers of Photography of Navajo." Portraits of photographers, followed by studies of 20th century modernist artists, ethnographers, and anthros comprise the central chapters. The work ends with a brief look at Navajo photographers "shooting back."[9] Throughout, Faris exposes, analyzes, attacks. Ethnographic photographers come in for a thrashing. Edward Curtis, long the focus of Native and non-Native attack (Huhndorf 2001), and Laura Gilpin (an icon of the "first wave" U.S. feminist movement and thus previously untouched by criticism) bear the brunt of Faris's well-aimed attack, but all the usual suspects among their colleagues appear as well. It is a rich work— multileveled, "heteroglossic," loaded with insightful readings, organized in provocatively eccentric layouts. The text is dotted with "portfolios," each of which collects a representative sample of one trope. These include "The Machine" (the camera), "Navajo Elected" (Navajos involved with the processes of filming), "Avoidance" (people hiding from cameras), "Navajo in Image, 1900-1950" (a history of tropes), "Church and State" (two tropes), "Hands-on Social Relations" (portraits of the physical appropriation of Native people by anthropologists, women tourists, and others), "Loom" (the weaving trope), "and "Mimesis" (Navajo photographers).

The book's design mimics various *genres* of "Indian" books. Portfolios recall exhibition catalogues. Toned in the sepias and grays of "old" photographs, the book's illustrations mimic both exhibitions and coffee-table "Indian" books. The cover's designer, Mary Shapiro, has broken up a background ethnographic portrait (titled, originally, "Navajo") with several images suggesting captivity: a box camera, in one upper corner, shoots "wanted posters," different profiles of the same head. Each small picture is differently colored, differently sized, and superimposed on the sepia seated figure of the large—original—portrait. The book's back cover reiterates this image. Here, enlarged to cover the entire book, the man is shown seated sideways, leaning against a chair back, his mouth slightly open. Here he assumes a different role, that of a model, posing according to the dictates of a (commercial) photographer.

Faris's readings of the pictures mirror the cover's complexity. One series, for example, shows Navajos pretending to take pictures of other Navajos; they, in turn, are photographed by "real" photographers. Such pictures rely for their effect on the juxtaposition of "primitive" Navajos, unable to use cameras, and sophisticated Westerners, who can. Despite Faris's anger at the racist implications of these pictures, he overlooks the equally negative gender relations revealed. It surely matters that the "pretend photographers" and their "pretend subjects" were all female while the "real" photographers were male. The "Hands-on" portfolio later in the book also cries out for similar analysis. The "hands-on" trope—the male anthropologist with his hands draped across the shoulders of male subjects or nonchalantly placed across the breasts of female Natives—is familiar to all readers of anthropological texts (See Haraway 1989, esp. chapter 3).

As with the "primitive/civilized" trope, however, Faris remains unaware of the sexual politics involved. Faris's analyses of the intersection of a visualist modernism with the proliferation of photos of Navajos deconstructs anthropological discourse. Photographs, he argues, reveal little about their subjects but much about the culture, methods, and values of the photographers and the acquisitive, appropriative world they serve. Moreover, texts accompany their pictures. "The West's real Navajo were not exactly what they appeared. Photographs could only tell the whole story if accompanied by anthropology's text" (16-17). Anthropology's words thus write the photographs. And these Faris demolishes, working from photographs to text and back again, tracking changes over time but marking the discursive systems of racism that shaped it all.

In the tropes that contain Navajos for the Western mind, "the same gestures appear again and again over time." Thus "despite the commentary of their partisans, Laura Gilpin looks like Edward Curtis, Marcia Keegan looks like Curtis, John Running looks like Curtis, Joel Grimes looks like Curtis...or Carl Moon, or Frederick Monsen"(19). And although the photographs containing these tropes are widely accepted as revealing "data" about their subjects, they do not. "Another Western truth at risk in this study," Faris notes, "is that images can expose human essentials, communicate something significant and non-trivial about us all" (308).

As he overlooks gender, so too does Faris neglect another vexatious problem haunting his text. Given the hegemonic power of this discursive system of representation and narration, one wonders how deeply Navajos, or other Natives, internalized the tropes, accepted the stereotypes ubiquitous in U. S. culture ("high" and "low") since the invention of the camera. To what extent can Navajo photographers stand outside the overculture's ethnographic images? Most non-Native scholars understandably skirt this potentially tendentious issue, but it remains present. Happily the problem is increasingly exposed by Native artists, writers, and scholars. Gerald McMaster and James Luna explode commercial stereotypes in performance pieces, Nora Naranjo-Morse and Simon Ortiz send up the tourist's Southwest in satirical sculptures, poems, and stories. Each enacts Ortiz's "existential Indian. Dostoevsky Coyote" (quoted in Penn 1996:231).[10]

Whatever his neglect of gender or of hard questions about colonized Indian minds, has Faris at least avoided the pitfalls of the Euro-centrism he condemns? Yes and no. Faris aptly limns and denounces practices of appropriation, but sometimes he goes too far, distorting his own perceptions. Sometimes, too, he skirts issues embedded in his narrative that would stop most Native readers in their tracks. There are occasions when self-reflexivity drives him into preposterous overstatement. One example: "Joe Toddy...at zoo in Colorado Springs, 1939" shows a laughing man holding up one arm of a cheerfully accommodating ape. The text explains earnestly that the snapshot was taken when Toddy visited the zoo with his artist son. Here is Faris's interpretation of this casual snapshot (in the deathless prose of anthropology): "This diversionary activity with an orangutan is undoubtedly innocent, but it is interesting that it is not a European-American photographed with the ape" (192). Huh? It's a group of friends and family, clowning around.

Humorlessness is not the only problem. Faris ignores what is potentially really interesting about this photograph, the fact that it is currently held not in a family album but rather in the collection of the Museum of New Mexico. What is it doing there? Who collected this picture for an historical museum? The presence of an informal family snapshot in a public museum archive surely prompts questions. Is it there because it is a 1930s era photograph, part of an historical record of that decade? Is it part of a collection depicting families of all races in the Southwest? Or is it there because Joe Toddy is a Navajo?

There are similar silences elsewhere. The first photographs of Navajos, we learn, were taken of the captives held at Bosque Redondo in 1864 after their forced march from their homes. That these first photographs (of what became, as Faris documents, an entire industry) were *prison* photos (like those on the cover, "jail" IDs) taken as signifiers of conquest, captivity, ownership, would certainly, I think, mark a Native intellectual's analysis of the subsequent photographic/anthropological discourse. But Faris gives this only a paragraph, couched in the passive voice familiar to Red Zoners: "the great majority of Navajo were rounded up in 1864 and forcibly marched...from Arizona to Bosque Redondo"(23). *Rounded up?* Wayward cattle in Faris's eyes, too? Who rode the horses, wielded the guns and whips? And *who aimed those cameras* at the prisoners, developed those pictures, labeled them, stored them away? The text is again silent.

So problems remain. To Native people, Faris has let his own embarrassment at the excesses of his profession bury important questions, thereby entombing the sorrows (Bosque Redondo) and egregious insults (the touch of white hands). Politics remain marginal. As is too often the case with cultural studies, analyses of how power is created, established, and implemented, as well as the means by which relations of power are stabilized and spread are restricted to those interesting but ethereal aspects exposed by the camera.

Leah Dilworth has written a much less visually and intellectually eccentric text but one with a similar subject—here *all* the Native peoples of the Southwest—and similar concerns about their representation by non-Native people. Dilworth's breadth is wonderful: ethnographers' versions of Hopi dances, Fred Harvey's Indian-starring tourist promotions, and the advertising campaigns of the railroads. Together these lured thousands of easterners to the Southwest: more ethnographers, then artifact collectors, bohemian artists, and the first flood of retirees. The book is replete with cultural criticism—explorations of tourism as spectacle, collecting as performance, ethnography as conquest. Dilworth concludes by locating this imagined Southwestern world within the broader context of the American modernism its creators helped produce, rereading "primitivist" painters and sculptors, poets and novelists. Once hordes of ethnographers and collectors and tourists had successfully appropriated the Native Southwest, reshaping its landscapes and peoples into objects of Anglo consumption, artists, dreamers of an indigenous national identity, began to deploy this periphery as "our past," claiming place and Native peoples as "our heritage."

Dilworth's book is a marvelously detailed account of these processes of appropriation and assimilation. As a history of the ways in which Indians were imagined and their images used throughout mainstream U.S. culture between 1880 and 1920, this is a splendid, original, and beautifully written work. It will be used, and should be, by all kinds of scholars of the Southwest, of U.S. culture (high and low, as Dilworth mingles Wild West Shows and World's Fairs, highbrow literature and dime novels, "art" films and B movies, ad art and Armory Show paintings), and of issues of representation, including those of gender which Dilworth treats with some care. (The introduction argues that "writers, artists, advertisers, tour promoters, collectors, and anthropologists created the Southwest as a backdrop for American virility"(1996:19) an idea that shapes much of what follows.) This book makes a fine companion to *Navajo and Photography*. Like Faris, Dilworth articulates ambitious goals. She, too, wants to "move the center," rendering Indians "constitutive" rather than "reflective," turning them from "subjects" into "subalterns" (8). Does she?

Unfortunately, there are no Natives in this text, however entertaining and interesting its invented Indians.[11] Perhaps Dilworth could not hear Native voices: she kept her distance from her subjects, spending but one brief research trip in the Southwest. Most of her material came from back East, from Yale, the New York Public Library, the Smithsonian Institution. Given the profound connection between Southwestern Native peoples and their land, I should think even a superficial understanding of their cultures would require a more extensive acquaintance with place. Her distance may also explain her uncritical reliance on anthrotexts, both as her major source of information about Native people and as the discourse most suitable for describing Indians. Consider, for example, these Navajos: "They were partially nomadic, practiced some agriculture, and raided the pueblos on either side of them for food" (10). Such statements, locking Native people into anthropology's familiar historical present, dot the work. This kind of objectifying language inevitably defines the readers: non-Native "we's."

Dilworth's condemnation of earlier anthropologists and collectors sometimes falters. Although she criticizes ethnographers' outrages that drove Hopis to close their ceremonies to outsiders in the 1920s, she uses their photographs. Why? She explains weakly that she wants to prevent "further mystification" (23). Then too, she thinks the theft and distortion of Hopi ceremonies weren't all bad. "Dissemination of [descriptions]," she writes, meant that "more and more non-Indians began to value and support the preservation of Hopi culture" (25). Two replies: why should ceremonies not be "mystified?" They are "mystified" in Hopi—and, like the religious ceremonies of, e.g., orthodox Catholics, should not exist at all beyond the world from which they come; and, why can't Hopis look after their own culture? (In fact, anthropologists and collectors—like the Spanish invaders of the 16th and 17th centuries—found the Hopis especially skillful at "preserving" themselves.)

The "we's" in this book are consistently obvious. One further example. After quoting Jesse Walter Fewkes's remarks about the

Snake Dance he "observed" in 1894, Dilworth writes, "the Indian problem in the 1890s presented a dilemma similar to that concerning incorporation of freedmen after the Civil War" (28). The *Indian* problem in the 1890s was survival: the Native population of the United States reached its nadir—fewer than 250,000—in 1900. The decade marked a rapid population decline. The *white* problem, on the other hand, was how to hasten this end, a "problem" they addressed directly, sending the United States cavalry to kill, capture, remove. This tactic culminated in 1890, at the last of the great U.S. cavalry massacres of Indian people, at Wounded Knee.

Dilworth's Western blindness also produces at least one historical howler. Explaining Anglos' preference for Puebloans over Navajos or Apaches Dilworth notes: "Because Apache and Navajo cultures had been more violently disrupted by European contact and were thus perceived as less purely 'primitive,' they did not fit the discovery scenario" (31). *What?* What about Oñate's invasion of the Pueblos in 1598? What about the 80 years of occupation— revolt, murder, desecration, and intermarriage—that followed? What about its consequences, the first American revolution in 1680 when Pueblo people drove the Spaniards out of their New Mexico? What about the ensuing reconquest?[12]

This ignorance of Pueblo political life expands as Dilworth locates 19th and 20th century Pueblos in a power neutral "borderland." "The relationship between ethnographers and Hopis was complex and locked in a process of continual negotiation," she writes (41). This word, "negotiation" (together with its twin, "exchange"), effectively dilutes centuries of powerful, violent, organized Pueblo resistance or Anglos depredation. Don Talayesva recalled the behavior of one missionary at Oraibi at the end of the nineteenth century:

> [We] remembered the Rev. Voth who had stolen so many of our ceremonial secrets and had even carried off sacred images and altars to equip a museum and become a rich man. When he had worked here in my boyhood, the Hopi were afraid of him and dared not lay their hands on him or any other missionary, lest they be jailed by the Whites. During the ceremonies this wicked man would force his way into the kiva and

write down everything that he saw. He wore shoes with solid heels, and when the Hopi tried to put him out of the kiva he would kick them (43).

Negotiation? Even Henry Kissinger would be shocked.

Dilworth misreads other Hopi texts, her understanding shaped by a combination of ignorance of Hopi political history and New Age stereotype—which, for all her efforts, she continues to accept. Discussing the secrecy of kiva societies, she quotes Nanahe telling John G. Bourke (from Bourke 1884) why he should not be privy to the secrets of the kiva: "its privileges are the property of its members and should be preserved with jealous vigilance; since, if they became known to the whole world, they would cease to be secrets and the order would be destroyed and its benefit to the world would pass away" (42).

"Nahane clearly explained why the members of the Snake and Antelope societies would not want Bourke or anyone else to witness their activities" Dilworth explains. "The knowledge these societies held was of benefit to the world" (ibid). But this is not at all what Nanahe is saying! He is explaining that secrecy is the essence of kiva social life. It is not the fact of the "knowledge" that matters (and matters here not to the "whole Anglo world" but rather, as Dilworth doesn't seem to realize, to the whole *Hopi* world) but rather the fact that this knowledge belongs only to kiva members. Acceptance into the kiva meant—and means—gaining little by little and with careful attention to the perpetuation of hierarchical order, knowledge of that society's secrets. Dilworth misreads, I think, not only because of ignorance but also because of twin desires: to believe that "the whole world" includes her; and that what Nanahe was saying is "universal" and "wise."

Such examples are, fortunately, relatively rare. However Dilworth does reproduce another anthropologists' habit, repeatedly removing agency from Native people by employing the passive voice, over and over and over. Here are a few examples: "the codes used in the construction of the ethnographic display were reinterpreted and new meaning was made" (54); "the visitor was transformed into the collector...he or she was educated in connoisseurship and authenticity" (85); or, "Indians were characterized as pure primitives, but people of Hispanic descent were figures who simultaneously perverted both the purity of Indian savagery and that of European civilization" (101). All over this text, in every context, agency vanishes. Perhaps only Native readers hear (Minerva's?) owl crying in the distance, "Who, who, who?"

Nevertheless, all this is not to dismiss the book. It is a fine example of what it is: an outsider's study of how other outsiders—boorish, arrogant, greedy—first invented then sold a fake Indian, setting him or her into an equally fake, thoroughly appropriated landscape. It is just the Indians who remain among the missing.

NATIVE AMERICA AND HISTORY

The final books in the group are historical and (preserving my discipline's reputation for keeping a wary eye on encroaching theories and methods) their authors use little from cultural studies. Wilbur Jacobs is one of U.S. history's most prominent eco-historians. One of the originators of ecological history—his *Wilderness Politics and Indian Gifts: The Northern Colonial Frontier, 1748-1763* was published in 1950—Jacobs has long campaigned for a recognition of the fatal link between genocidal (the term is his) Indian displacements and the continent's despoliation. He has also written critically about two of the giants of Western history, Frederick Jackson Turner and Francis Parkman, in book length studies and essays, some of the latter reprinted in the collection discussed here, *The Fatal Confrontation: Historical Studies of American Indians, Environments, and Historians* (1996). Each piece in this volume is driven by this critical eye, what the writer of the book's "Introduction," his former student Albert Hurtado, calls an "inclusive, conscience-driven historical view"(xv). Though admiring Turner and Parkman, though aware that he—a member of Southern California's ruling class—had benefitted directly and indirectly from the westward invasion of Anglo Americans, Jacobs never avoids seeing the frontier as, again in Hurtado's words, "a series of holocausts. For Jacobs," Hurtado continues, "this was the dark side of the triumphant Turnerian march of American civilization, the truly savage story hidden behind the Parkman narrative"(xiv).

This collection treats not only invaders and frontiers, Indians and historians, it also details the ecological disaster that accompanied European invasion. One stimulating essay compares American Native-white relations with those accompanying the European invasions of Australia and New Guinea. In every case, Jacobs is unfailingly gentlemanly *and* unfailingly polemical. His critical revisionism was shared by other radicals of his generation interested in Native America: Francis Jennings, Robert Heizer, Henry Dobyns, Sherburne Cook. Following in the brave and much-ignored footsteps of Oklahoma's Angie Debo, these men recast America's celebratory master narrative (Parkman's romance, Turner's tragedy) into something rather less boastful. All shunned euphemism—"contact," "culture clash," "negotiation," "exchange," "settlement"— in favor of starker terms: invasion, theft, genocide. The "Afterword" in this collection reveals Jacobs's lifelong devotion to such truth-telling. Here are three examples of many: "my accumulated evidence consistently revealed a history of depraved Anglo behavior toward Indians" (1996:192); "I examined evidence that indigenous peoples were swindled and brutalized by colonial profiteers, missionaries, and their offspring" (186); and Native people died of "malevolent...germ warfare" (192).

As his invention of ecohistory and his foray into comparative indigenous-white history both suggest, Jacobs eagerly embraces new ground. In one essay he describes "Parkman's rapturous emotion in shooting and watching the agonizing deaths of bison bulls at the waterhole" (126), and then suggests in a footnote that Parkman may well have experienced the same "orgasmic" pleasure attributed to Theodore Roosevelt by one of his feminist graduate students (n.17, p. 134). Whatever their motivation, the relentless slaughter of animals, white "settlers'" rapid ruin of every landscape, haunt Jacobs's prose. John Muir, Thorstein Veblen, and Rachel Carson are his constant companions as he voyages across a pillaged world.

Still, the erudite Jacobs never really engages contemporary methodologies. Nor does he try to "give the Indian point of view," though he does note its absence from his own work (except for references to M. Scott Momaday and Vine Deloria Jr.) as well as from that of those he cites throughout. This book, like the works of his contemporaries, is an Anglo's polemic, a polite condemnation of that history where the gentlemen conquered a people, savaged a land, and then proceeded to write self-exculpatory celebrations of their victory. The conquerors and their historians were white. Most were male. They were all privileged—denizens of places like the Pasadena where Jacobs was reared, where "my father had known Turner as a fellow member of the Pasadena Neighborhood Church, a Unitarian congregation that also included the famed Robert Milliken, founding father of the California Institute of Technology" (185). (This was the Milliken who announced in the 1920s that Southern California "is today, as was England two hundred years ago, the westernmost outpost of Nordic civilization [with] a population which is twice as Anglo-Saxon as that existing in New York, Chicago, or any of the great cities of his country" [quoted in Hilden 1994: 21).

But Wilbur Jacobs makes no bones about this. He says who he is as clearly as he states the terrible truth of U.S. history. Who can quarrel with this? Given the neoconservatism of much recent U.S. history (where words like "exchange" have returned to disguise the brutal facts of invasion and conquest as in Karen Kupperman's (1992) euphemistic version of the invasion written for the American Historical Association's 1992 celebration of what it called "the Columbian Encounter," and where negative portraits of Native people more closely recall Walter Prescott Webb than Francis Jennings), Jacobs continues to serve as a beacon, a barrier against still more "organized forgetting" (Kundera 1980).

The 1994 Sandos-Burgess book, *The Hunt for Willie Boy: Indian-hating and Popular Culture*, accepts the anti-Anglo premises of Jacobs's work, but moves beyond, into a territory pioneered by a group within another generation of historians of Native America, led by the influential Calvin Martin. Beginning in the late 1970s, Martin proposed an essentialized Indian world whose utter difference from the European world inevitably inhibited Euro-American attempts to depict Native America. The sole solution, Martin insisted, lay in accepting "Indian epistemology," characterized by a highly eccentric, fluid sense of time, a time that was distinct from "anthropological" (Western) time, and was, instead, "biological time." In his edited collection, *The American Indian and the Problem of History* (1987), Martin offered an example of why "Westerners" failed to accept this "Indian" epistemology: "we are derelict by our silence on the memory of our sacred relationship to the Bear—the biological sphere that embraces and courses through us..../we need to discard anthropological time for biological time, which means finding ourselves in the bear in biological time" (1987:219-20).

Although there are certainly cultural differences between Anglos and Indians—with nearly endless permutations in both cases as well—most Native people (excepting those men who, like Martin, cherish images of themselves as highly masculinized grizzly bears) find Martin's and others' efforts to enter a world of "Indian time" very funny indeed. Countless jokes depend upon fooling whites by pretending that all Indians "understand" via some sense carried in the blood, just "when" something "is meant to happen" (see, for example, Henrietta Whiteman's essay, in Martin 1987:162-70).

To some extent, Sandos and Burgess have attempted to achieve one form of this problematic transformation in their revision of accepted narratives of one 1909 event: Willie Boy's three killings in the southern desert of California (of William Mike; of Mike's daughter, Carlota, who eloped with Willie; and last, of himself, after Carlota was dead and he was alone in the desert, hunted by various well-equipped Anglo posses led by Indian trackers). The cover's two contrasting photographs set the stage. From a tiny framed jail photo ID stares a black, white, and grey-faced Chemehuevi Indian, his eyes wide: Willie Boy. Next to him, sheriff's badge on chest, rifle in hand, arrogance shaping his features, looms a much larger, much *lighter*, Robert Redford. Willie Boy is real. Redford is an actor playing the real undersheriff of San Bernardino County, the man who led the "hunt" for a fugitive Willie Boy and his runaway Carlota. Throughout, a binary tension—between "real" and "unreal," between "white" and "red," between something similar to Martin's "anthropological time" ("ours") and "biological time" ("theirs")—plays itself out in the authors' analyses of the press treatment of Willie Boy, of Henry Lawton's 1960s "non-fiction" novel *Willie Boy: A Desert Manhunt* (the 11th of 34 publications about the incident), of the 1969 Hollywood Western, *Tell Them Willie Boy Was Here*, last, of the Native versions of the event.

Sandos and Burgess are keenly aware of the problems inherent in the task of outsiders trying to write Native history. "As America confronts the quincentenary of...the Columbian exchange, we think it self-evident that Indians must be sensitively included [note the passive voice here, too] in telling the history of the multicultural world Columbus left in his wake" (1994:7). But here lies the problem. The Americas have always been a "multicultural" world, since hundreds of distinct Native nations spoke very different languages, inhabited very different landscapes, and participated in many different—though often interlinked—economies. But this is not what is meant here. What is clearly being said here is that "we" (European American historians) must allow some space in "our" histories for some of those small handful of Indians and their descendants, those left after the devastation unleashed by the "exchange."[13]

Still, Sandos and Burgess do provide readers—and film goers—with a fresh look at western history, using one relatively insignificant event to demonstrate the ways in which Native people have been created as portable backdrops for the white occupation of the West. The contributions of the press to the hysteria that followed Indian-on-Indian violence, the presence in the area of so many Indian haters, the activities of the Bureau of Indian Affairs agent (typically for the time, a European-American woman), and the panic among Anglos because their "last frontier" was closing, shaped both the tragedy (a chase across miles and miles of desert, Carlota's death, Willie Boy's suicide) and its interpretations, invented then and later by journalists, novelists, anthropologists, and then by a film producer (Abraham Lincoln Polonsky) and an actor (Robert Redford). Throughout, Sandos and Burgess argue, the self-serving perfidy of nearly all the Anglos involved blocked any chance that the Native story would be heard beyond reservation borders.

This work aims to draw this Native narrative into public view. And here is where *The Hunt for Willie Boy* provides a mirror for the other works. Unlike Faris, Dilworth, and Jacobs, these two authors have followed a Native scholars' map, albeit with Martin as their guide. They have gone to the elders, to the tellers of the Chemehuevi and Cahuilla stories, giving "equal space" to "real" indigenous voices, to the "biological time" that purportedly shapes Native life. Nevertheless, there is disappointingly little from Chemehuevis or Cahuillas and much from the ethnographic record. How did Willie Boy live? Ethnographers tell "us." How did he survive, running over 50 miles of desert without water or rifle? Again, ethnographers explain that Willie Boy must have been one of a special group among the Chemehuevis, the runners, who knew how to lengthen their strides to great lengths and run and run and run (an explanation confirmed by a Chemehuevi descendant of runners). Further "we" learn that Willie Boy was a Ghost Dancer, part of that resistance movement that spread across the West at the end of the 19th century.

Sandos and Burgess signal "Indian" voices by italics. This technique is meant to suggest alternative readings of events. Carlota's whole family, we learn, not just her father, was opposed to the union, not, as whites said, because of her youth, but rather because Willie and Carlota were too closely related in the clan system that governed tribal life. Many Chemehuevis, moreover, continue to believe that the bones found by the posse were not those of Willie Boy at all. They believe he escaped and died many decades later, of old age. Not all the trackers were Cahuillas, as the text suggests. One, at least, was Chemehuevi, a man who later married William Mike's widow, Maria. Conflicts between William Mike and Willie Boy were not simply personal. Rather, Mike, an older, traditional Chemehuevi, was hostile to the modernity Willie Boy, and (*pace* the anthropologists) Ghost Dancing, represented.[14] Whereas the latter might readily abandon the tradition prohibiting distant cousins from marrying, the former could not and did not. Such are the different versions spoken by tribal people to these Anglo historians.

Two of the concluding three chapters, Rashomon-like, pose contradictory tales, the Indian story a page and a half long (representing, the authors tell us, "biological time"), Sandos and Burgess's tale (in anthropological time so twelve and a half pages plus pictures), and last, a series of post-writing musings. Here the authors turn to Richard Drinnon (1980) and to Herman Melville (1987/1857) to condemn, once again, American history's obfuscated structure, found in the "metaphysics of Indian hating." When they discover evidence that this Indian hating was internecine, however, they are profoundly troubled. Their research uncovers the fact that Native people from the Morongo reservation, members of the Cahuilla nation, aided in the hunt for Willie Boy and then in the writing of Lawton's novel (which describes Willie's dead face, "the lips curled back in an animal snarl" [1960:175]). Lawton's book became a bestseller and negative images like this characterizing Willie Boy spread. By the time the movie version of the book appeared in 1969 (*Tell Them Willie Boy Was Here*) it drew much local press interest, both because many local Native people played roles in the film (*The Daily Enterprise* for Wednesday, May 22, 1968, in "Willie Boy film-makers to Return to Scene of Murder," by Evan Maxwell, noted: "a large number of Indians from the Morongo Indian Reservation will be used as extras... and in scenes depicting a festival that preceded the shooting.... 15 local Indians also would take part in a depiction of an Indian game called peon and authentic Indian singing for scenes in the movie" [B-1]. Anne B. Jennings published a similar article headlined, "'Willie Boy' Rides Again in Banning," in the *Press-Enterprise*, once Lawton's employer, on Sunday, June 23, 1968) and that participation—in a film based on a viciously anti-Indian novel—shattered many whites' romantic notion of pan-Indian solidarity. How do Sandos and Burgess explain the willingness of some Indians to join in the novel's and then the film's negative portrayal of another Indian? The authors write, "through both the novel and the film, Ben de Crevecoeur [one of the original posse organizers and a virulent bigot] sucked the Cahuilla at Morongo Reservation into the vortex of his Indian-hating." Later, "Jane Penn, a member of one of the first Cahuilla families at Morongo...[even befriended] Lawton." Though the authors admit the "importance of filming on the reservation for the Cahuilla economy," they conclude, sadly, that through "Cahuilla endorsement of the novel and participation in the film..., native peoples sadly have been drawn into Indian-hating"(131).

Here, again, the outsider/insider problem evident in each of these works lurks behind this text. From the Red Zone come other voices: "Why can't some Cahuillas loathe some Chemehuevis? Why are their choices to help present a negative version of people they dislike so incomprehensible? What's the difference between this kind of behavior and some Britons' "Hop off, Frogs," campaign against the Channel Tunnel?

Why assume that Indians all love each other? Or that their historical memories are short, even if one believes that they inhabit biological time? Why are the Cahuillas—or the Chemehuevis—of our era any different from those 1980s Dutch people who, recalling that one of the Nazis' first gestures after their invasion of the Netherlands was to steal bicycles, celebrated their European football championship over the Germans by holding up vast signs facing the German fans' side of the stadium: "Grandma: We Found Your Bicycle!"

Dostoevsky Coyote....

CONCLUSION

None of these scholars, then, speaks from the Red Zone. Problematic as they are, the texts from anthropology and cultural/literary studies come closest to reading through to the "inside," abandoning some of the West to visit the Rest. If only James Faris and Leah Dilworth had linked their cultural studies to politics, acknowledging the power relations supported by the phenomena they analyze, hearing and narrating the voices of resistance and assimilation, their books would have been models for future work. For now, however, we should depend on voices from the Red Zone and its equivalents, reading scholars who *begin* from "inside" racial politics and culture, their perspective innately that of the present periphery. Their work holds a whole new world wherein the center no longer lies somewhere between Paris, London, and New York, but rather (like the California of the year 2005) sits culturally and intellectually astride Africa, the Americas and the Caribbean, the Pacific Islands and Australia, and Asia.

CHAPTER 2

RACE FOR SALE: NARRATIVES OF POSSESSION IN TWO "ETHNIC" MUSEUMS

INTRODUCTION

For Ngugi wa Thiong'o, East Africa's greatest writer and political thinker who, for 22 years, has lived in exile from the neo-colonialist Kenyan state, the role of intellectuals among the once colonized peoples of the world demands that they work to "move the center" from Europe to their own centers. He dates the beginnings of such moves to the 1960s, when "the centre of the universe was moving from Europe [...] when many countries, particularly in Asia and Africa, were demanding and asserting their right to define themselves and their relationship to the universe from their own centres in Africa and Asia"(1993:2). This movement is complicated, not least because moving centers demands that previously colonized people undertake lengthy and sometimes painful "decolonization processes" in order to relocate to their own centers. At the same time, as Ngugi explains, "It [is] not a question of substituting one centre for the other. The problem [arises] only when people [try] to use the vision from any one centre and generalize it as the universal reality" (4).[1]

Both processes remain incomplete—both decolonizing minds occupied by the colonizers' various cultural presumptions *and* getting those who occupy the Euro-center to allow for the existence of other, equally legitimate centers rather than simply extending their center outward until the whole world is sucked into a universalist void. Here I shall use two sites of contemporary cultural contestation, the Museum for African Art (formerly the Center for African Art) and the George Gustav Heye Center of the National

Museum of the American Indian, to examine some aspects of both problems. I shall explore the Museum for African Art first, beginning with its texts, including catalogues produced both before and after the opening of the SoHo museum space on Broadway in New York City. These include *Perspectives: Angles on African Art* (Baldwin et al. 1987); the record of the museum's traveling exhibit, *ART/artifact: African Art in Anthropology Collections* (Vogel 1988a); and the provocative catalogue of the subsequent exhibit, *The Art of Collecting African Art* (Vogel 1988b). I shall then look carefully at a publication that is both a catalogue and a critical work, *Exhibition-ism: Museums and African Art* (Nooter Roberts and Vogel 1994), published to celebrate ten years of exhibitions in conjunction with a 1992 symposium, Africa By Design: Designing a Museum for the 21st Century. I shall conclude by touring a 1998 exhibition, *"African Faces, African Figures: The Arman Collection."*

From the Museum for African Art I shall then move farther downtown, to one of this museum's sister institutions, the National Museum of the American Indian (NMAI), which opened its Manhattan doors in 1994. The first two of three inaugural exhibitions (*"Creation's Journey"* and *"All Roads Are Good"*) borrowed some of the same curatorial techniques employed by the pioneering African art museum. The second half of this chapter compares the two museums by analyzing the Heye Center's inaugural exhibition, its published texts, as well as its constructed narrative. Throughout, I shall consider the extent to which these museums "move the center," from the overculture's national history of the United States, in one case, or from Europe to Africa, or even the African diaspora, in the other.

In recent years, museum curators and others have quite thoroughly deconstructed the once obscure practices of museum exhibitions so that their collective complicity in the "invention," celebration, and dissemination of national identities is by now well established. Others have theorized space and the ways in which museum space has been "produced," to use Henri Lefebvre's terms (1974) as a venue for what Aimé Césaire called "the [Europeans'] forgetting machine" (Césaire 1972:9-10).

The racialized (and gendered) nature of such "exhibition-ary complexes" (Bennett 1995) have also received considerable scholarly attention. I think, however, that two problems remain: first, museologists have not succeeded in moving the center, not least because their well-intentioned efforts to "deconstruct" and thereby "deracialize" their museum practices have remained mired in a "universalist" discourse that remains hopelessly Euro-cen-tered despite the fact that their "universalism" and practices *have* assumed fresh shapes, as Richard Schechner (1999) has noted:

> These "new museums" are not new in their underlying assumptions, but they offer "performative experience" that replaces the "I brought them back alive, or stuffed" [...] dioramas of older-style museums [...]. What these "new museums" do, in fact, is combine approaches of the American Museum of Natural History, the Metro-politan Museum of Art, and Disney. In other words, the strategies of hegemony have shifted toward the experiential and the performed.

A second dilemma in these "new museums" emerges from the fact that some communities of color, the purported objects of such museological good intentions, have themselves sometimes ignored the ways in which participation with such museums col-laborates in their own continuing colonization. Of course how Native Americans and other "others" are convinced to join tourists in enacting the narratives of what might be called (with some exag-geration) their "reconquest" by a new, equally hegemonic "plural-ist" Euro-culture poses a complicated problem, one that deserves more attention than I can give it here. Simplifying madly, I am arguing that one problem—identified so long ago by Frantz Fanon (1967))—stems from practices grounded in cultural essentialism. Many involved in purveying such messages argue that overcom-ing Eurocentric practices of all kinds, moving the Euro-center if you will, requires little more than a simple inversion of hitherto negative ethnic stereotypes. "Bad," in other words, simply becomes "good." In the case of ethnic museums, objects once called "arti-facts," representations of "the primitive" or "the savage" other, are now designated ART, described by European aesthetic criteria, and, by the by, assigned a more profitable niche in the museum marketplace. The Martiniquan surrealist René Ménil, writing in the 1930s, issued a warning:

> If we think we can recapture the image of us that has resulted from colonial culture and use it for our own benefit simply by reversing its colours and qualities, we are making an error. The fact is that if we are not what the white man, in his colonial delirium, would like to think us, we are no more the contrary of his idea of us. We are not the 'opposite' of our colonial image, we are *other* than this image (1996:81).

But it is something other than Ménil's clear recognition of genuine otherness that links these two museums. Instead, both triumph a new "universalist" aesthetic, couched in the seductive words of "multiculturalism." In other words, both museums attempt to show that there is room for all at the art table, and both therefore exhibit their works insistently as "great art," defined in European aesthetic terms—terms that, of course bear considerable commodity value. Although a certain overstatement lends a defensive tone to both museums' efforts to include African or Native American objects in the Western canon, neither interrogates the canon itself. No one in these museums questions the truth of Western absolutes upon which all such aesthetic judgments depend.[2]

And yet many scholars have delineated the extent to which all such "universal" aesthetic judgments rest squarely within a history of profoundly racialized practices. David Dabydeen, poet, story writer, and lecturer in Caribbean Studies at the University of Warwick, has made a television documentary that, following Eric Williams's earlier *Capitalism and Slavery* ([1994/1944), uncovers some of these. *Art of Darkness* (1987) explores the extent to which all the "high art" and "high architecture" (England's "stately homes" so beloved of American tourists) that characterized 17th and 18th century British high culture were materially *and* aesthetically embedded in the slave trade and in the practices of racialized "forgetting" that long pre-date "modernity," the condition with which such racism is more usually associated in ethnic art criticism.

[A word about such forgetting. The publicity brochure for the Museum for African Art features a figure from Zaire (Fig.2.1), loaned by Mr. and Mrs. J.P. DePannemaeker-Simplelaere. The

Fig.2.1. Double Bowl Figure
Collection of Mr. and Mrs. J.P. DePannemaeker-Simplelaere
Photo courtesy of the Museum for African Art

photographed figure hides a terrible history. Belgian conquest and imperial rule, the cruelest in Africa, made these collections of Zairean art possible, as the Belgian name of the owners of this figure would tell museum visitors if only they could read beyond the brochure's silences.]

THE MUSEUM FOR AFRICAN ART

The Center for African Art was founded in 1982 by a group of wealthy collectors who served as the first board of directors. The Center was quasiprivate, supported by a combination of public and corporate funding, but, unlike the National Museum of the American Indian, it was privately governed. Like the NMAI, however, this Center (later Museum) also originated in a muddle of identities and purposes that continue to trouble it today. First, its original location: in two side-by-side mansions on the Upper East Side of Manhattan (some of the most expensive real estate in the world), the museum readily represented those on its board of directors, collectors for whom African (and Native American) art offered both an outlet for their commodity fetishism and a route out of modernity, a personal escape from the urban, cold, competitive capitalist world that provided them their art-buying fortunes. These collectors, together with a staff of ethno-art curators, intended that the museum would "increase the understanding and appreciation of African art." To that end, the Center held several exhibits, each of which "explored facets of the art itself." An early statement by Susan Vogel, one of the founding directors, underscores the extent to which this Center intended to remake African art, hitherto the domain of ethnographers, anthropologists, or collector/visitors to what Vogel called "the nightmare-dream of dark otherness," into "real art." "The time has come," Vogel insisted, "to accept what Africa really is [...] to look at African art the way we look at all art."(Baldwin et al. 1987:10) Despite this universalizing determination, however, some of the early exhibitions mixed this "new" art appreciation with familiar "old" anthropology (*"Igbo Arts: Community and Cosmos"*1985) and others made no pretense of engaging the former at all, eagerly embracing the world of "folk" ethnography (*"The Essential Gourd: From the Obvious to the Ingenious"* 1986).

By 1987, however, museum directors found this mixture unsatisfying. Led by Vogel, prompted by new work in critical museology, the Center announced that it would add to its initial "art appreciation" methods those of a "forum," a place in which challenges to traditional ethnographic museum practices, including the Center's own, might unfold. That year's second exhibition, *"Perspectives: Angles on African Art,"* launched the Center into a new arena, "invit[ing] the public to look at African art anew" (Baldwin et al. 1987: frontispiece).

Here is where ethnic art entered the arena of performance. As visitors moved around various exhibits, invited to look from many angles, their experience of objects—once limited to that of the viewer peering through a glass at carefully posed, captioned artifacts—shifted. "Action" became "interaction" as seeing demanded that viewers fracture their usual museum viewing practices by looking from above, from below, behind, around, *and* by seeing objects as art, as artifact, as object, as cooking pot. Richard Schechner's 1999 analysis of such new practices is cogent: "I have a feeling that this shift is part of the 'market economy' ideology: it is necessary to create in the museum-goer a desire to touch, be in, be included, to perform along with—all as part of arousing the 'need to own' that drives a market economy."

So what were, in the last century, public expressions of a collective bourgeois consciousness, celebrations by Europe's new, mass ruling class of their accession to power that remodeled the old private, aristocratic *cabinets de curiosité* into publicly owned imperial exotica—now assumed a fresh form. This allowed the sensation (if not the experience) of a reprivatized, reindividualized ownership of still-imperial commodities. Thus in these two museums, a new need, born from the excessive private wealth of late 20th century U.S. capitalism, is emerging: to own for oneself what were (and still are) the stuff of public museums.

These overt and covert critical projects continued, gaining momentum through five years of experimental exhibitions[3] and culminating, in 1992, when the Center changed its name to the Museum for African Art and sponsored a symposium, "Africa by Design: Designing a Museum for the 21st Century." This event was followed by a move from uptown to downtown into a new location. A highly self-critical exhibition soon followed: "*Exhibitionism: Museums and African Art*," opened in 1994. A "heteroglossic" text accompanied the show, featuring not only the exhibition's internal narratives but also comments made by symposium participants and several other notable ethnographers and cultural studies scholars later interviewed by Susan Vogel (Nooter Roberts and Vogel, 1994).

All these texts (the catalogues from "*Perspectives*" and subsequent exhibitions, as well as the book *Exhibition*-ism) raise several intriguing and troubling questions. The most important of these stem from the ways various commentators consistently elided

"African art" (and, by implication, the material cultures that produced that art) and the cultural identities of people of the African diaspora. The collected remarks from both *"Perspectives"* and *"Exhibition*-ism"—uttered almost exclusively in the passive voice: "It was discussed mainly...," "It was certainly not seen...,"[4]—suggest the extent to which the Museum for African Art continued to see itself as representing and exhibiting what might be described as a white version of the much debated decades-old African assertion of *négritude*, here called merely "blackness," a quality neither geographically nor historically African. Here, for example, are words from the Museum's founding manifesto (again, note the passive voice): "The Center is founded in the belief that traditional African art, an eloquent testimony to the richness of Black culture, is one of mankind's highest achievements" (Baldwin et al. 1987:11).

Although indicative of the Museum's laudable intention to shift African art work out of its long-time Western role as primitive objects of voyeuristic anthropologists, these remarks are nonetheless replete with difficulties. One need only ask Lenin's questions: "who? whom?" Who is speaking here and to whom? Who, in other words, needs to be convinced of the "richness of black culture"? On what scale are "mankind's highest achievements" measured? Who does the measuring? And—perhaps most important of all—what constitutes the "traditional African art" that represents "blackness"?

These kinds of questions troubled the Center's 1987 exhibit, *"Perspectives: Angles on African Art,"* problems that were reflected in the catalogue accompanying the exhibition. The catalogue tells us that the Center for African Art began its curatorial task by choosing ten guest "co-curators," each fitting into one of ten categories Susan Vogel and her team had identified as those characterizing African art. They were also selected, Vogel tells us in the catalogue, because they were "individuals who are far from the old stereotypes about Africa as obscure and unknowable." How have they defied this pervasive Western stereotype? All "have made African *art* part of their *intellectual* and *aesthetic* lives" (Baldwin et al. 1987:11, emphasis added). A prime difficulty, though unrecognized by the Museum's officials, was thus immediately explicit. To know Africa, the exhibit implied, one need only know—aesthetically and intellectually—African art. And therein lay one of many problems.

The ten co-curators included white Americans—Nancy Graves, Ivan Karp, David Rockefeller, William Rubin, Robert Farris Thompson—and black Americans—James Baldwin and Romare Bearden. Two Western-trained African museum professionals, Ekpo Eyo and Iba N'Diaye, together with one African artist, Lela Kouakou, filled out this nearly all-male and heavily North American assemblage. The center's director, Susan Vogel, treated nine of the ten "curators" identically, offering each a set of 100 photographs of objects from which they were asked to choose a few for exhibition. Strikingly, however, the tenth curator, Lela Kouakou, a sculptor from Côte d'Ivoire, was treated differently. Vogel's own words explain: This Baulé artist, though not the only African, or the only artist, was the only one, in Vogel's judgment, "familiar only with the art of his own people." In her eyes this meant that he could not select any but Baulé objects. Why? Here is Vogel's explanation: "Field aesthetic studies, my own and others, have shown that African informants will criticize sculptures from other ethnic groups in terms of their own traditional criteria, often assuming that such works are simply inept carvings of their own aesthetic tradition" (Baldwin et al. 1987:17).

I am not the only one to be startled by such arrogance. This selection process—and the resulting exhibition—drew an immediate, hostile reaction from Anthony Appiah, published in *In My Father's House* (1992). It is not necessary to recount the whole of Appiah's very sophisticated argument, but suffice it to note here that what most offended him was Susan Vogel's "Eurocentrism." He does a lovely job of satirizing the words recorded above—by quoting David Rockefeller and others who, needless to say, always and everywhere "criticize sculptures from other ethnic groups" without the least concern that their criteria are drawn from "their own traditions." As "we" all know, *these* criteria are "universal."

This abbreviated version of Appiah's much more complicated reactions exposes some of the power relations present within this Center from the start. Another example comes from the symposium, "Africa By Design," some of its deliberations recorded in an accompanying text, *Exhibition*-ism. Although I saw the subsequent exhibition, and was troubled by the problems of perspective I saw reflected there, I visited only as a tourist, not then involved in writing about ethnic art museums. I shall therefore restrict my remarks here to the published text.

Marking the planned move from the Upper East Side to a downtown location, the symposium drew several participants including some who had been co-curators in 1987—Ekpo Eyo, Robert Farris Thompson—as well as three new African voices— Ayuko Babu, dele jegede, and Jean-Aimé Rakotoariosoa. Other U.S. museum professionals (this time including more than one woman)—Carol Duncan, Labelle Prussin, Enid Schildkrout, and Fred Wilson—joined in the project to delineate a collective version of the "ideal" "black" museum. Shortly after, Susan Vogel and Mary Nooter Roberts produced a text describing these discussions, adding a handful of new voices to the symposium's "dialogue." Taken from interviews conducted by Vogel, fragments of the ideas of Michael Brenson, James Clifford, John Conklin, Arthur Danto, Maureen Healy, Ivan Karp, and Barbara Kirshenblatt-Gimblett formed a counterdialogue, printed in bold type alongside the main text. All were the voices of well-known museum critics or professionals with the exception of that of Maya Lin, the architect chosen to design the new location's interior spaces.[5]

Despite the intention to provide readers with a provocatively multivocal conversation, between white and black, African (and Asian?) and American, the project evidently proved untenable. Throughout the text, African scholars and critics contested the textual siting of the museum's "Euro-center," while its representatives reiterated its "universality." Here, for example, is an African commentary by Jean-Aimé Rakotoarisoa:

> The problem is, who decides that such and such an object is a good object and is representative of African art? [...] There is very little effort given to ask *Africans* what they might think of such displays. [...] We have to rethink our vocabulary—for example, the opposition between what is religious and what is secular.[...] As a matter of fact, this ratio could be inverted. For example, for me a Christian would be a secular person

as far as my religion is concerned (quoted in Nooter
Roberts and Vogel 1994:38).

Carol Duncan, an American art historian specializing in the
period of the French Revolution, replied, patronizingly, "You're
talking about a museum in New York City and not a museum
in Africa.[...] In our culture," she explained as though to a child,
"when you build a big building and call it a museum and you put
things in it, that means you [?] respect those things a lot" (quoted
in Nooter Roberts and Vogel 1994:53).

Here's another, similarly pointless, exchange in which James
Clifford, trapped in his own cultural predicament, declared himself
part of another Euro-space, that of universal aesthetic experience:
"Everyone," he announced, "has a dream of being alone with a
great show. [...] Take all the other people out and encounter a kind
of sublime response." Ayuko Babu tried again, tactfully, to shift *his*
center: "Well, there's always a struggle, you know, between cultural
consumption and cultural experience. You want to make sure that
you give experience as opposed to cultural consumption, because
the people with guidebooks are into cultural consumption. You
want to be able to stop them so they have the cultural experience"
(quoted in Nooter Roberts and Vogel 1994:48). But his words, too,
fell on deaf ears. Throughout the symposium, white participants
and black participants, Americans and Africans, continued to
dance around every single issue, one side trying to suggest that
there *are* other ways of seeing, the other trying to explain that "we"
all really see the same.

In the same period, a much less slickly produced work offered
an alternative to claims about African art's "universality." *Museums
and the Community in West Africa*, a collection of reports from the
West African Museums Programme, includes a compelling essay
by Alpha Oumar Konare that pleads for the maintenance of ties
between objects and their worlds, as well as between museums
and their communities. "To conserve an object," writes Konare,
"means to preserve it, but it also means keeping the language that
surrounds it. An object is conserved when its continued use is
assured (1995:8).

There are other, similarly problematic exchanges and statements throughout the catalogue. Ivan Karp (anthropologist and long-time curator of African art at the Smithsonian Institution) joined his voice to Carol Duncan's to describe what he believed to be a common experience of contemporary "shock" museum exhibits. Both had previously visited an exhibition held at Washington, D.C.'s American History Museum, a narrative "about black migration from the South to the North." Karp recalled: "At one point in order to go from one room to another, you have to go through a door marked 'Colored' or a door marked 'White.' You have to. And people back up, they pause, they hesitate. They don't know whether to make a gesture or obey the rule—they have to confront 'Why am I doing this'"? (quoted in Nooter Roberts and Vogel 1994:52). Duncan agreed, adding, "I have never been more moved in any exhibition anywhere than by that exhibition." Her subsequent remarks suggest, however, that it was less the choice of doors that affected her than it was another scene in the exhibit:

> There was a cutaway of an actual train from the 'teens or '20s, and in that train was a mannequin of a single young woman asleep. [...] It was very, very quiet. There was just one figure and I suddenly got scared—I felt frightened. I realized that, God, I just [fell asleep on a train and the exhibit] made me [re]live an experience of traveling, of being alone, of there not being any noise [...] I have never had such a real experience before in a museum (Nooter Roberts and Vogel 1994:53).

Such fatuity, lying there naked for all who can see to see, is surely far more painful than either of these moments experienced by two highly privileged people in a national museum in their nation's capital! Does Ivan Karp *really* believe that "we" all hesitate before such doors? What statement would any person of color be making by not walking through the door marked for their forbears? Could Karp imagine, too, that *some* people of color would much rather walk through a door marked "colored" than one marked "white" (not to mention "anthropologist")? And does Carol Duncan really consider her 1990s journey from New Jersey to a Washington, D.C. museum to be even remotely similar to that employment-seeking trip undertaken by the isolated young black female figure depicted

Figure 2.2. Altar exhibited in "*Face of the Gods*" (1993)
Susan Vogel and Mary Nooter Roberts write that these altars "were treated by their public as if they were sanctified - indeed, they had been. The interactions of visitors with the works on display added a new spiritual dimension to the museum experience of African art." (Nooter Roberts and Vogel, 1994: 50)

Photo courtesy of the Museum for African Art.

in this diorama of segregation's truths? Did no one interviewing these museum scholars notice these articulations of North America's vast racial divide? Evidently not. Both lengthy quotations are printed without comment on facing pages of *Exhibition*-ism.

The main text is similarly fraught. Mary Nooter Roberts's long essay includes a discussion of a 1993 museum exhibit, curated by Robert Farris Thompson. "*Face of the Gods: Art and Altars of Africa and the African Americas*" offered "twenty or so [!] altars, from diverse centers of Afro-Atlantic worship." Some, she explains, were "real"—"originally made for use and transported from their sites"—others were commissioned by the museum "from artist practitioners of the religions in question," and still others were "re-creations of both historical and contemporary but untransportable altars, designed and fabricated, from photographs, by the museum's exhibition team" (Nooter Roberts and Vogel 1994:52).

The curators anticipated two problems, that of displaying publicly objects of religious practice and that of juxtaposing widely differing religions. Preexhibition debates apparently raged among Museum staff, debates about "authenticity," about "the aesthetic and ethical implications of activation and desacralization, and about the presentation of living religious works for museum presentation." In the end, however, curators satisfied themselves that presenting religious artifacts from religions such as Santería and Candomblé was acceptable since both were highly syncretic religions anyway.

Curators soon discovered (to their evident relief) that the exhibition altars were quickly transformed from "dead" museum exhibits into "living" altars by museum visitors who made offerings to all three kinds of altars indiscriminately, thus giving them, in the curators' words, "life" (see Fig. 2.2).

Of course Mary Nooter Roberts could not leave it at that, respecting practices of which she had only a remote understanding. Instead, she had to bring these gestures into her world, making all this *art*. Hers is the familiar language of art gallery sale catalogues: "These offerings were not merely visible signs of engagement," she concluded, smugly, "but also acts of innovation —contributions to the creative process."(Nooter Roberts and Vogel 1994:53) But were the people who added coins or objects to the altars *really* "contributing to the creative process"? Or were their acts those of believers whose god (unlike the god of New York's Upper East Side) manifests everywhere, even inside the Museum for African Art? Even more chillingly Eurocentric were the similar misapprehensions of Robert Farris Thompson, the exhibit's main curator. According to Nooter Roberts, Thompson agreed with her observation that in Africa such "'exhibitions' [sic] [...] are staged in the spaces of everyday existence, of which they are often a part.[...] This practice," Thompson assured Roberts, "extends to the African-Americas where altars can be found in laundry bins, closets, beaches, yards, and vehicles—a range of sites different from but no less startling than that on the African continent" (Nooter Roberts and Vogel 1994:58, 77 n2).

"To whom, to whom?" cries Minerva's owl, hovering over lower Broadway.

Still, despite the Euro-blinders worn by its officials, the Museum for African Art *has* succeeded in some of its project. Vogel and her cocurators have disturbed the comfortable world of African art collecting and display, challenging some of the "exhibitionary complex" of most African art museums. One traveling exhibit, "*ART/artifact*," designed by Vogel to demonstrate "how the installation makes the African artwork," or "where you stand influences what you see" (Vogel 1988:111)—aroused considerable hostility from Dallas museumgoers and newspaper critics because its "contrived purposes" "hid" beauty from would-be beholders. Vogel is right to be proud of having elicited such a strong response with an exhibit aimed to do just that although this readily caricatured "Dallas aesthetic" was perhaps an easy target.

But interestingly, Vogel has published nothing critical about the next exhibition's strikingly revealing catalogue. *The Art of Collecting African Art* (Vogel 1988b) unveils the stories of the weird and, to my mind, perverse relationships between wealthy collectors and "their" African artifacts, individual pieces that they possess (and display in their home galleries, neoaristocratic *cabinets de curiosité*) detached completely from African people, African time, and African place. In the process of preparing this exhibition, Vogel encouraged the lenders to accompany their chosen objects with narratives of possession, which she then edited and published at the time of the exhibit. These testimonies document an extraordinary degree of commodity worship. George and Gail Feher confessed their "obsession." Over the years of their collecting, they tell us, "the objects themselves [became] the ultimate satisfaction!" Daniel and Marian Malcolm admitted that "The discovery of new objects in unexpected places is continually a high! [...] It was insidious," they continue, "somewhere around 1963 we realized that seeing and getting pieces was very meaningful for us—we began to look forward to the next piece"(in Vogel 1988b:16, 22).[6] (I am reminded of one Native American's response to this shopping mall ethos: "Americans," said Robert Thomas in 1994, "confuse consumption with experience.")

This compulsive desire to own *things* underlay all the collectors' remarks. More tellingly, each of their statements underscored the extent of their appropriation of African material culture, an appropriation that the Center, at least according to much of their publicity, intended to challenge. These collectors' African possessions, as many photographs accompanying various Museum catalogues show, inhabit their Upper East Side New York world, completely isolated from origins. Nowhere in these testimonies did any of the collectors so much as imply that a knowledge of Africa, of the realities of the people who made *their* objects, mattered. Ernst Anspach, for example, blithely admitted that he had "never been to Africa." He explained that he didn't think "going is very important to collecting." "For Mr. Anspach," Vogel explained,"the African context is not important at all for an understanding of the objects *except where it helps inform him about the probable authenticity* [read "market value"] of an object"(Vogel 1988b:40).

Is it hopeless? Is the Euro-center unmovable? Well, the Museum's oft-repeated claim to a diasporic identity is not entirely unjustified. Despite the foci of its many exhibitions, despite the behind-the-scenes control of the space and its contents, despite its many Euro-centered texts, the Museum for African Art, like the altars displayed in *"Faces of the Gods,"* has, to some extent at least, been re-appropriated by the African diasporic communities of New York City. These communities use the Museum to see, discuss, and experience some of the material cultures of Africa. Many black New Yorkers, as well as tourists visiting from elsewhere, come to use the space, often in ways Vogel and the other founding directors probably did not anticipate.

Some of these (mildly) counterhegemonic practices come about because of the nature of the SoHo space to which the Museum moved in the early 1990s. Although not designed by someone from the "rich black culture" of the Center's universalist dreams, the long, wide vestibule space originally held—scattered about on benches and on floor mats—dozens of African objects for touching and close observation (and purchase: everything here is for sale at modest prices). I should note that things have changed. By 1998, the open displays of goods for sale had been joined by locked cases, where more valuable goods are now kept. There is also a space where books—for children and adults—are for sale—or for reading on the comfortable chairs provided. I have been there when African American parents were reading African storybooks to their children, when children by themselves were choosing and buying books. The last time I visited, a small boy, Haitian by his very shy French, had spread out his drawings of Haitian scenes, of birds and trees and people, portrayed, I thought anyway, with considerable subtlety and sophistication. I was moved by his presence there—and more by the fact that the four people "in charge," two African American women, one African American man, and an African man, did not do what the guards (almost all African American) at the National Museum of the American Indian would without question have done and have done very very quickly: that is, throw him out.[7] Instead they let him use the small space among the children's books to roll out his drawings and attract buyers.

To some extent, then, *people* have re-created this space into a kind of "counterspace" that defies the control of the wealthy collectors and scholars who sit on its board and create its exhibitions. But a problem remains here, shared, though in a slightly different way, by the National Museum of the American Indian. Those of the African diasporic community who come to this Center seeking "roots," seeking identity, those who bring their children to see black culture, to buy black books and artifacts, participate, whatever their intentions, in the "timeless, a-political Africa" decried by Jean-Aimé Rakotoarisoa (quoted in Nooter Roberts and Vogel 1994:53). To oversimplify, an Afrocentric appropriation of Eurocentric displays of African art ignores, I think, what Manthia Diawara calls "the texts" [...] "the lived experiences of black people." Without such texts, all objects, every representation, stand isolated from history, symbols only of a romanticized, uncomplicated, and, most importantly to Diawara, hopelessly *ahistorical* Africa. Such appropriations Diawara sees as just another twist on ethnocentrism: this he calls "Americocentricity" (Diawara 1992:289).

This Africa, then, is not very different from the Africa "collected" by rich white collectors, ethnographers, modernist artists. It serves not to transform, not to transgress, the marginalized identity of "otherness." Rather, as Diawara and others argue, it merely perpetuates the cafeteria approach that characterizes contemporary

U.S. "multiculturalism." Here, the gazes of diasporic black people, as well as those of white museumgoers, fix an Africa as invented as that created long ago by European imperialists. So Gina Dent asks, "Do we, peoples of the African diaspora, any longer have the right to invent an Africa?" (1992:7). Coco Fusco adds: "For black peoples [and, as I'll observe shortly, for Native American peoples], at this historical moment, the postmodern fetishizing of the exchange of cultural property seems less like emancipation and more like intensified alienation" (quoted in Dent 1992:7). Or, as Richard Schechner might put it, more like a leap into a *global* turn-of-the-20th century market economy (1999).

ONE EXHIBIT OBSERVED

All these aspects of the Museum for African Art's exhibitionary complexes cry out for a more thoroughgoing deconstruction. But there is space for but one more analysis, this focused on the Museum's spring 1998 exhibit, *"African Faces, African Figures: the Arman Collection,"*[8] an exhibition that postdates Susan Vogel's 1994 departure from the Museum. Here is *The New York Times*'s notice (Fri. March 20, 1998:38):

> The excellent collection [...] that the French artist Arman has amassed and carefully culled during the last 40 years is one of the season's best exhibitions. High points among the 180 works from Central and West Africa include dense accumulations of nearly identical objects, creating a revealing dialogue between tradition and individual interpretation

This "clustering," of many objects of the same kind is meant to allow viewers to perceive the "universal" aesthetic pleasures embodied in them. But such an exhibition plan not only replicates that mark of contemporary capitalist culture, the plethora of similar commodities available to avid shoppers, but it also reproduces all the dozens of "timeless Africa" exhibits I have already mentioned. How could it be otherwise when objects from all over sub-Saharan Africa, "typed" by anthropological categories, are "massed" into a single case, a single room? Still, I was curious so I paid my money and went in.

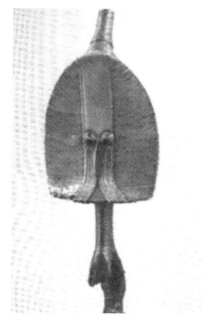

Figure 2.3. Reliquary guardian from Mahongwe, Gabon
Exhibited in 1990.
Photo courtesy of the Museum for African Art.

In the entryway hung a vast, 12-foot glass case full of brass faces. They were identical: round, wearing crowns and earrings, standing on triangular "bodies." Some were very large: three or four feet, some smaller. Each pair of eyes—"clustered" for aesthetic effect—stared from the case at the viewer, supposedly crying "we are beautiful," "we represent Africa" or some similar claim from the exhibit's brochure. But not every museum visitor heard these words. Some knew, some others, surely, read the signs mounted next to this first case: these were *reliquary objects*, faces made to live in homes, commemorating and honoring ancestors. They once belonged to (were made by) "ancestral societies."

So how did Arman "collect" them? No word here, or in the following "clusters," though more wall placards explained, in familiar ethno-speak, the origins, the meanings, and the "universal" qualities of the objects. From all over "sub-Saharan Africa," the placards tell us, four kinds of objects had been seized, sold, and

59

then massed, initially in Arman's home, now, temporarily, in the Museum for African Art (where they are "massed" to reflect not their African contexts but rather the site of their current possession). First are more funerary objects, all once belonging either to ancestor societies or to family memorials or graves (see Fig. 2.3); second, sacred masks made and used by secret women's and men's societies; third, divination figures; fourth, power figures. These latter included fecundity sculptures plus stools and other objects, each of which, we were duly informed, (formerly?) legitimated the authority of chiefs, elders, and so on.

Many questions are begged here: how and why were so many sacred objects sold to Arman or his predecessors? By what right, beyond the naked right of victorious conquest, were they removed from their time and place? Where were the members of those bereaved families, those no-longer secret societies, those ruling elites whose ceremonial objects no longer lived in Africa? What effects had such a significant loss of material culture had on those people all over Africa commemorated in this funeral procession, this parade of "victor's spoils"? (I overheard only one visitor's comment during this visit: an African woman, peering into a case full of ceremonial masks from a formerly secret women's society, exclaimed to her companion, "How did they *get* these?") But what an irony, too. This Arman show unselfconsciously opened and closed with its own damning visual commentary: the final case, too, held "reliquary objects," clearly marking, at least for some of us, the funereal character of Arman's "obsession."

INDIAN COUNTRY, U.S.A.

The rather subtle narrative of death told through the Arman exhibit brings me, finally, to the National Museum of the American Indian, first named, significantly, the National *Memorial* Museum of the American Indian. Here death wears no disguises. At the George Gustav Heye Center in lower Manhattan, the Museum seizes *its* role in the funeral procession, indeed much more straightforwardly. In no way a site of resistance, a counter-space, or even a place where Native people come seeking roots, this "national" museum, explored in depth in Chapter 3, is little more than a vast mausoleum. Its spatial and ideological narratives tell the story of the murder, burial, and resurrection of survivors, now "our" Indians, America's quaint and exotic past. As in the Museum for African Art's many exhibitions, hundreds of artifacts assume multiple roles in a vast performance, though here the stage set is less like a shopping mall and more like Disneyland. Rather than evoking the desire to possess commodities, this museum's exhibits let visitors experience ethnicity. In a mockery of decades of Hollywood's white Cochises and Geronimos, "braves," and "squaws," non-Native visitors come to the NMAI to spend a few hours playing "Indian."

I'd like to demonstrate this part of my argument by taking a brief tour of the inaugural exhibitions, linked together in a metaphor of movement. *"Creation's Journey: Masterworks of Native American Identity and Belief"* is first, followed by *"All Roads Are Good"* and *"This Path We Travel: Celebrations of Contemporary Native American Creativity."* (Each exhibit is further divided: visitors move from one exhibit to another without always realizing it.) I begin outside the building. In stark contrast to the SoHo space that then held the Museum for African Art, the Heye Center's building *began* as a monument, one celebrating the high capitalism of the gilded age. Opened in 1904, the Alexander Hamilton Customs House sits, appropriately enough, just behind the three-quarters' life-size Wall Street bull. The neoclassical building's friezes, its vast sculptures of the four continents, its heavily ornamented and painted central dome all celebrate the "discovery," the conquest, and the resulting profits. Male Indians, all alike in their half-nakedness, their feathers and paint, decorate both the outside and the interior spaces of early 20th century building.

The Heye Center itself is a result of the 1989 merging of two Indian collections: that of the quasi-private Museum of the American Indian which housed George Heye's vast personal collection of art, artifacts, and human "remains," and that of "America's Museum," the Smithsonian, which had long owned a considerable Indian collection also including some 20,000 Indian skeletons. Both bones and millions of symbols of cultural destruction thus lie at the heart of this "new," this "Indian," this "American" museum. Here in the Heye Center the objects (no one mentions the bones) inhabit a spatio-temporal tale of conquest and recuperation, a

Figure 2.4. The photograph, captioned "Beaded Moccasins, ca. 1860. Upper Missouri River" appears in the *Creation's Journey* catalogue (Hill and Hill, 1994:7). Photo courtesy of the National Museum of the American Indian.

spectacle of death and reincarnation. In this museum, Native people emerge from their historical graves as Indians, denizens of America's historic theme park, essential cogs in the vast machine of forgetting that here, like Kafka's penal colony punishment mechanism, inscribes the master narrative of "our" United States on the bodies of tribal people.[9]

Briefly, then, here are the stages in this Museum's narrative. First, monuments to mark the dead. (A bitter irony: Many of the artifacts here are, in fact, *from* graves, stolen by grave robbers who continue to pillage Native burial sites wherever objects of market value—including bones, which are still collected on a black market—are thought to lie.) The opening exhibit, *"Creation's Journey: Masterworks of Native American Identity and Belief,"* lays out a vast cemetery of exquisite objects, what the Museum calls its "Masterworks": a Crow war shield, a stunning Pomo basket, an exquisitely beaded bandolier bag, an intriguing Zuni bird figure, two beaded buckskin moccasins. The accompanying catalogue, in the glossy style of the most expensive coffeetable art books, illustrates many of these "masterworks" in exquisite, large scale photographs (see Fig. 2.4).

Who selected *these* objects? Although the curatorial machinations of this museum are considerably less transparent than those behind the much smaller Museum for African Art's exhibits, visitors to "Masterworks" are told that many Native people were involved in choosing and annotating exhibits. As is the case throughout the Museum, each such person is authenticated by tribal identity, marked in the parentheses familiar to every Native American. Despite such obvious efforts to lend the exhibition (and the Museum) a clear "Native" identity (the stated *raison d'être* of this "new museum"), most of those involved here bear no such authenticating markers and are, in fact, non-Native.

Each selected object, each "masterwork," sits isolated inside a heavy glass case, background draped with expensive fabric, lighting focused "boutique" fashion. Every design element cries commodity value—and tells of the utter isolation of each object from its own time and place. These rooms constitute a vast monument to the murder of Native peoples, of their bodies, their cultures, their world views. "We" killed them, reads the subtext, and now look at us recuperating them as "art." In other words, "we" have rescued, collected, and preserved all that was valuable of "theirs." (When I walk through these rooms I cannot help thinking of the invasion as a great neutron bomb, that dream weapon of the Cold War, technological teleology of the Cartesian revolution, a device

Figure 2.5. The Appeal to the Great Spirit (1909)
Cyrus Dallin's statue stands in front of the Boston Museum of Fine Arts.
Photo courtesy of the Museum of Fine Arts, Boston, c 2000, (all rights reserved).

that kills all living things but leaves everything else untouched and ready for collection.)

Next we encounter the ideological justification for the conquest, an exhibit titled "Growing Up Indian." This display is set in a long, narrow, dark hallway. Here stand six human-sized glass cases, each containing, at eye level, "Indian" toys. Behind loom huge twice-human-size photographs of tribal children: an Apache adolescent, a pair of Comanche girls, an Osage child, and so on. In contrast to the carefully posed "beautiful" Edward Curtis photographs familiar to most Americans, these are "before" pictures. Individuals here are unkempt, still "wild." These are savages. But the fact that such children played with these crude little dolls and tepees and toy ponies just as white children play with *their* toys shows that inside all the savagery they possessed "universals," the capacity to become "us" once "we gave them our civilization.

Beyond this "before" exhibit lies another problematic stage. Here is Indian resistance, represented by its most famous manifestation, the Ghost Dance.[10] Of course here this movement, which swept the Plains and much of the West and Southwest (though in different forms) in the final quarter of the 19th century takes the form created by anthropologists.[11]

It is not a vast, organized movement of pantribal political resistance but rather a quaint and atavistic manifestation of despair, the feelings "we" think Indians *must* have been feeling as they watched the destruction (by whom?) of their world, feelings constantly represented in the public art of the period in sculptures like the huge bronze, "Appeal to the Great Spirit" that stands today outside Boston's Museum of Fine Art (see Fig. 2.5). (There were lots of others, each bearing a chilling title: "End of the Trail," "The Last Brave," and so on.)

The Ghost Dance itself, I learned in an obligatory anthropology class in the early 1960s, was a slightly mad dance of "near-ghosts," a collective expression of the utter despair Plains Indians felt once they became aware of their complete defeat at the hands of the whites. This version of Ghost Dancers' stupidity explained why all those poor hapless Indians died in the Army massacre at Wounded Knee in 1890. The ignorant Indians, according to subsequent ethnographers and historians, believed that if they danced, white bullets couldn't kill them. If they danced, and kept dancing, the white invaders would disappear while the buffalo returned. Thus all those nearly 300 unarmed women, children, and old men, whose bodies were first stripped of saleable artifacts and then photographed before being dumped into hiding beneath the earth, had refused to surrender to the cavalry because they foolishly thought they could

Figure 2.6. This image shows a girl's dress (ca. 1850, Northern Plains) exhibited at the Heye Center, NMAI, though shown here without its cement occupant.
Photo from Hill and Hill (1994:39), courtesy of the National Museum of the American Indian

not be killed. By killing them all, the cavalry demonstrated to other Ghost Dancers that this primitive superstition did not work.

What was it about this Ghost Dancing that so threatened the U. S. government that they sent the cavalry to kill old people and children suspected of participating? A few recognized that the dancing was not merely the pathetic attempt of a broken people to resume their old, "savage" ways. Some army officers and a few Indian agents understood that its practice constituted a pan-Indian rebellion against the invading whites. As most Natives knew, Ghost Dancers were combining religion, ceremonies, and theater with politics just as Native people had done before the invasion (see Schechner 1993:35). By dancing, by worshipping in an intensely *Indian* way—and in public, in the face of white agents, white cavalry soldiers, and white invaders ("settlers")—Ghost Dancers were challenging both the invasion and its consequent white hegemony which on the Great Plains in the 1870s and 1880s showed itself in constant government-issued, Indian agent-enforced prohibitions.

Trapped on reservations, Native people were forbidden their holy people, their ceremonies, their religious objects, and even the rearing of their own children, as this was the era when attendance at federal boarding schools became compulsory, as "memorialized" at NMAI and discussed below. The Ghost Dance rituals, which drew together hundreds and sometimes thousands of related Indian bands and nations for days-long public ceremonies, were as "in your face" as possible, evoking the sort of terror of masses of "wild savages" Laura Ingalls Wilder and dozens of other white female writers were depicting in their hundreds of best-selling, pioneer celebrating narratives (Hilden 1994:59-63). The point of these ceremonies was not only confrontational, however. Native people believed then, and believe now, that painstaking attention to one's ceremonial life always accompanies the kind of careful attention to one's political and moral life that constitutes a good journey through this world. By dancing, and undertaking the other essential ceremonies they were *creating*: an *Indian* world, an Indian self, a Native people, a Native politics (see Ostler 1995).

The version of the Ghost Dance presented here in the "Indians' Museum" makes no mention of the political nature of the Ghost Dance, or of the facts of the government's bloody suppression of its practice.[12] What **is** here is a carefully gendered grave: grey colored cement figures of two girls—one an adolescent, one a child—stand facing one another, smiling. Behind, looming over their grey cement braids, hangs a ghostly symbol of masculinity: America's favorite Indian, the generic Plains warrior, represented by a large, elaborate eagle-feather war bonnet. It is empty, its noble owner now, no doubt, "vanished." A burglar-proof plexiglass box shields this diorama of death—from thieves, but also from viewers who might want to look through the beads and quills and feathers of the ghost dance dresses for bullet holes (see Fig. 2.6). (One German visitor, an Internet designer from Dusseldorf, was less moved by the Museum than his fellow tourists: "I miss something about the destruction of Indians by the European conquerors," he wrote guardedly on his visitors' questionnaire.)

So much for resistance, then, in "our" museum. Here, visitors pause to mourn just another "famous last stand." The Ghost Dance movement thus becomes yet another marker of the tragic passing of America's "wild" past. Thus these grey cement figures, together with the empty Ghost dancer's war bonnet, mark another tomb in this cemetery of Native America.

Just around another corner lies another stage, this a transition, from "blanket Indian" to "progressive," assimilated capitalist Indian. There are two representations: first another grey cement figure, an adult female, clad in traditional Osage clothing and blanket and carrying a traditional Osage cradleboard. This figure is dead. Surrounding her are others, however. Some 150 people are presented "live" in a vast wall mural photograph from the 1920s that encircles the diorama. Here are white people as well as both "blanket" and "progressive" Osages, the latter marked by modernity: bobbed hair and cloche hats for the women, three-piece suits, wing collars, and fedoras for the men. The people are engaged in some commercial transaction—probably the buying and selling of the Osage's oil. These Indians, then, belong to the "modern" capitalist world. Still, the forgetting machine operates here, too. There are the assimilated Osages who led the tribal council in the 1920s, who made the oil deals with white corporations, who accumulated vast personal fortunes infamous across the white Oklahoma of the time. But here are also those traditional Osages whose oil and land and, too often, lives, were stolen by some of these same white people—in a rampage of murder and fraud that ultimately drove Washington bureaucrats to send in the FBI, though, as both John Joseph Mathews and Linda Hogan have suggested in their novels, not in time to bring the murderers and thieves to justice (Mathews 1988/1934; Hogan 1990).

The second exhibition marking this inaugural event is "*All Roads Are Good*." Museum visitors learn that the things they are seeing were selected by 23 prominent Native Americans invited to New York by the Museum directors. These selectors were taken to the vast Bronx warehouses storing George Heye's vast collection from which they chose those objects they wanted exhibited in the first displays. These selectors are listed in the inaugural brochures and catalogues. Their names, together with edited clips taken from the videotapes of their Bronx visits, appear throughout the Museum, their tribal identities "legitimating" both the exhibits and the Museum itself. The variety of their origins (Gerald McMaster, Cree, from Canada, Edgar Perry, White Mountain Apache, from Arizona, Miguel Puwainchir, Shuar, from Bolivia) testifies to the Museum's inclusiveness, its commitment to, in the words of the founding director, Richard West Jr., "the many voices that are Native America" (quoted in Hill and Hill 1994). One voice is not heard, however. Victor Masayesva, Hopi filmmaker, was in fact one of the original invitees, the 24th selector. He had accepted the invitation and had come to New York. He had gone to the Bronx. While in the warehouses, however, he had failed to select any objects for exhibit. Frustrated, his "minders" (each Native was accompanied by at least one non-Native museum curator as well as a video team) had asked him why he was not choosing. According to gleeful eyewitnesses, distressed by the revelations of the storehouse's previously hidden record of theft and destruction, Masayesva replied: "Oh, I'm not here to select things to show in your museum. I'm here to find out what you have so we can get them back" (Huhndorf 1994). Nowhere does the Museum tell *this* story, the fearful possibility of repatriation—now prescribed by law—that threatens this and every Indian show with the loss of all ceremonial and sacred objects (as well as the seldom-acknowledged bones). Thus the disappearance of repatriation-minded Victor Masayesva's voice from most Museum texts is not surprising.[13]

So behind this National Museum of the American Indian monument to the triumph of capitalism over tribalism lies yet another hidden tale, another story of death, another notice that when Indians die (even metaphorically, as we shall see) it will be whites who take over.

Another stage continues this saga of death, though here it is the death not of peoples or cultures but rather of "Mother Earth," here altered to suit more Western ideas into "Father Earth." A Great Plains burial scaffolding divides one exhibition space from the next. Atop lies what at first looks like an Indian man's body. Non-Indian Museum visitors may "read," may grasp the intentions of, this display more quickly since they are not shocked by what the scaffolding or the invitation to walk under it represent to Indians. They may see that the body is meant to represent capitalism. They may quickly see that this body does not wear traditional Plains clothing but rather is covered in bits of the US flag, in dollar bills, in gas masks, and so on. They may recognize the message: that what capitalist white America now needs from its dead, its vanished indigenous people is drawn from the Indians of positive stereotype. It is their lack of materialism, their spirituality, their ability to live *with* the earth that once again made Indians popular in what was then America's *fin-de-siècle* distress. (Of course here, too, Native America offers much willing acquiescence, many tribal people claiming a special relationship with Mother Earth, and embracing those New Age tourists who venture into Indian Country seeking solace and solutions.)

Just in case anyone passing beneath this burial scaffolding (or beside it, since the Museum offers an alternative route for squeamish Native people or their friends) wonders, the next displays carry the viewer straight through a death and spiritual re-birth of white capitalist America (which re-shapes itself around Indian spiritual traditions) while at the same time narrating the successful re-birth of the Indian as a white man. "*This Path We Travel*," in other words, offers a universalist rebirth, created by Indians for their non-Native friends. Here, the market value of Indian spirituality is on show, exhibiting the value of Indians as New Age tourist destination. These spaces comprise the metaphysical side of the artifact coin—the side inviting non-Indians to take whatever they like of the Native spirituality they so admired during the course of the conquest. (Tourists are glad to possess this, too. Here are samples of visitors' comments left recently at the Heye Center. A professor from Amsterdam: "we could feel/hear the heartbeat." A New York actress: "entrancing, a little sad." A businessperson from Silicon Valley was "left with a sense of peacefulness," while a N.Y. social worker gushed, "wonderful, peaceful, serene, enlightening, spiritual." Having read all the Museum's propaganda about how this was an "Indian" museum, she added, "Thank you for sharing!")

Next, Native artists, 3 women and 3 men, all chosen, assembled, and paid by the Museum's directors, offer the results of their year-long collaboration. The women give us birth, represented as though they had all spent too much time at Judy Chicago's infamous *Dinner Party*. Wombs are everywhere in the "women's space": in the circles of text surrounding each portrait of an "important Indian woman"; in the little cave structures through which visitors pass as they follow a long sinuous snake figure winding along the floor; in the spiderwebs of light that form sacred circles on the floor and through which each visitor must pass; in the endless procession of big round clay pots, tilted on their sides, spilling fake food and water onto this women's floor, in the "ecofeminist" goddess shrine. A caption reads: *Deep within our souls/the Goddess awakens/ Changing, Shifting/a new time nigh/Now the Sister rebirths/ and our hearts/know the story unfolding...*

Once reborn, bodily and spiritually (flute music, brought to life by a step on the floor snake's large, glittering glass eye, sounds this latter moment), we then enter the male world, a forest of vast, 10-foot-tall phalluses, each marked at eye level by the clichéd detritus that signal "Indianness" in the contemporary world. Tied on with rawhide are dream catchers, feathers and beads, bone, and so on. This space is Donna Haraway's nightmare patriarchy. In the context of the contemporary U.S., it celebrates the rebirth of the Indian as a multicultural Euro-patriarch, a gigantic phallic presence clothed in the kitsch of the New Age. What *is* left of "Indian," then, here in this resurrection scene, is a male cartoon Indian, tellingly provided by Native artists trapped in their own colonized minds.

Stage six brings us at last to the final victory wherein "the Indian" is the multicultural modern subject. The exhibit walks visitors through two sites of celebration: first, a turn-of-the-century schoolroom. Individual slanted top wooden desks, lined up in neat rows open to reveal schoolbooks and paper, pencils and pens. Inkwells sit empty on desk tops carved with initials, hearts and arrows, and other such *universal* childish symbols. In front a familiar set: teacher's desk, chalkboard, U.S. flag.

Still, this *is* an Indian museum. Some tourists may even know that few Indians (of the 250,000 remaining in 1900) attended local public schools. There were strict segregation laws in some places, bigoted school boards in others. So the exhibit bows in two directions: tourism and truth. The room, wall placards explain, is a reproduction not of an ordinary public school but rather of a "typical" Indian boarding school classroom. Oh. But the sunny McGuffey's Reader design of this space is a disguise, hiding what only a fraction of the Museum's audiences know, the terrible history of the compulsory education of Indian children, wrenched from parents and home and shipped hundreds, sometimes thousands, of miles to federal Indian boarding schools where they either died of white diseases or survived by becoming white (though some only temporarily). The motto of the most famous of these schools, Pennsylvania's Carlisle Indian School, opened in 1879, tells the missing story: "Kill the Indian and Save the Man."

The second marker of the victory celebration is another interior, this of a "traditional" late 20th century Indian house, popularly known as HUD houses after the government agency that built thousands of identical grey concrete-block squares all over Indian reservations. Here, though with a sparsity that accurately reflects contemporary reservation poverty (though before reservation casinos, in many cases), lie all the appurtenances of modern American life: a comfortable sofa and chairs facing a TV, a kitchen complete with stove and refrigerator, pantries and bookshelves, rag rugs and carelessly scattered Pendleton blankets in the *faux-*Indian designs popular with American consumers. Many symbols of late capitalist life are here, in fact, including the most trivial: cola cans and Mickey Mouse toys; wall clocks and cereal boxes, baseball banners and cooking powders. But here, too, is an Indian kicker: most of the commodities selected to represent modern America *also* represent the final reincarnation of a reified Indian subject. Calumet baking powder, Mazola margarine, Atlanta Braves baseball team, Sioux Bee Honey...each bears an Indian "logo," evidence, finally, that "Indians 'R' Us."

So this is "our" Museum. Some hoped it would be revolutionary. Tom Hill, Seneca, and one of the Museum's guest curators, insists that the Museum is "no longer [a] monument...to colonialism" but rather "a truly new world in which cultures have genuine equality and creators and creations [will] be seen whole"(quoted in Hill and Hill, 1994:19). But to me and many others, this statement seems little more than an expression of the false consciousness René Ménil warned against decades ago (1996). Far from detonating history's buried bombs, far from exploding myths or rewriting narratives, this National Museum of the American Indian in reality just sings another, very long, very elaborate death song for American Indian people.

CONCLUSION

And so both venues for the playing out of contemporary racial politics are little more than elaborate theme parks, Disneylands where members of a hegemonic overculture can perform, can play "Indian," or play living in "Africa."[14] Both museums are, as well, sites for liberal white redemption though the NMAI is more visibly so. Indeed, NMAI officials are quite open about it. Here is a letter from the Secretary of the Smithsonian, pleading for donations to support the new Museum:

> Handle this letter carefully. Because you may be holding a powerful spirit in your hands. The spirit of brotherhood. The spirit of compassion. The spirit of understanding among all the peoples of the earth. According to the traditional religions of many American Indians tribes, human beings aren't the only ones who have spirits inside them. Animals, physical objects, and even the forces of nature are imbued with spirits as well. [...] Is it possible the letter you are holding in your hand is imbued with just such a spirit? And if you believe sufficiently in the moral rightness of the project [...] is it possible you can make it come true?

He concludes with even more shamelessly New Age rhetoric:

> Is there a voice inside you telling you it is only right and fitting that the American people build this Museum? [...] Release that spirit. Let it mingle with those of thousands of other people throughout our nation. And let it further the momentum already begun to create the first national museum dedicated to Native Ameri-

cans. Become a Charter Member today (solicitation, Smithsonian Institution, n.d.).

Richard West Jr., the Museum's (Southern Cheyenne) founding director, is no less dependent on New Age stereotypes, and no less embarrassed to link white salvation to white donations:

> When the Museum on the Mall [...] opens [...], you'll understand why we've been calling it 'the Museum Different.' From the moment you walk through its doors, you'll hear the sound of drums. Smell the scent of sweetgrass. Feel the warmth of ceremonial fires on your face and the cool mist of falling water on your skin. [...] It's exciting, isn't it? And you can take pride in knowing you were among the first Americans to step forward and say that such a Museum was long overdue" (NMAI, n.d.).

I shall close by returning us briefly to Africa. *Parade Magazine* several years ago headlined the news that Disney's new Animal Kingdom is now open in Florida, a 500-acre theme park where, a featured article tells us inside the magazine, visitors can "Step Into the African Wild," where "on safaris, riverboat rides and jungle trails, visitors can observe animals in natural settings." No people, of course, no Africans, just Mickey, dressed up like the hegemonic little mouse he is, here a Great White Hunter, the Bwana who is going to escort you and your children through the "wild." Like Mickey, the park is only "modeled on" something else, a place, Africa, all dressed up in its requisite representational gear. Mickey gets his "authenticity" from his "real mouse ears." Safari Village, in its turn, wears "real "Africanesque" figures on "its many facades," carved, the magazine assures us, "by real Balinese woodworkers" (Ciabattari 1990).[15]

And so we have it: postmodern muddles dressed up in global disguises. But underneath the postcolonial, globalized skin breathes the same old Euro-body carrying the same-old Euro-defined ethnicity through familiar Euro-designed spaces, where history is rewritten into scripts for the untroubled performance of the neoliberal (neocolonial?), multicultural project.

CHAPTER 3

PERFORMING "INDIAN" IN THE NATIONAL MUSEUM OF THE AMERICAN INDIAN

with Shari M. Huhndorf

> *Chinua Achebe speaks: The only place where culture is static, and exists independently of people, is the museum. [...] Even there it is doubtful whether culture really exists. To my mind it is already dead. Of course ad good curator can display the artifacts so skillfully that the impression of completeness or even of life can be given, but it is no more than the complete skin which a snake has discarded before going its way* (Achebe, 1969).

PROLOGUE

Because this text is a "hybrid," somewhat fractured and as heteroglossic as even the most critical Bakhtinian might demand, we[1] shall begin by "mapping" a path through the chapter. It unfolds in three broad sections, each of which mixes theory with examination of practices, centered on the National Museum of the American Indian (NMAI). The focus of our attentions here is the New York branch of the National Museum, one of three Museum sites. (A second site—the Museum's center—opened in September 2004, on the Mall in Washington D.C. A research/storage center in nearby Maryland completes the trio.) The George Gustav Heye Center in New York was the first Museum site to open to the public. We begin with its setting. From there we proceed to "tour" the inaugural exhibits, reading them in more detail than that offered in Chapter 2. Here, they appear as the multifaceted texts they, in fact, are. We then conclude with a brief reading of the Museum's "exits," including some analysis of the messages carried from the Museum by its visitors.

Three of us—Shari Huhndorf, Carol Kalafatic, and Patricia Penn Hilden—toured the inaugural exhibits together, seeing through indigenous eyes, the eyes of those born in the Red Zone. This first journey to the Museum began suddenly. Together with Dean Curtis Bear Claw and Chris Eyre, the authors were invited to a British Broadcasting Corporation interview on the occasion of the Museum's opening, in November, 1994. In preparation for the subsequent interview, we visited the George Heye Center (joined by our friend, Carol Kalafatic, whose comments on that occasion and subsequent visits appear all through this chapter) and reviewed the Museum's various published statements, including the Charter Members' Guide. This inaugural document, written "in-house," articulated NMAI's dual purpose: to counter stereotypes, to give voice to hitherto silent American Indians. The Guide identified the communities the Museum intended both to serve and to signify: "When you visit the George Gustav Heye Center...you won't see the usual museum interpretations of Native Cultures. Rather, this is a place where American Indians tell their own stories in their own words" (n.p.). This claim quickly became familiar as dozens more such assurances of "authenticity," of "real Indian control," were reiterated in every Museum publication available at the time of the opening: in exhibit catalogues, in the first monthly newsletter (*The Smithsonian Runner*), in every subsequent fund-raising letter or brochure. This museum, we read over and over, would counter stereotypes, give voice to the mute.[2]

That these preliminary publications had the desired effect of reassuring the non-Native public of this museum's difference from its predecessors became clear as we listened to the broadcaster sent by the BBC's Radio 4 Programme. Questioning Dean Bear Claw, Chris Eyre, Patricia Hilden, and Shari Huhndorf at a hotel in uptown Manhattan, his words echoed both NMAI's claims and some of the confusions common to contemporary museological debates about ethnographic displays. These debates fall on two sides: On the one hand, museums are educational and thus, when created not by ethnographers but rather by their subjects—here American Indians—and when free and open to the public, they can offer both stereotype-countering perspectives and evidence of a more tolerant, multicultural United States. Skeptics—among them many American Indians involved with museums—argue that regardless of the ethnic origins of curators or boards of directors, most ethnographic museums remain memorials to wealth and privilege, educating a public to accept the relations of power extant in given societies. Proponents of either side of these debates would probably agree on one thing: "Indian" museums possess an important potential. By producing an entirely new narrative, they might indeed clarify national histories, revealing aspects obfuscated in more celebratory narratives, but only if they painstakingly avoided the simple construction of an alternative, but still equally triumphal, master narrative of the nation's past.

Our interviewer arrived carrying bags of such ideas as well as notions gathered from other museum "Indian" exhibits, from Hollywood movies, anthropological texts, and the Museum's own publications. It was soon obvious that his reading of this inaugural propaganda had not prepared him to hear "real Indians" criticize "their" museum. Surprised by our unexpected criticisms, he floundered amid various museological problems. Tentatively he ventured:

> Thinking of it as a museum of East Coast Americans, or even just New Yorkers, don't you think that any good purpose is served by holding up intensely beautiful objects for the general public to admire? It might be only a little thing but it might encourage someone who hadn't really thought of it before to come to admire and respect what are...a very wonderful set of cultural products.... If that makes somebody think of Native American culture that was destroyed and even...feel guilty on behalf of white America that might not be a bad thing, might it not?

Chris Eyre replied:

> I went through the museum real briefly but it didn't
> feel right, it felt really synthetic. Much of it is [made
> up of] stolen artifacts and if that's something people
> in this country want to see, well....It seems real inter-
> esting to me that the concept of the museum is that
> [for] America this is *their* history, but it really isn't,
> it's Native history. They are artifacts that are gathered
> and stored here for the populace, for the immigrant
> majority or however you want to put it. But...those
> [are] other peoples' things....They're commodities. If
> you want to learn about Sioux or Crow or Cheyenne,
> that [knowledge] is a commodity....You should travel
> around and see. If the government wants to put money
> into economies it would be interesting to give those
> things back and if you want to see them, then come
> out and see them as we would show them...[3]

The BBC's man objected: New Yorkers are a long way from the
centers of *what's left of Indian life* [emphasis added]. Is there not a
case for bringing aspects of Native American culture into the lives
of New Yorkers?" Chris Eyre, accepting his role as Living Remnant,
explained again: "It has to do with dominant culture...and wanting
everything delivered to that dominant culture."[4]

Despite Chris Eyre's patient efforts, and despite the interviewer's eventual desire to be accepted as "one of us" (leaving the hotel
he draped an arm around one pair of shoulders and confided, "I
know something about tribal life. My grandparents were poor Irish
farmers"[5]) we failed to convince him that this National Museum of
the American Indian was not "new" but rather only a glossy retake
of an old film. The sets are new, the production values impressively
high, but the plots and the actors are all the same.

THE MUSEUM

A Spatial Map: **Figure 3.1**

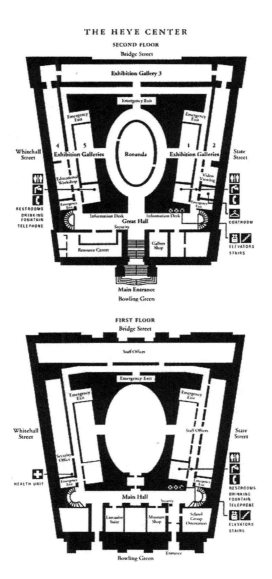

THE HEYE CENTER

An Ideological Map

Two incidents from the authors' first visit to the museum. Near the entrance to the second stage of the exhibition, we encountered an African American museum guard who, as he passed us, spoke loudly into his walkie-talkie: "This is Indian 23 calling Indian 2. Come in, Indian 2."

Later, a man, who had been watching us writing in our notebooks and discussing exhibits, approached us. "Are you gals doing some sorta anthropological study of these Indians?" he asked. "We *are* Indians," we replied rather rudely, "and we're doing an anthropological study of white tourists." Visibly distressed, he hurried away.

Most tribal people come to Indian museums carrying generations of memories. It was Ishi, California Native, "last of his stone age tribe," who walked with us, his haunted black eyes scanning the words mounted on walls, explaining objects in cases. We heard his voice from *his* museum captivity, his final years when he was displayed as "the Last Yahi" by the Department of Anthropology at the University of California.[6] Ishi's dark history, emblematic of Indian relations with America's museums, quickly complicated the George Gustav Heye Center's—or the BBC's—attempts to reshape our memories, and it was with vivid memories of our ancestors' humiliation walking with us, Ishi's captive eyes guarding our steps, that we headed for the Heye Center at the bottom end of Manhattan Island. What we found was not the Native voice promised to Charter Members. Rather, everything was eerily familiar: more feasts for the collectors whose avarice had helped accelerate the U. S. government's legislated murder of cultures; another World's Fair Midway, replete with children's games, here updated to include "interactive" video displays; another theme park; more Natural History Museum dioramas; and even—and this was most shocking—living exhibitions in the persons of the tour guides (called "cultural interpreters") and of other Native people hired to sit in a "Talking Circle" located at midpoint in the exhibits, ready to answer tourist questions—and, in keeping with long tradition, to embody authenticity, to "be a real Indian" for Museum visitors.

Although the Museum presents *these* living spectacles entirely without irony, Guillermo Gómez-Peña and Coco Fusco have recently deconstructed such familiar museum practices, presenting themselves in a cage, their performance called "The Year of the White Bear: Two Amerindians on display for 3 days at Columbus Plaza, Madrid, 1992." They explain:

> We presented ourselves as aboriginal inhabitants of an island in the Gulf of Mexico that Columbus had somehow overlooked. We performed "authentic" and "traditional" tasks, such as writing on a laptop computer, watching television, sewing voodoo dolls, and doing exercises. Interested audience members could pay for authentic dances, stories, and Polaroids of us posing with them. More than half our visitors thought we were real (quoted in Tomassi, et al. 1994:76-7).

What concerned us at the NMAI, however, were not the non-Natives, duped by their own images of exotic Others into accepting the most evidently preposterous performances of aboriginality. Instead we wondered about those who willingly occupy museum spaces, living displays of "real Indians"? Gómez-Peña has considered the processes by which colonial subjects internalize their own subjugation, noting sorrowfully that "real" displays of Native peoples, "in zoos and circuses...concert halls and contemporary museums...living dioramas and festivals," have caused some Natives to "absorb...this identity as the object of European contemplations and at times still cater to that desire... presenting ourselves...frozen in certain historical moments" (1994 1996).[7]

Evidence of a similar absorption, a similar internalization of colonial dreams of savage others, was everywhere evident in "our" Museum. NMAI's complicity with traditional Euro-American expectations began at the entrance. As noted in Chapter 2, the Museum is located in the vast *beaux-arts* Alexander Hamilton Customs House. The edifice sits monumentally alone at the apex of triangular Battery Park, the Hudson River flowing along the park's western edge. Over each of the doorways on the building's sides and back are generic Indian heads, each a mixture of tribal insignia so it is impossible to know whom they represent (Chingachgook? Hiawatha?). In front of this imposing *faux-baroque* pile sit four enormous sculptures, each female, each representing one of the continents. They are all appalling but "America" may be the worst.

It features a vast seated female, (Indian) corn stalks in her lap, her foot on an Aztec figure (Quetzalcoatl?). A Northwest Coast raven mask hangs over one shoulder, and, kneeling to peer humbly from behind and below at the woman's face above, an adult male Plains Indian, war bonnet and all.[8]

Inside, everything is set in splendid, cold marble. In the middle of a vast rotunda sits an oval space, fenced off by waist-high mahogany railings. Eight *faux*-Egyptian brass lamps mark a center square. Although the riot of exotic building materials and design motifs should have satisfied even the most floridly imperialist *belle-époque* tastes (returning from England to New York in these years Henry James famously exclaimed, "So much taste! and all of it bad"), there is still more excess. The great domed skylit ceiling is *faux*-Renaissance. Frescoes circle this space, beaming scenes of triumphal U.S. commerce, great vessels coming and going, goods loaded and unloaded, Indians paddling below, ready to attack from canoes dwarfed by Europe's huge seagoing ships. *Trompe l'oeil* sculpture niches separate these narrative scenes, each holding Italianate portraits of one of the "discoverers": Columbus, Vespucci, Hudson, Verrazano, and the rest. The effects of this choice of site are not lost on tourists. Two ladies from Westchester gushed in the visitor's book: "We haven't seen the exhibits yet, but we're thrilled that the 'Museum' brought us to see this magnificent building!—like the Sistine Chapel!!!"[9]

("Oh capitalism," we wondered, reading their words. "Where is thy hegemonic weakness?")

Tucked inside the atrium of this temple of capitalist worship were the first signs that nothing in the exhibits within would challenge the assumption that Westernness is the norm, these are the Others (Haraway 1989; Rydell 1993; Bennett 1995; Wallis 1997). "Language videos" showed Museum patrons how quaint primitives coped with Western technological wonders. On the screen was a puzzle game: one side showed drawings of radios, trains, cars, airplanes, washing machines. Players could try to match these with "Indian" terms: "box with sound inside," "smoking pony," and so on. As they matched these curious Indian terms with the white objects they identified, tourists were invited to marvel at how creative, how "poetic" all those primitives were in the face of overwhelming European and Euro-American superiority.

Such "interactions" are an integral part of the "new museology,"[10] created by a new generation of museum curators and a self-described "new" generation of anthropologists anxious to transform a sorry history into practices meant to be less triumphal, more inclusive of those colonized by Europeans and their descendants in the Americas (Karp and Lavine 1991; Leone and Little 1993). And evidence of this new museology was in full public view in the multimillion dollar Heye Center of the National Museum of the American Indian. But alas, as with the language videos, we discovered that the displays inside merely replicated—though with more sophistication and considerably more obfuscation—all the tired clichés long familiar to "Indian museum" visitors. In other words, nothing about the newly refurbished Alexander Hamilton Customs House muted the customary triumphal sounds of the victors' celebratory choruses.

Still, the Heye Center's planners did not set out to fail in their project to retell Native stories, to reconstruct Native museum practices. In the early days, hopes were high. Many believed that with the 1989 merger of the old quasi-public Museum of the American Indian with "America's Museum," the Smithsonian Institution, tribal people *could* assume control of the destinies of the more than 1.5 million Native objects left in George Heye's rapaciously acquired collection. That collection had once held many more artifacts, more than 4.5 million, in fact. But the avidity of collectors, fed first by Heye himself and then, after his death, by compliant Museum directors, played itself out by decimating the collection. So great was the loss from that museum that a 1975 inventory, ordered by the New York State Supreme Court, found that fraud and theft by curators and museum directors had "lost" three quarters of the original collection![11]

That few noticed the shrinkage is not remarkable given the fact that only a small fraction of the objects—about 10,000—was ever displayed on 155th Street. For decades, these relatively few cultural artifacts of the continent's first peoples were packed together in old-fashioned, funkily crowded glass cases, tribes and times muddled so senselessly that they resembled nothing so much as Borges's famous Chinese Encyclopedia in which animals were divided into fourteen [Western] mind-bending classifications, among them: (a) belonging to the Emperor, (b) embalmed..., (e) sirens..., (i) frenzied..., (k) drawn with a very fine camel hair brush..., (m) having just broken the water pitcher, (n) that from a long way off look like flies (quoted in Foucault, 1966:7).

After the merger, all the cases, all the storage vaults in the Bronx, were thrown open, potentially liberating at least some of the artifacts to play their role in what the new Museum's planners described as "an attempt to redress a long history of unbalanced and ethnocentric presentations of American Indian history and culture." They promised that they would use these lost symbols of forgotten material cultures to "achieve an internationally visible reinterpretation of past conceptions pertaining to American Indian culture" (NMAI Working Paper, n.d., n.p.).

To explore the success of such challenges to everything Native people know about museums, we left the lobby and started into the first exhibit, the first stop on the tour: "*Creation's Journey: Masterworks of Native American Identity and Belief.*" We pulled open two elegant, heavy glass doors, one bearing a spiral Anasazi motif, designed to draw us in, to announce "Indians." Just inside, appropriately, stood a list of the "special donors" who shaped this exhibition. We knew where we were straight away: one foundation, eleven major corporations, two "Indian Art" galleries, and several famous private collectors (including two Rockefellers and Tom Brokaw). All had donated money and loaned objects. Below and in smaller lettering, the "development team" was named, tribal identities lending legitimacy to Museum claims. There were, in fact, just two Indians among the ten team members, one the "photo researcher."

Exhibits of individual objects came next. Here, in these first two galleries, the museologists' efforts to claim Native objects for the "highbrow" art world met the materialism of those who collect—invest in—such artifacts. Here lay a complication inherent in the museum-as-temple model.[12] What remained hidden, however, were the real creators of Indian museums: the thieves who robbed graves of their "beautiful" artifacts, the "collectors" who bought from those thieves, or, only slightly more respectably, from the "field agents" alert to the acquisitive possibilities left behind by government removals, imprisonments, famines, or by lengthy "reeducation" processes that carefully taught Native children to loathe their own cultures (Hilden, 1994).

As we quickly discovered, this National Museum ignores this troublesome history, opting instead for a curious cacophony of museum sounds: the whisper of fine art boutiques, the laughter of the Midway at the fair, the hushed seriousness of educational history narratives, the quickly indrawn breath of the practiced shopper, recognizing the extraordinary monetary value of objects seen.

"Masterworks of the Collection" assigned Native artifacts to the hallowed temple, the fine arts museum. Each object sat in isolated splendor, posed against expensive fabrics, bathed by a circle of soft light, transformed into a commodity bearing "connoisseur value." (Nearby, a schoolchild cried out to his friends, suddenly comprehending: "These things is worth MONEY!")

Just inside the entrance to "Masterworks," a tribal voice, her words printed on a large wall placard, intervened, complicating visitors' responses and announcing the pluralist theme of the entire inaugural display. "There Are Many Ways of Seeing," the placard proclaimed. "These objects, because they are in a museum, stand outside their own cultural contexts, and different people bring different ideas and values to their interpretation of what the objects mean."

Then, disingenuously, she confessed:

> The ways in which [objects] are displayed demonstrate how museums can influence the viewer's perceptions....The beauty...will appeal to most people. The skill of their construction will interest some. They way in which they were used in daily life will be of interest to many. Their special significance to the Indian people who made them *may* become apparent, but in many cases it cannot be known because the people who created the objects died long ago and took with them the knowledge they possessed....

So: art or craft appreciation, *National Geographic* education, and... the objects' meaning for Indians? Well, no: "we" cannot know, evidently, what the objects mean to Indians because they come from an historic time, a time long ago and all their makers are dead (or vanished, as the stereotype more commonly asserts). Still, "the different voices that surround...the objects speak for them," the words continued, "since they cannot speak for themselves. Listening... you will experience different ways of seeing different objects."

Despite sincere intentions, problems lurked. Whatever their source, such wall placards, or the smaller captions, overhead speakers carrying "real" voices into the spaces surrounding the objects, or even the "real" people (the Indian guides hired by the Museum to inform visitors and add local color), did not answer essential questions: to whom were these words addressed? Who is the "you" who would "experience different ways of seeing?" Surely the "you" is not a tribal person? Surely the "you's" to whom the Museum purportedly belongs are not included here? But wait! As the placard reminded us, the writer *is* a tribal person, one of the Native voices hired to reclaim the Museum for "us"! But here she had quite clearly assumed another, more familiar voice—that of the objective, scholarly viewer of "their" objects from "their" culture. This discursive move from the tribal world—that world that grants this voice its authority to speak here—to the Western scholarly one (whose language validates cultural judgment) occurred again and again in the opening exhibit, as Indian authorities assumed the voices of non-Native art historians or even anthropologists (Berlo 1992).

Having read the voice speaking from this wall, we peered expectantly into the first case. But though "boutiqued" in familiar shopping-mall fashion, this object was not for sale—nor was it silent or even multivoiced. We heard its cries, felt its trembling. Torn from its life among the Crow nation, "sacralized as an object of abstract contemplation, a frozen archive" (to paraphrase Charles Mereweather (1994) Sore Belly's prophetic war shield hung behind glass). "Remarkably well-preserved....The shield *possessed* magical powers," the caption assured us, erasing its presence, assigning it to a safely vanished past. But this shield defied containment by its case or by its caption and sounded its going-home song.

Lest visitors pause overlong here, other voices quickly intruded. From overhead speakers came the sounds of drums, of Indian voices. Their words were obscured by the noises of the schoolchildren who crowded into the Museum that morning. Most of these children, reared in a universe of consumption, were, as one of their number, quoted above, demonstrated, alert to the money messages all through this boutique of valuable Indian artifacts. But if spotlighting, glass show cases, heavy cloth drapery, and glitzy backgrounds failed to attract some of the children to the excitement of the marketplace, an alternative attitude was quickly provided in the next display, more open about its Boasian intentions (Jacknes 1985). Around a corner, near the end of the "Masterworks" opening gallery, a display entitled "There Are Many Ways of Seeing" reiterated the first placard's admonition. Here was another large glass case, this divided into three sections forming a triptych displaying on either side a kayak and some Eskimo clothing, and, in the center, a video screen (lit up by an "interactive" touch) narrating aspects of Arctic life.

Three discordant voices captioned the three cases, each generic, each speaking in instantly recognizable languages: those, in turn, of anthropology, of art history, of "the Native." First, the anthropologist: "Constructed of light wood frames and covered with sea mammal skin, kayaks were fast and seaworthy, and *were preferred* over wood boats in icy waters." (Emphasis added. The passive voice, universal in anthropological writing though here that of anthropologist Edmund Carpenter, again removed agency from the subjects of the observer's attentions.)

The art historian—this time one of a special sub-category, an "ethno-art-historian"—offered ignorant passersby (those who hadn't seen Robert Flaherty's 1922 documentary, *Nanook of the North*) the requisite viewing lens. "Theirs is a world which has conquered with each act and statement, each carving and song—but which, with each accomplished, is quickly lost." Ah! both conquest (of nature, not of people) and evanescence distinguish Eskimo art from "modern" art. But then how do carvings and song reach the market, the museum, where their peculiar fragility renders them rare, still more valuable? *How did these objects climb into their glass cases in the National Museum of the American Indian?*

The third voice echoed a hundred movies, endless coffee-table book "translations" of famous chiefs' speeches, countless children's books. It spoke in the images of poetry, its Wordsworthian tones here "indianized" into monosyllabic simplicity and laid out in the brief, repetitive lines that every schoolchild knows signals "this is a poem." It was the voice of the nonbloodthirsty cousin of Robert Berkhofer's *White Man's Indian* (Berkhofer, 1978). As that historian has argued, those Natives not whooping and grunting with savagery are serene, harmoniously at one with nature. So familiar was this stereotype that any one of the three of us, Arctic native or not, could have written something very like the "Native" caption to this exhibit of Arctic hunting:

> I was out in my kayak
> I was out at sea in it
> I was paddling
> very gently...
> ...on the water a petrel
> turned his head this way that way
>
> ....
>
> He plunged but not for me:
> huge head upon the water
> great hairy seal
>
> ...
>
> and the seal came gently toward me
> Why didn't I harpoon him?
> was I sorry for him?
> was it the day, the spring day, the seal
> playing in the sun
> like me?[13]

Here yet again, the gentle, nature-loving, happy Eskimo, this one murmuring poetry through his cheerful grin.

The next stage in "Creation's Journey" left "Masterworks of the Collection" and moved, in the third exhibition gallery, to "The View From Within." Here non-Natives (the vast majority of Museumgoers) were invited to pass through an archway into a series of twists on the familiar natural history museum diorama. The gatekeeping voices at this entrance replicated the first triumvirate. Reading—as most Westerners would—from left to right, anthropologists came first: William Sturtevant and Franz Boas trumpeting their universalist, "Family of Man" message. Under the skin, their words reassured visitors, everyone is really much like everyone else. Second spoke two fine art museum curators, Frederick Douglas and René d'Harnoncourt, the first of their snooty profession (or so the placard informed us) to transform "historical Indian objects" into "real art" by exhibiting Indian artifacts at New York's Museum of Modern Art in 1941 (Douglas and d'Harnoncourt 1941; Rushing 1992). Here, too, their words from that exhibition's catalogue validated the objects we were about to see: all "high art."

Last, again a Native voice, here to lend authenticity. This voice, that of a Native art historian, was conciliatory. Although Native representations had not always employed universal ideas, motives, or imagery, her placard told us, the Western idea of "aesthetically pleasing art," once absent from Native America, had now entered contemporary Indian culture. Thus NMAI's "view from within" would not elude non-Indian visitors since everything in *these* rooms (or, we could not help wondering, only those things made after "westernization"?) reflected universal aesthetic "wonder." The exhibition's design elements reassured as well: Here, as in the opening display, each object stood alone, splendidly lit, cloaked in the requisite fine textile backcloth: a beaded buckskin shirt, a quill horse mask, some paintings, a ledger book, all from different Native cultures but all "beautiful."

This universalist multiculturalism was not, however, the entire message of this "insiders' view." Just beyond this fine arts display lay another, "foreign" space, a room made up to represent those exotic Pueblo kivas familiar to everyone from countless postcards and pictures, movies and coffee-table photography books(Faris, 1996; Dilworth, 1996).

And herein lay more lies.

This "kiva" drew tourists into a "secret" *Indian* world, a place of difference, a place that cleverly mingled the authentic and the counterfeit: fake sandstone, fake sand, fake adobe, "real" tribal voices wafting from nontribal sound speakers, and even a fake blue corn painting on the floor. This, like the spiral design at the entrance, was at least vaguely familiar to most readers of *National Geographic* Southwest Indian articles. It was an emergence design, used in Pueblo ceremonies that are no longer open to any public gaze, whether those of avid anthropologists—of whom the Pueblos have surely had more than their fair share?—or those of the tireless eastern tourists in hot pursuit of "exotic" spiritual experiences in a desert landscape (Hughtie 1994). (So invasive were these non-Native intruders that many Southwestern Native nations began to close ceremonies to outsiders early in the 20th century. Today, visitors to these pueblos and communities must be invited to witness ceremonies and dances sacred to the group.[14])

This "kiva" was a starkly simple space, appropriate to the Southwestern aesthetic. On the right, a fake fire pit held a single large red clay pot. Tourists, prepared by the art boutiques through which they had just passed, saw commodity values everywhere, found themselves plunged into "the kiva experience," and even invited to "interact" by touching a real Pueblo pot, prime symbol of Anglo collecting. This interaction was another illusion, however, this of possession. Would-be holders quickly discovered that the clay vessel was glued tight to its cement "sand" base. So it held some value, but not the kind of value held by the "real" beautiful pots, those "collected." These were isolated, protected, lit up and swathed in desert-textured fabrics, inside security-wired glass cases set into the "kiva" wall.

Messages lurked here in confusion. What should visitors understand? That the people of the Southwest did not distinguish pots for use—represented by the careless tilt and illusory accessibility of this "interactive" display - and pots desired by collectors? That until connoisseurs found and "rescued" or "preserved" them, beautiful pots were carelessly used in quotidian tasks by "primitives" unaware of their monetary value, without regard to their potential place in the market (1994)? Does the fake kiva—complete with muted singing Pueblo voices—hint at those ceremonial secrets once so greedily sought by career-making anthropologists, avid collectors, and hungry spiritual tourists but now frustratingly closed to outsiders? Was this fun house kiva meant to fool viewers into thinking that they were being allowed to sample this forbidden ophiolatrous world?

Or was the emergence design painted on the floor signaling a transformation, a shift from fine art boutiques through the mysterious underground world of the kiva to what lay around the next corner, a display that might have been captioned "capitalism rampant in Indian Country"? Leaving the kiva we turned another corner to find ourselves plunged into the Southwest created by turn-of-the-century Anglo intruders.[15] Here more Southwestern artifacts stood before a giant wall photograph of the impossibly cluttered interior of an early 20th century trading post. Walls dripped baskets, blankets, masks. Shelves sagged beneath the weight of heavy silver and turquoise jewelry massed together with beadwork, drums, and dozens of other objects, sacred and secular, all "collected" from the peoples of the Southwest and for sale to touring Easterners. This picture records the tracks of the inexorable juggernaut beneath whose heavy treads Pueblo people (or their material culture) were dragged, devil (or the US cavalry) take the hindmost, into what another museum caption, later on, would describe as the "capitalist art market."

Although resisting Pueblo voices were absent from this display, there *were* cries of outrage against this process. In 1882, while collecting for the Smithsonian, Frank Hamilton Cushing recorded his fear of Hopis who did not want to relinquish their material culture. "They beg for war," he wrote home, "and say, 'When the Caciques of the Americans sit on our decapitated heads, then they can dress our bodies in their clothes, feed our bodies with their victuals, then, too, they can have our things to take with them to the houses of their fathers...' We can make no collections here, save by force," Cushing concluded, then fled (quoted in Hinsley 1981:11). More questions begged here, too: Were these objects collected by force? Did the market represented here change Native life? Did collectors' tastes, curators' desires, anthropologists' dictates fix the most salable techniques, designs, colors, and materials, those elements that had once changed more freely in precapitalist times? Did tourist demands begin to shape what Native artisans made, how Hopis *acted*?[16] The Museum's many voices were silent.

Following the Museum's footpath, we next passed through several small exhibits to emerge in a womblike niche. Hidden around another corner lurked the first natural history museum diorama. Coming suddenly upon such a life-sized figure in "our" museum was bizarre. We knew, of course, that such dioramas were nothing new, especially in Indian museums. Such lifelike figures had been used to commemorate nationhood at the 1876 Philadelphia World's Fair. After their success there, organizers of Chicago's World's Columbian Exposition, scheduled for 1893, hired the Smithsonian to create similar displays of life-sized, costumed Indians to illustrate that fair's evolutionary race ladder.[17] (That there was little concern for authenticity then was underscored by the fact that Franz Boas "posed for the Kwakiutl Hamatsa dance, and [Frank Hamilton] Cushing posed for several Zuni and Plains figures..." Dilworth, 1996:46; also Rydell, 1984; Greenhalgh, 1988; Sherman and Rogoff, 1994:xii-xiii; Stewart, 1995:44; Fernandez-Sacco 1998.)

The sculptor Casper Mayer invented the method followed later by the NMAI. He had taken plaster casts of faces and various body parts of Indians located "in the field," in "visiting circuses" (where Indians were often featured performers) and at Pennsylvania's Carlisle Indian Boarding School (Moses, 1996; Huhndorf, 2001; Deloria, 1998). When Mayer's Chicago Fair exhibits proved wildly popular, the directors of New York City's American Museum of Natural History commissioned more "life groups"—figures that soon represented "Indian" to countless generations of America's children and their parents. (Indeed, so normative have such displays become that the Pequot Nation's new museum, located on its reservation in Connecticut, employs many such "living" dioramas, each illustrating some feature of a "vanished way of life," although as with the NMAI, nothing hints at who or what made that life disappear.")

We were familiar with such lifelike "Indians" from childhood. And here they were—again. This first figure, one of several to come as we soon discovered, featured a traditionally garbed Osage woman standing in the center of another near-life size photograph circling the walls. This figure wasn't quite as "fun" as its World's Fair or Museum of Natural History predecessors, which would have included several feathered and painted "Osages," posed in the "living" positions made familiar by hundreds of paintings, photographs, and Wild West show performances. But both figure and picture were "real," a real face, a life cast of a local New York City Indian, though not necessarily an Osage, and a "real photograph." "Real" except for the fact that this Osage face was not like the stereotypical, generic "Indian" posed in museums, imprinted on coins. Instead, "her" skin was utterly *un*real, made of cement, an unhealthy and eerie grey. We discussed this strange color choice, finally agreeing that the only reasonable explanation must lie with the designer's wish not to offend anyone. Knowing that the public carries a stereotypical red-skinned, black-haired, black-eyed Indian in its imaginary, those who made this and the other Native figures in the Museum must have addressed the fact of Indians' varied phenotypes by choosing the one color no one (alive) has.

And the photograph? There was no context provided for the image, though the clothing and hairstyles of a handful of nontribal people or "modern" Indians mixed in with traditionally garbed Osages suggested the 1920s or 1030s. Was it, as suggested in Chapter 2, a group portrait of those Osages depicted so movingly in John Joseph Mathews's *Sundown* (1988[1934]) or Linda Hogan's *Mean Spirit* (1990)? Are these the Osages whose oil-laden land produced so much fraud and so many murders that the FBI (at the behest of the tribe) finally got involved in the investigation? Who knew? This "Indian" museum, "our" museum, was again silent on "real authentick historical facts."

There was still more to *"Creation's Journey"* —more *faux*-Indian rooms, more "fine art" objects, more grey-peopled dioramas. There were lots of "interactive" videos and Indian toys, all chained in place, for children to handle. There was more occlusion of history, most strikingly in a curious "Ghost Dance" exhibit (discussed in more detail in Chapter 2), set inside protecting plexiglass. Here, grey-skinned Indian children wore dresses described as those once belonging to Ghost Dancers. From the ceiling above them hung a feathered "headdress." All stood within a strange timbered space.

Outside the case and chained to a post hung a "real" buffalo robe with which visitors might once again "interact."

Captions affixed to the case described the late 19th century Ghost Dancers, followers of the prophet Wovoka. instructing visitors that the prophet had promised his thousands of followers that white people would eventually disappear if they kept dancing. The caption neglected the rest of the story, how Wovoka taught that whites would be vanquished and the life-giving buffalo return only if Ghost Dancers kept the ceremonies faithfully, only if they lived their lives in accordance with very strict rules of personal responsibility and behavior, shunning the culture destroying materialism and decadence of the whites. The exhibit also failed to inform the public about the government's (and vigilante white settlers') violent efforts to quash the practices of the politically subversive (though entirely peaceful) Ghost Dancers. There was no whisper of the Seventh Cavalry's 1880s mission to kill all those who persisted in their dancing, no word of the corrupt Indian agents who used the accusation "Ghost Dancer" to get rid of tribal members they feared or whose land or possessions they coveted. It said nothing, either, of the rest of the story, the U. S. Army's 1890 massacre of some 300 old people, children, and women—Big Foot's band of Ghost-Dancing Sioux—at Wounded Knee.

Unlike most of those standing outside the plexiglass exchanging breathless admiration of the dresses' artistry, the headdress's feathered beauty, we *knew*. We peered more closely at the girls' dresses. Did bullet holes attest their provenance? Were they, like hundreds of other "artifacts"—cradleboards, dolls, dresses, shields, bows and arrows, pipes, bags, medicine bundles—robbed from the bodies of Wounded Knee's dead and sold to George Heye's field agents (Hilden 1994:34-5)?

The Museum held two more sections, each of which continued to insist that Indians were everywhere heard here, controlling each step in this multicultural tour. "*All Roads Are Good: Native Voices on Life and Culture*" was next, followed by "*The Path We Travel: Celebrations of Contemporary Native American Creativity.*" Both continued the practices on display from the outset, distinguishing high art from low and entertainment from education, all the time carefully detaching artifacts from any historical context. The twinned conceits that "we" were on a journey, that Indians were "our" guides continued as well. The *faux*-kiva's subtheme, linking Indians with Anglo spiritual quests, grew more apparent, satisfying one of the most strident of contemporary public demands. Two examples, both from the final section of the exhibition's narrative of travel, must suffice.

Between displays in the final section, "*This Path We Travel*," lay two interactive *faux*-spiritual experiences. The first involved a large rope spiderweb, spotlit, suspended from the ceiling so that an intricate circular pattern fell on the wood floor and altered the image of all who lingered beneath. The wall instructed visitors: "The balance of life in this earth and universe is represented by the circle and the symbols of Father Sky and Mother Earth ..." (The most phenotypically "Indian" of us stepped into the light, held her arms aloft and gazed soulfully at the ceiling while the other two collapsed in laughter. Our amusement soon drew the attention of two white women who angrily informed us that we had no right to interrupt the spiritual experience of "the Indian.")

The Museum offered still another circle, this labeled "The Sacred." Here, again, tourists were invited to play, to experience "Indian," this time by stepping inside a sacred circle drawn on the pale wood floor. Like the earlier rope web, this circle was lit from above so that a halo of light surrounded those who stepped inside. A soft heartbeat sounded from above. Words painted on the facing wall reassured. "By walking into the sacred circle, you acknowledge your part in Creation." So this pause in the Museum's narrative was a religious experience, a chance for the disconnected, the alienated non-Native to meld into the vast, romantic myth of earth-embracing (earth-accepting) Indians. We stood quietly nearby for some minutes, watching people walk reverently into the circle, some standing unabashedly for the prescribed several seconds, others hurrying, slightly embarrassed. One man reached out a foot, letting it fall inside the circle as if accidentally. He then hurried away. We wondered: Who are the Indians here? Overwhelmed, we hastened through the last of the inaugural displays, at once amused and horrified by this pandemonium of messages, some pandering to New Age consumers, others crying out the extent to which some Natives have internalized those pernicious stereotypes that lock

Native America into cases as secure as those holding their "fine art" artifacts.

And then we were finally at the exit. But before the Museum let us go, it had one final statement. By now we had realized that this Museum was not merely another in New York City's stellar lineup of fine arts galleries, or even just another kiddie museum, a quasi-educational substitute for the dinosaur room at the Museum of Natural History. It wasn't only a theme park where children and adults could play with "their" Indians, or even a narrative of "our" national heritage. It was also an Indian mall, and Indian malls mean collecting *and* shopping.[18]

All through the exhibitions, the Museum had provided for all, though significantly the "all" hitherto had not been divided by those distinctions of class and power and privilege that underpin this and other museums. Such divisions, like those of race, had so far remained veiled, hidden by confusing shifts in this Museum's discourses, between "high art" and "low," between education and entertainment, between wonder and hilarity. Just beyond the exhibition's exit, however, both inside the main floor's marble-columned lobby and directly downstairs, amid the Museum's staff offices, Pierre Bourdieu's "distinctions" asserted themselves—preparing the travelers for their reencounter with the New York City beyond the Customs House doors. What had been occluded all along, Bourdieu's structures that disguise "taste and its consequences for maintaining inequality in society," stood suddenly revealed—marked by spatial location as well as by content (1984:175).

We began on the main floor. Off to one side of the ornate entrance hall, alongside the Museum's main doors, stood a "fine arts" gift shop. The lighting was muted, the carpet thick, the colors southwestern. On sale were those lovely objects—pots, bracelets, carvings, fetishes, necklaces, blankets—still produced by Native artists and artisans for the upper end of the vast Indian art market. They were displayed in locked glass cases. They were very, very expensive. In this distinctly up-market art boutique, the objects for sale were, almost without exception, much, much too costly for most tribal people's budgets. It was an irony one observes everywhere in contemporary North America: Exquisite necklaces, earrings, rings, and bracelets, carved from silver, inlaid with turquoise, coral, and turtle shell, ornament the bodies not of those whose culture produced such fabulous beauty but rather the bodies of descendants of immigrants to these shores. In their immigrant homes—styles, tastes, forms, and structures similarly brought from "old worlds"—rugs and blankets, pictures and artifacts, proclaim their owners' "love" of Indians, their recognition that Indians' possessions are very good investments, indeed. And it was to these buyers that the upper floor Museum gift shop addressed itself.

IT'S INDIANS! BRING THE KIDS!

But there were others invited into this museum, too, those for whom tribal people are fun, are a leisure activity. These had been provided a second shop, a souvenir shop, appropriately lower down, in the basement of the Museum, out of sight of those who might take offense at the transformation of Museum Indians, makers of "investment quality" fine art, into exotic, funfair entertainers. This shop, department-store lit and decorated in primary colors, sold "the Indian experience," mostly to children. Here were plastic, made-in-China, bows and arrows, tin drums and drum sticks, little vinyl "medicine bundles," plastic headdresses with dayglo pink and green feathers, Indian ball and stick games, and the inevitable "Indian princess" dolls. Arts and crafts kits promoted America's history-shifting master narrative, calling on young painters to "discover the history and lore of *our* Native American ancestors," or urging builders of ersatz tipis and igloos to "touch a piece of *our* Native American heritage." After our collective visit, Carol Kalafatic wrote a description of this shop and sent it to us:

> To nurture the nascent adventurers/archaeologists in the milk-tooth market, there are "discovery kits." A blond boy—"us"—wearing an Indiana Jones fedora smiles from the photo on another kit called "Native Americans of the Southwest." Urging the presumably eager child buyer to "learn about Pueblo Cultures while excavating *your own* Anasazi artifact," the kit is modern museology's "finders-keepers" ethos in a box.[19]
> In turn, Dover Books offers "Little Woodland Indian Girl Paper Doll," a creature who not only replicates the ownership/guardianship mode of the Museum's collections but who also presents the contemporary

children's world's favorite image—a vanishing, pan-Indian female. Children can dress their own "Nellie" in eight different paper outfits, each simulating the clothing of a distinct "woodland tribe." The first page of the accompanying book explains the plethora of tribal outfits. "The woodlands of the present day northeastern United States...were home to dozens of Indian tribes...Nellie, our little Indian girl, is proud of her kinship with many of these tribes." This bizarre paper image of a multitribal child sports two braids, medium brown skin, and nondescript turquoise-dot "jewelry." (Yes: turquoise, a stone quite foreign to those same Woodland tribes but nevertheless, the stone—accompanied by silver work—that always signals "Indian.") (Kalafatic 1999).

The shop encouraged parental participation. "Indian popcorn" was microwave ready. Recipe books, videos, postcards, cheap blankets and rugs (many made in India in a riotous semiotic confusion) and a dozen coffee-table books of photographs and ethnographic "facts" about the quaint customs and habits of America's endlessly "vanishing" Indian peoples loaded the counters. And, in mad pursuit of the "authenticity experience," the gift shop offered..Fry Bread Mix! And thus a fitting conclusion—excess commodity flour, lard, and sugar, offered to starving reservation people as partial payment for the millions of acres of treaty-stolen land, transformed by Native ingenuity to disguise mold and rancidity, here become portable artifact of Indian authenticity for tourist consumption! It was a final, and appropriately ironic, statement in the multitude of words heard in this Museum.

CONCLUSIONS

So here we were, leaving "our" museum, sad, but also troubled. If the National Museum of the American Indian was really "our" museum, if Native peoples helped construct it, helped choose each exhibit, helped write the brochures and placards, the advertising copy and the Museum's fund-raising appeals, why did it sadden us? Who were we to reject it? Indeed, the BBC interviewer had wondered the same things. Like us, he'd read the Museum's congratulatory propaganda. He'd watched Museum videos of various

Native artists involved in selecting and designing these inaugural exhibits. After listening to our criticisms, he wondered whether we or they were "authentic" Native voices. "Some of the quotations that appear in the literature and surrounding the objects and, of course, in the video material and so on sound pretty affirmative," he told us. "Are we to assume that these are inauthentic responses on the part of these Native participants in the exhibit process" (BBC Interview, Nov. 1994)? Shari Huhndorf, speaking for all of those present at the BBC interview, explained that it isn't so straightforward:

> There is one section with a video of a Tlingit art historian looking at a button blanket, and there are mixed messages there. On one hand, she was talking about the blanket as she was asked to talk about it: she was explaining it to people who didn't understand it. And on the other hand, she was saying how this blanket belonged to people at home, and what having this blanket would mean to that particular family. I think that in the context of this exhibit these words meant something different from what I think is the message that people take away. I think she is saying that maybe these things shouldn't be here and that they mean something different to us. And I'm not sure that's affirming.

To our collective sorrow, then, we find ourselves agreeing with one Native scholar who, more than 24 years ago, condemned "Indian museums," and specifically the old 155th Street Heye Museum of the American Indian. "We don't want the typical white man's thing that they can see in New York," he insisted (Anon. 1987) Well, that's just what we've got here, Achebe's empty snake skin, offering only the illusions upon which white appropriations of "Indians" rest. Nothing is new. And we don't want it, either.

Anyway, that's what we think.

PART II
HISTORY, RACE, AND POLITICS

CHAPTER 4

‖ RITCHIE VALENS IS DEAD: ‖ *E PLURIBUS UNUM*[1]

State of California. Proposition 187. General Election, November 8, 1994
Section 53069.65:

> *Wherever the state or a city or a county, or any other legally authorized local government entity with jurisdictional boundaries reports the presence of a person who is suspected of being present in the United States in violation of federal immigration laws to the Attorney General of California, that report shall be transmitted to the United States Immigration and Naturalization Service. The Attorney General shall be responsible for maintaining on-going and accurate records of such reports, and shall provide any additional information that may be requested by any other government entity.*

1970: Newspaper reporter to Native American elder: "Do Indians think the United States should get out of Vietnam?"
Elder: "We think the United States should get out of North America."

"YOU ARE *ALL* ILLEGAL ALIENS"

Debts:

Part of the me born in Los Angeles in 1944 is illegal, anyway. Sometime in the 17th century these ancestors arrived, from England, from Holland. They carried no documents, no permits to land on the shores occupied for millennia by my other ancestors.

These European adventurers sought much: wealth, land, adventure, a new way of life.

Though they would not speak of these things until much later, and then not about themselves but only about those whom they, with an arrogant dismissal of history, labeled "aliens," these forebears of mine from Europe inhabited an underground economy: without documents, on land that belonged to others, they lived precariously, often stealing what they needed, sometimes killing, capturing, and selling into slavery those whom they were rapidly displacing. They carried foreign diseases. They spoke strange tongues (and refused to learn the languages of this place). They brought a knowledge of merciless, technologically sophisticated war making (Jennings 1993:44 [1976]).[2] Their strange religion prescribed huge families, and they obeyed. When they couldn't feed all their children, or treat all their illnesses, they depended upon the kindness and generosity of those *indígenas* they encountered.

As time went on they formed gangs, forcing the narrowest conformity among members. Nonconformists were exiled as heretics, hanged as witches, pressed to death beneath the heavy rocks of collective disapprobation (thus beginning a long tradition of majority social tyranny in North America). Their gangs, led by autocratic, vain, and utterly hypocritical men, justified their pillage in the baroque language of 17th century Christianity, protected their stolen territory, appropriated more and more resources. Driven by avarice, they soon discovered where the real money lay, and organized an increasingly lucrative slave trade, seizing and selling natives. Sometimes they kept captive girls and women to satisfy their lusts, and the first "mixed bloods" (the first "tragic mulattos") were born. (Natives resisted: Edward R. Castillo [1978] reports that the rape of native women trapped in mission slavery was so common that the people took collective action and "every white child born among them for a long period was secretly strangled and buried.")

At first, most *indígenas* followed ancient tradition and welcomed the new arrivals, overlooking their curious habits, their murderous intentions, their deviousness, their odd-sounding languages, the awful smell of their food and their unwashed, pale, hairy bodies. Bemused, they tolerated Europeans' inept and aggressive attempts to live against the land by unceremoniously tearing down forests, damming rivers, slaughtering animals, ripping and moving the earth.

In the early days, only a handful of prescient tribal people resisted. They warned that these Europeans were not like others, not simply people to be welcomed into their world as custom demanded. One elder warned that these predators in human form, "as numerous as the leaves upon the trees," would "eventually crowd [you] from [your] fair possessions" (Calloway 1994:40). But few listened. Time passed. Whole nations vanished before guns and disease, before the lies, the inhumanity, the unbridled—and to most natives, incomprehensible—greed.

> Walt Disney's version neatly captures the pervasiveness of the historical lie. His *Pocahontas* improbably—but oh, how the overculture wants to believe its master narratives?—falls madly in love with the English hero of this plundering expedition, a bland and blond John Smith. (As England disappears behind the billowing sails, Smith roars his purpose: "For riches and freedom!" "Yes!" cry his shipmates, "for riches and freedom!") A cunning raccoon, a clever hummingbird, and a wise old (Grandmother) willow tree join with a cartoon Pocahontas to smooth the conquest. Though the rest of Disney's Powhatons aren't initially thrilled (two of them—but none of the English—soon lie dead), the efforts of the hopelessly perky animals and talking trees together with those of Disney's Indian Barbie doll, the raven-tressed, sexually precocious Pocahontas (Ready to sacrifice her people for love), soon win out. The pillage begins...(see Reddish 1995:22-33)[3]

The people took note. They tried to assess these "foreigners," so frantically ruining life on this earth, overrunning the land, draining resources, and, when they weren't killing the local populace or each other (guns provided the sport of these cruel men), purposefully destroying the traditional values of those there before them. They were not good: not for the land, not for social relations, not for spiritual life. Nearly everyone began to fear them.

How to drive them out? How to keep more from coming? The people built borders, set warriors to watch, to capture and punish transgressors, to send them home. Many retreated behind nature's fences—vast stretches of desert, towering mountains, wide rivers. Still, the invaders came. "What if we starve them out?" someone suggested at last. "What if we refuse to help them when they're sick? Refuse to feed them when they're hungry? Refuse to teach them how to live in this land that mystifies them so?" One 17th century Micmac elder even tried reason: "If France...is a little terrestrial paradise, art thou sensible to leave it?" he asked the invaders. "Why venture thyself with such risk...to the storms and tempests of the sea in order to come to a strange and barbarous country which thou considerest the poorest and least fortunate of the world? ...We scarcely take the trouble to go to France," he remarked, "because we fear..lest we find little satisfaction there, seeing,....that those who are natives thereof leave it every year in order to enrich themselves on our shores. I must open to thee my heart," he concluded gently, "there is no Indian who does not consider himself infinitely more happy and more powerful than the French" (quoted in Calloway 1994:50).

Too late. Still illegal, without any documents save the visible European origins of the pale colors they bore—of skin, eyes, hair—backed by superior weapons and the will to use them ruthlessly against people, animals, land, they kept on coming. They overran the continents, killing savagely until they were millions and Natives were few. A strange, restless avarice drove them on. They took. They possessed.

The East filled: my illegal forebears moved West, from land "bought" from an earlier (French) conquest onto land seized in the war with México when Aztlán became "New" Mexico (i.e., "ours"), West Texas, Arizona, (Alta) California. Now "ours" (personal pronouns swarmed with ambiguities), the West began to fill with Anglos. Then at mid-19th century, catastrophe: material desire, driven by the discovery of gold, exploded all over California. Where once native populations had offered rape victims, slave labor and (on paper) converts for the wicked mission padres, or cheap labor for the Mexican landowners who replaced the Spanish church fathers, now their very presence began to threaten those who had seized the land from Mexico, Anglos, "Americans," who intended to own all of California, especially those thousands of acres of the land that contained, or might contain, gold.[4]

That a real Indian threat lurked mostly in greed-maddened Anglo minds meant little. Neither their traditional gentleness nor the scarcity of those tribal people whose land they yearned after slowed the spread of a violence even more terrible than that already familiar to native people across the continent. Anglos viewed the courtesy and politeness of the native populace with dismissive scorn. "Yankees," David Banks Rogers boasted,

> fresh from contact with the natives of the plains who were prone to fight to the death in defense of their rights, treated with contempt the quiet, unresent-ful slaves of the Spaniards, in derision dubbing them "diggers," in common with all other coastal tribes.... Woe to the hapless native who, under the influence of liquor, attempted the terrorism that had been the dread of the "paisano." If he tried his violence upon one of the newly-arrived Anglo-Saxon lords, the chances were very slight of his ever again appearing before an accredited judge for sentence" (quoted in Hurtado 1988:22; see also Owens 1992:39).

How slight? For the tribal people who remained in California (of the 310,000 natives who had occupied California when the Spanish arrived, only 150,000 remained in 1848), the Gold Rush meant near-certain death.[5]

The 1850s were hideous. Whites—"Americans" or "Yankees"— killed, raped, mutilated, and sold natives with utter, utter impunity. Only a few among the Anglo-Saxon lords objected. In 1861, after a decade of unbridled gold greed, an editor at the Marysville (Calif.) *Appeal* recorded the appalling facts: "from these mountain tribes," he explained, "white settlers draw their supplies of kidnapped children, [who are] educated as servants, and women for purposes of labor and lust" (Castillo 1978:109). As for tribal people who resisted, or who happened to get in the way of white vengeance (no one was very particular about identifying the victims, a red skin was a red skin, after all), merciless slaughter awaited. One gold miner, Edwin Franklin Morse, confided the gory details of one typical event to his diary. Two Grass Valley brothers, Samuel and George Holt, "were in the habit," he wrote, "of enticing the Indian women and girls into their [saw]mill and insulting them." [Remember: in this era, "insult" meant physical assaults, including rape, and thus this tale tells us that the play of sexual power relations, present from the first moments of "contact" between male Europeans and female natives, continued unabated.] "When the bucks[6] learned of this they rose in their wrath and, attacking the mill one night, killed one of the Holts and severely wounded the other with their arrows, and burned down the mill." Soldiers—stationed here and throughout the West to protect settlers from Indians—responded immediately, "and, joined by some of the miners from Grass Valley, went down and killed several Indians in retaliation." Morse, bearing the European patriarchy that transformed relations between tribal women and men, expressed sympathy for those most offended in such events: "This always seemed most uncalled for to me, as the Indians were perfectly justified in resenting the insult to their women" (Morse 1927:234-5; Hurtado 1988:1; see also *Klanwatch* 1995:7).[7]

But these same Anglos tried—how they tried!—to "civilize" the natives. When, soon after his arrival in Mexican California in 1839, John Sutter discovered a need for cheap labor to build and serve the colony of Anglo settlers he brought to Sacramento,[8] he quickly "gain[ed] ascendancy over the tribes by persevering, by kindness and the exercise of skill and well-timed authority." He even "supplied [poor] Mexicans and Indians with clothing, hats, and every thing necessary to humanize and civilize them," though to little avail. Most Indians, complained one Euro-American contemporary, persisted in their barbarism, dancing "a dance for the dead in which they are horribly disfigured with mud and tar and paints...." The poor Mexicans in their turn, all *vaqueros* in the stereotype of those days, were initially not quite so despised. Unlike California's Indians, they were horsemen, cowboys, real *men*, the envy of recently arrived Eastern "greenhorns." They could work cattle better than anyone, better, even, than Anglos. Lest this pose an ideological challenge, however, Anglos soon offered an explanation: Mexicans' ranching skills were not acquired, but were, instead, a gift of nature. One gold miner explained that cattle ranching was "the life, and sport of the Mexican, who is almost born upon a horse [and] can accomplish daring feats upon his back." He "is absolutely good for nothing anywhere else," this writer was quick to add (Jones 1927:240-1, 242).[9]

There was a brief moment around the turn of the 20th century, when some Mexicans and some Indians even achieved heroic roles in the spectacles of popular culture when "real Mexicans," together with representatives of a completely vanquished people carrying "pure blood," were featured players in Wild West entertainments, roping, riding, warring, and hunting in endless re-enactments of Western frontier myths. The key to acceptability had two sides. First, Anglos had to believe that you were either no threat (the contented citizens of another country or members of a vanishing—assimilating—race). Second, you had to live somewhere else. Thus indigenous "Mexicans" and "half-breed" Indians continued to threaten Anglo hegemony and in these popular entertainments, they joined "white renegades" to portray villains. Not many years of the 20th century passed before indigenous people of any color disappeared both from California and from the white imagination. The 1900 census counted only about 20,000 tribal people remaining (Hurtado 1988:195). The "new West's" boosters published a magazine to attract Easterners reflecting this new reality. *Out West: A Magazine of the Old Pacific and the New* (its motto? "The Nation Back of Us. The World in Front") illustrated the myth beckoning more Anglo settlers: "The genius of the West" showed (white) peopled covered wagons appearing over the rim of a broad mesa, empty of inhabitants. Below and in the foreground lay a broad, shining, equally empty valley. In the sky, however, skirted by roiling white clouds, rose a naked Anglo woman, pointing West with her raised left arm[10]

Endless public outcries, then as well as now, attest: out of sight was the only way nonwhites stayed out of mind. Thus "Home on the Range," beloved of presidents and schoolteachers since its appearance at the beginning of the 20th century, included forgivingly agentless declarations of possession and dispossession: "Oh *give* me a home where the buffalo roam,/Where the deer and the antelope play,/Where seldom *is heard* a discouraging word/And the skies are not cloudy all day....Where the air is so pure, the zephyrs so free,/The breezes so balmy and light,/That I would not *exchange* my home on the range/For all the cities so bright." The cheery tune ends with an even more ominous passivity: "The red man *was pressed* from this part of the West,/He's likely no more to return/To the banks of the Red River where seldom if ever/Their flickering campfires burn."

Well, the Indians were gone, vanished, or safely locked away on reservations. And soon, even the most grudging admiration of Mexican *vaqueros*, even of those "safely" foreign-born, dissolved in the face of fears that the Anglo Saxon world was being overrun: by non-Anglo Saxon Southern and Eastern Europeans in the East, by the descendants of Africans in the South and by Mexicans and Asians in the West. And when cattle ranching yielded its economic dominance—to gold mining, farming, commerce (and, in the higher reaches of the Sierra Nevada, sheep ranching, which called for the skills of Basque herders, not Mexican cowboys)—non-white cowboys (black, as well as brown and red) became obsolete. The threat that they and their descendants might choose to settle in white cities intensified. Unable to force most of them (or those of Chinese or African heritage) onto arid North American reservations, Anglos passed Chinese Exclusion Acts and began to exile Mexicans "home"—to the nation now south of "our" California. And this meant a bigger and better border.

All was not well. Though most Indians stayed on their reservations,[11] though most Chinese and Japanese stayed in their urban ghettos or in isolated, invisible rural communities,[12] and though African-Americans remained but a tiny minority of urban populations (they, too, invisible, locked into race-defined ghettos), Mexicans kept coming, across the Rio Grande, across to New Mexico, to Arizona, to California, to Aztlán, called by agriculture, by industry, and—eventually—by war[13] (Freedberg 1995:1).

So a Republican congressman, frenzied in his racist xenophobia, declared in 1995: "I don't want to see the sons of Hispanics burning the flag that white men's sons fought and died for in World War Two and Vietnam." Was he color blind or is he an idiot? Did he really not know that Latinos —and African- and Native-Americans— fought in both wars? dying in vastly disproportionate numbers in Vietnam? And how horribly this history repeats itself: Latinos, African Americans, and Native Americans are today dying in even more disproportionate numbers in U.S. wars in Iraq and Afghanistan[14] (*SF Chronicle* Dec.20,1995:1; Trujillo, 1994).

Here, in our West, brown (and red, Mexicans are Indios, too) immigrants just kept on coming. More borders. More guards, these deliberately the cruelest they could find to confront the frighteningly permeable line that ran east to west along the southern reaches of Angloland, this place they had begun to believe belonged to them by birthright. The "Texas Rangers" reigned supreme, their utter ruthlessness celebrated, justified by the nation's premier historians. Listen to Walter Prescott Webb (1965 [1935]: "The Mexican has a cruel streak, which, in turn, must be dealt with cruelly."

A 1942 Los Angeles County sheriff reported on the barrio violence that resulted from the arrival of the first thousands of *braceros*: Anglo-Saxons, he noted, preferred to use their fists in fights while Mexicans wanted knives. "His desire is to kill, or at least to let blood. It is," he insisted, "an inborn characteristic" (Sánchez 1991: 177).

Of those Mexicans who ignored their Anglo guards, who braved the cruelty to cross into their ancestral lands (still often at the behest of California's rich Anglo settlers, unable to work the fields, clean the houses, tend the gardens, care for the children) it was okay as long as they were content to use up their youth doing work no one else wanted at wages no one else would accept. But then they began to settle—whole families. Anglos began murmuring in their Brentwood, their Westwood, their Beverly Hills mansions. Listen: "First we got rid of the Indians and now this!" Listen: "They are taking our resources, overrunning our land. They won't learn our language. They have too many children. They don't eat our food. They smell funny. Their music is foreign. Their religion is not our religion. They have brown skin, hair, eyes. They are destroying our traditional values" Listen: "They are *undocumented aliens.*"

They sought variations on the solutions of their ancestors. I wrote to A.:

> Home again in L.A. after 30 years. Not my neighbor-
> hood, of course, this one for the rich, this Gringoland

for sure. But, homesick after years in alien Manhattan, I strolled this morning, all unknowing, through the shiny streets of vast lawns and tall trees and sweet flowers—"bougainvillea, hibiscus," I practiced names recalled from childhood, "star jasmine, honeysuckle"—that climb the hills around the U.C.L.A. campus. The houses we remember seeing from a distance, from our childhood across town. In that tradition of historical forgetting, of the entire transformation of a genocidal past into a romantic nostalgia, most houses here are built to look like California missions, with red tile roofs and arched doorways. To our eyes trained by childhood poverty and to mine trained more recently by years of New York crowding these are vast dwellings, made still larger by the whitewashed walls looming between passersby and the privacy within.

Stunned by so much color, so much, yes, beauty, I did not at first see the markers. But after a time I began to note. Each house bore a tiny blue sign anchored firmly in the sea of grass visible from the street:

"White People's Stuff Protection Agency"

Below this message, sized to disguise the truth of the sign's purpose:

Armed Response"

ARMED RESPONSE!? I read it out loud, shocked as I went on walking, sadly less unknowing, up and down the hills, still smelling, feeling, but no longer *thinking*, "home."

So who provides the guns this time? No Texas Rangers here—too gross, too, well, "white trash." So who? I began to watch as I walked. Then I saw the first of what became dozens of cars, each marked with the logo of the White People's Stuff Protection Agency. Driving the cars were...not Mexicans, not Indians...African Americans—mercenaries, black-skinned people (men) hired to keep the brown/red skinned people from stealing what they cleaned, moved, watered, tended, pruned, dusted, washed, polished for the people who evidently did nothing at all. They cannot imagine, these empty, greed-driven gabachos, that those who work for them do not long to own the appurtenances that spell American wealth, that constitute their identity as surely as it formed an identity for their ancestors. "White people," Robert Thomas once said, "confuse consumption with experience." Too bad.

"WE HAVE BORNE EVERYTHING PATIENTLY FOR THIS LONG TIME"

—Joseph Brant, Mohawk leader, speaking to a council in an Onondaga village on Buffalo Creek, April 21, 1794 (quoted in Vanderwerth 1971:50)

The atrocities we've committed against each other haven't been on a grand scale. (As [Richard] Hofstadter noted, there is nothing in our history to compare with the slaughter of some 10,000 French Huguenots on St. Bartholomew's Night in 1572, or the massacre of more than 100,000 Indonesian Communists in 1965, let alone the official horros of Stalin, Hitler, or Pol Pot.
—Sean Wilentz (1995:40-41)[15]

In 1500, the population of Native North America numbered between 12.5 and 15 million people. "In 1890 [when]the federal government declared the period of conquest...officially over...only 248,253 identifiable Indians remained alive within its borders, with another 122,585 residing north of the border, in Canada...The census conducted in 1900 revealed only 237,196 Indians in the U.S., barely 101,000 in Canada.
—Stiffarm with Lane (1992:36-37)[16]

Proposition 187

Section I: Findings and Declarations

Listen:

The People of California find and declare as follows:

That they have suffered and are suffering economic hardship caused by the presence of illegal aliens in this state.

That they have suffered and are suffering personal injury and damage caused by the criminal conduct of illegal aliens in this state.

That they have a right to the protection of the government from any person or persons entering this country unlawfully.

Therefore the People of California declare their intention to provide for cooperation between their agencies of state and local government with the federal government, and to establish a system of required notification by and between such agencies to prevent illegal aliens in the United States from receiving benefits or public services in the state of California.

Section 113

Listen:

Any person who manufactures, distributes, or sells false documents to conceal the true citizenship or resident alien status of another person is guilty of a felony, and shall be punished by imprisonment in the state prison for five years or by a fine of seventy-five thousand dollars.

Section 114

Listen:

Any person who uses false documents to conceal his or her true citizenship or resident alien status is guilty of a felony, and shall be punished by imprisonment in the state prison for five years or by a fine of twenty-five thousands dollars.

A SHORT HISTORY OF HATE

> *1517: Jaguar priests of the Yucatán Mayas: "The offenses of the white people are all alike....Gradually we discover that the Christians are great liars. Little by little we realize that they are cheats."*
> —quoted in Jara and Spadaccine (1992:29)

The legacies of European genocide in the Americas are many and bitter. Two spread through everything, twisting all our lives here in the West. One we have seen. This is the continuous barrage of fear-driven efforts to keep California white—to keep, in other words, every material advantage gained by warfare and pillage in the grasping hands of the Anglo "us." The other is mixed blood.

The first produced oddities both serious and ridiculous. And its essentials were never consistent. Both Mexicans and Indians played good, played bad, played "indigenous," played "foreigner." No attitude was consistent, no official policy firm. But by the close of the 19th century, Californians knew at least one thing clearly. There, people of several ethnic origins lived too close to keep an endemic Anglo fear—perhaps of their own history—at bay. Together these people of color bore the brunt of Euro-America's hatred. Public policies were fear-driven, inconsistent and random, aimed now at one group, now at another. But always directed by Anglos, those self-styled ("real") Americans.

Listen: In 1871, Chinese men living in that part of Los Angeles known as Chinatown were massacred (Raftery 1992:7). A few years later, purportedly terrified of the "yellow peril," the U.S. Congress passed the Chinese Exclusion Acts, and even the wives and children of those men imported to work the railways and mining camps of the West were forbidden to enter the country. So scary were the "yellow devils" that the California legislature in its turn decided that while black and Indian children could begin to attend public schools, those "Chinese" children who were already in the state would be taught in segregated schools.

But this exclusive focus on Chinese and Chinese Americans was short-lived. Whiteness requires constant vigilance, and there were other threats to the racial purity of Anglo California. In 1916, for example, the good Anglo folks of the Sherman School District in East Hollywood petitioned to have "Mexican" children excluded from their schools, on the grounds that they carried communicable diseases (an ironic recognition of how quickly European diseases became "theirs"). Alas for these worried parents, however, the school board's physicians soon reported that the "Mexican" kids carried no illness not familiar in every Anglo school population. This didn't reassure parents, since they were less concerned about disease than about racial mixing. But it was some time before this school board hit upon a satisfactory solution. Only in 1921 did they figure out how to segregate "Mexican" children from their "American" peers. Claiming that they were being helpful, they set up special "ungraded" classes, for all the nonwhite children, defined as "non-English speakers" (Ibid. 1992:112).

Ironically, these segregated classrooms were born in an era of frenzied "Americanization" efforts in the Los Angeles Schools, aimed at transforming those "foreign" children who couldn't be got rid of into imitations of the Euro-American ideal. Central Junior High had its fairly anodyne "junior citizenship program" for both white and nonwhite working-class families. School children and their parents, led by Euro-American teachers (there were no others), were taken all over the city and invited to observe (and presumably to learn to desire) the appurtenances of white, middle-class "American" life. Oozing racial stereotypes, one participating teacher noted that "Mexicans, Polish, and Russians enjoyed rehearsals of the Philharmonic," while "Chinese, Korean, and Japanese students received the most pleasure from a visit to the different departments of the Hall of Records" (Ibid.:112).

Other such programs were more pernicious. Los Angeles public schools also aimed to humiliate "foreigners" into assimilating. School "christening days" made "Orientals" assume "given names the teachers could pronounce"[17] (Ibid.:94). "I.Q. tests"—utterly dependent upon cultural knowledge held tightly in Anglo hands—became segregationist school boards' next weapon; classes began to be assigned not only on the basis of language, but also by intelligence quotients.

When schooling failed to create children of color in a white image, policing took over. Then, as now, the Los Angeles police were unsubtle racists. During a bloody suppression of a Wobbly strike on the San Pedro docks, reporters discovered (purportedly to their liberal horror) that many of *their* policemen, including the chief, Louis Oaks, were active members of the Ku Klux Klan (Ibid.:103). For those would-be cops who hated "foreigners" but couldn't find employment among the white-bedsheet-hidden police of Los Angeles, that hate-filled decade created a second possibility, the Border Patrol.

This new police force was ready when another crisis, the Depression, struck. They were there when Anglos decided—again: they never tire of this sport—that they were in economic danger because of "Mexicans." Legal or no, Mexican-born or not, these "foreigners" were quickly "repatriated" to Mexico. (Not surprisingly, then—as now—particular victims of this race-driven exportation were those on public assistance.)

Listen: Former governor Pete Wilson's mythical "Californians" are those who "have always answered adversity with bold thoughts...always dared to dream." With a straight face and a stunning tolerance for 8th-grade social studies textbook cliches, the then-governor celebrated his Californians who "followed a dream," pioneers who went "west in wagon trains across a desolate prairie and over frozen mountains....These early settlers risked their lives crossing the mighty Sierra, till one day they crossed a ridge to find themselves gazing down from the heights upon a golden valley that held the promise of California."[18]

(If that prairie they crossed is really so desolate, then give it back: to the Lakotas and Dakotas, to the Omahas, the Winnebagos, the Cheyennes and Arapahos, the Osages and Mesquakies whose high-grass prairies those were once, before...Frozen mountains? the Sierra Nevada, the Rockies? OK: give them back too!)

With unusual candor Pete Wilson admitted that "most of us are not the lineal descendents [sic] of those pioneers. We (!) came later. We came by ship from Asia and by station wagon from Ohio. We came during the Great Depression from the Dust Bowl in pick-ups piled high with our possessions."[19] ("Pickups" has a nice, friendly, Chevy ring to it. But these migrants from the Midwest, these who had been sharecroppers and tenant farmers, didn't drive shiny new trucks. As Dorothea Lange's unforgettable photographs show, as John Steinbeck's prose tells, they came in ancient brokendown cars and trucks—and anything else that moved. Wilson also neglects to mention that those "we's," those "Okies" and "Arkies," were met by gun-toting Anglos, all too ready to shoot if the newer "we's" protested the nighttime burning of their Hoovervilles, their migrant camps.)

And the Dust Bowl refugees were not the same "we's" who came a little later to serve Anglo farmers who found themselves suddenly short of labor. Those we's were *braceros,* Mexicans imported to plant, weed, tend, and harvest California's crops in the absence of sufficient earlier "we's," the, "poor white trash," pickers of John Steinbeck's *Grapes of Wrath*, who, only a few years before, had replaced the Mexicans "repatriated" south of the border. But however essential to feeding the Anglos of California, to sustaining the vast profits of what was even then a sea of agribusinessmen, these *braceros,* like their predecessors before them, soon posed a problem. Unlike the Okies and Arkies, *braceros* were visible; they spoke a "foreign" language, they had dark skin (they worked hard and without complaining), they were *different.*

Once again, the Los Angeles County Schools leapt into the breach, commissioning studies, then holding special workshops for Anglo teachers forced to confront brown-skinned, Spanish-speaking children in their classrooms. One commission report informed the teachers (with characteristic muddle): "Several investigations pertaining to the adjustment of Mexican and Spanish-speaking pupils in the various school systems disclose facts similar to those which follow: On the average they are retarded and over age for the grade, the retardation ranging from 50% to 86% of the enrollment." Still, there was hope. This stunning "retardation" was not due to race. "There are no significant inherent racial differences in mental endowment" (Hughes and Palm 1942:12). So what to do?

> We—my sister and brother and I—know exactly what was done. We were children in those schools, children in heavily "Mexican" neighborhoods, first in downtown Los Angeles, then in the north San Fernando Valley (in a brand new housing tract planted atop a dry desert wash just south of Roscoe Boulevard). In elementary school we learned about being Americans, Mexican-style, as we danced "La Jesusita," "La Cucuaracha," the "Mexican Hat Dance." We sang songs: "Come break the Piñata, come scatter the toys," "For we are humble pilgrims, Jesús, María, y José..." WE SPOKE SPANISH, *caló,* the soft language of our suburban *barrio.* BUT we were not Mexicans. We were even half-white. We were "smart kids," not sufficiently least to spend our days in Spanish-speaking classrooms. So, when we finished 6th grade, they put my sister and me on buses and drove us far across town, to an Anglo school where we

learned the language of "civilization," French. Soon, the Spanish we all knew from our street play was gone, buried beneath the pluperfect, buried inside the throat-stripping 'r's' of a new language, a better language, a *white* language. When Ritchie Valens was killed in the terrible plane crash that devastated our neighborhood in 1959, we two could still dance the *pachuco*, but we could barely remember the words of his signature song, "La Bamba," at our school's memorial assembly. Ritchie Valens—who crossed over, but only after Valenzuela was Anglo-ized—was dead.

"And we came by jet-liner last year, last month, and last week."
—Pete Wilson (1995)

Well, it was the American dream all right, though "we" no longer skulk across borders in the night; "we" are white; "we" are not Mexican, or Salvadoran, or Guatamalan families dodging searchlight-waving helicopters or the traffic rushing along the 6-lane, 8-lane freeways we must cross, "free"ways posted with signs "PROHIBIDO"[20] (Arteaga 1994: cover photo). Nor are we black-skinned Haitians, running from murder, from anarchy, from fear, paddling, sailing, swimming, desperately, desperately toward Florida. "We" have plane tickets; "we" are white.

But still "we" are dissatisfied. Still the dream eludes "us." Pete Wilson tells us why. Listen:

"Ours is a generation that cannot take for granted the good life, the historically generous bounty of California unless we are prepared to make dramatic change...." Change?

Listen: "The People agree....They ask 'Why should federal law reward illegal immigrants for violating the law and punish California taxpayers and needy legal residents?'"

Here it is: Proposition 187 in a paranoid nutshell. American politics, driven by greed. We have heard it before. We shall hear it again, and again, and again.

What to do? Well we can become like the "Thems" who own the place now. We can assimilate (or at least perform respectability). Or, we can kill our all our children who "look" white.

But that's me.

MIXED BLOODS

Charges and (Partial) Payments

> *Their relationships with other human beings are just a tactic, not a need. They are pilgrims in the world. Their search is directed either by utopia or nostalgia. Their present is always imperfect, made of change and doubt. The subject is always alien, exiled."*
> –Jara and Spadaccini (1992:86)

> *I remember one later shame-filled day when I was living with my mother in Butte, Montana. A number of white classmates relentlessly made fun of my last name, and that filled me with shame and guilt. I believed that being an Indian was no good and countered them by saying that although I did have Indian blook, a full ¼ of my blood was French; therefore I did have some value. I said that often and even believed it. It was shameful.*
> —George P. Horsecapture (1991:203)

Twentieth and twenty-first-century Californians have depended upon two kinds of borders to keep "their" state Anglo. One is physical, symbolized by the barbed wire of the 19th century West (collected now by aficionados of a past romanticized and cleansed by myth of its blood). The other is less visible; terror and self-hatred fence "alien" minds, converting people with brown and red skins to whiteness. For mixed bloods, for George Horsecapture and all of the rest of us, the process has been devastatingly simple: our "white" blood forms the core of respectability, of an authenticity created to define insiders to the American Dream.

The techniques developed to instill such identification in those not purely white were first practiced on all Indians, mixed or "pure." As the Board of Indian Commissioners explained in 1875:

> It is the aim of the Government of the United States to reclaim the Indian from his rude, wild, and savage state by the kindly influence of just dealing; by an undeviating observance of good faith; by a firm, but kind and paternal rule over him; by protecting him from wrongs and aggressions; and by educating him and his children in letters, arts, manners, and religion...in this way lead them up to citizenship and absorb them as we are absorbing men of all other races and lands and climes,

into this Christian nation" (*Annual Report of the Board
of Indian Commissioners* 1875:6).

Of course authentic whiteness could not ever be achieved, not
even among those whose mixed genes provided all the requisite
visible characteristics. "Blue eyes are like money," Alica Walker
observed at Emory University in 1990. The buy your way in." But
not all the way in.

Always in exile from themselves, then, these "alien" children.
The cross blood Indians among them discovered that some treaties had exiled them; some had kept them in. The earlier treaties,
those of the Sauk and Fox (1830), the Poncas (1858), the Kansas
(1859), the Omahas (1865), and the Blackfoots (1865—unrati-
fied), provided for their children whose blood was not whole.
But many later ones (affected by the blood policies of the federal
government) did not. As a result of this muddled history, Russell
Thornton writes, "The status of these mixed bloods has often been
problematic: sometimes they have been considered American
Indian, sometimes not....Generally, mixedbloods who accepted
tribal ways of life were welcomed, whereas those who preferred
non-Indian ways were not" (1986:41-2).

Whatever the efforts and policies of various Native nations,
however, numbers of mixed-bloods increased steadily. In 1830, 46
percent of American Indians were "full-blood," 42% mixed blood,
and 11% unspecified. By 1980, the majority of those identifying
themselves as American Indians were mixed blood, while some
"6-7 million [other] Americans had some degree of American
Indian ancestry" (Ibid.).

Sherman Alexie
1.
I cut myself into sixteen equal pieces
Keep thirteen and feed the other three
to the dogs...
2.
It is done by blood, reservation mathematics, fractions:
Father (full-blood) + mother (5/8) + son (13/16) (1992: 36-37).

So what does this mean?

PAYMENTS (SUBSET: *DESIRE*)

Frantz Fanon: "I marry white culture, white beauty, white white-ness." (1967:63)
Sherman Alexie: "There is nothing as white as the white girl an Indian boy loves." (1992:18)
Wendy Rose: "Step softly.
She is not of this world
And no one rides to the rescue."(1994:99)

So we drown.
Suburban tides run clear before Fanon's confession,
Scrubbing the red.
Luna to Moon. Lunada.

Pulling the water
Pouring the
Washing the
Color. Gone.

Lacunae:

"White Women are nothing without their mirrors," Frances's grandmother tells us, gently.

I Hold Up a Red Mirror:

A pale statue of Ohio, Iowa, Kansas
(Names remember mine her ancestors slaughtered.)
She fits her colorless moon lines around your brown body,
Mud yellow hair, disarranged by the lust her holding flaunts,
Hangs firm, bronzed not by the exigencies of her mythic inherit-ance

But by white Europe's aversion to that clean that startled dirty Columbus...

("They were strange men," tribal people recall, "smelly and sweaty, ignorant of the delights of a frequent bath, hungry for gold and precious stones.")

No Medusa, then: No power. No passion.

And you, ése?
What can she (re)make of you?
Your hair—vanishing more surely than any Indian—worn long, tied back,
Defiant,
One silver earring marking culture.
You know, mi carnal. You know.

Seeing me
You circle, turn your back to my dismay. Amor de lejos, amor de pendejos.
You take Miss Middle America's beige, Burberry-shrouded arm
Hold your mirror before her pale face
And walk away.

MI MIXED BLOOD VIDA LOCA

Más vale que haiga un tonto y no dos. (Much better to have one idiot and not two.)

R. shows up at the American Film Institute's Award ceremony for the famous Indian film maker shunning us, toting HIS prize: a woman whiter than white, albino nearly. However trendy in SoHo these days (and *au courant* with black), to us it is the look of near-death and frightening.

Skin color matters, we know. My father used to criticize a self-conscious 15 year old over and over and over:

"You are so pale. You look sick. What's the matter?" Near naming my mixed blood's adherence to the European side....For him, my blue eyes, paying my way in to the overculture (like Wendy Rose's cousin, the "green-eyed boy/everyone loves" [1993:47]), shut me out of his world. ("It's your blue eyes, not your brown hair," my sister says. "Get brown contact lenses and see how everyone native treats you then.")

PAYMENTS (SUBSET: "REAL AUTHENTICK INDIANS?")

That famous filmmaker, meeting all of our talking circle, reacts to blue-eyed Shari and me:

> Summoned to swell the nearly all-white crowd with some *indígenas*, a group of us went together. There, we joined a line heading into the auditorium. The film-maker was standing outside the door, nodding graciously, willingly receiving accolades from his dozens of admirers circling around. Without speaking, he watched those who passed carefully. Dean, tall, black haired, black eyed, was first of our group. At the sight of him, the filmmaker grinned happily and leaned over the heads of several admirers to grab his hand. Then Carol, also dark but much shorter. He had to reach across several people to reach Carol's hand. He did. He shook it joyfully, enthusiastically, still smiling. But Shari and I were next. The smile disappeared. He took in our blue eyes, nothing more. His face went cold and still. His eyes moved rapidly past us, aimed at a spot just above our not-quite-black hair, came to rest. Smiling again, he recognized our next friend, Chris, black of hair and eye, red of skin.
>
> Who *were* we to Mr. Princeton Indian? Mr. Rich New England Indian?
>
> Are we, Shari and I, both blue of eye and light of skin, the same objects of desire as white women? Not blonde, of course. And (as A. wrote once, trying to explain our connections), blonde or brown or black, we share souls, we know race rage, we share, as Dean says, "blood." Does this complicate the straightforward assumption of our Lady Whiteness? Or does it make

us safer for those men who understand the peculiarity
Fanon named so long ago? "There IS nothing as white
as the white girl an Indian boy loves."

NEW CHARGES (SUBSET: RACISM)

So, I admit to a curious potential landlord, I am American
Indian. His face closes. He mutters mostly to himself. "Parties,
alcohol, rent due...." His wife freezes with embarrassment, chats
mindlessly to cover what I realize only slowly. His Navajo jewelry,
I see now, is about loving dead Indians, vanished—but quaint—
people. It's about anthropology. It's about book learning and Hiawatha. And, of course, as Tim points out, it's about owning the
material cultures of the conquest...the victor's spoils.

NEW CHARGES (SUBSET: TRAGIC MULATTO)

Week after week I call A. from New York, asking advice.
Always it is the same. A professor, a colleague, has telephoned. The
requests are varied, endless. "Could you: (1) Come to party? There
will be some Native Americans there and you always make everyone so comfortable; (2) Help me understand why X isn't doing the
work for my class? Her term paper doesn't explore all the readings
assigned so I don't think she's even done the reading, I think for
her own good I'm going to have to fail her; (3) Explain why Y is
having trouble with the financial aid office? We've offered all the
help any student should need but he still seems to have problems;
(4) Bring 'your group' to an event we're having on Friday? We want
a Native American presence; (5) Meet an aboriginal film maker
who is visiting New York for a semester? I know you'll all have a
lot in common."

So I sit in rooms, hang on telephones, write, explain, tell,
explain—all the time, though, swallowing a reaction not unlike D.'s
pulling away when those Anglo women pet him and pet him. I am
angry. I am horrified that I must do this. But what is the choice? It
is, A. tells me over and over, the condition of *la frontera*, life on the
border, mulatto life.

So, keenly aware that this act patronizes a good friend, betrays
a sister, I explain (though with tongue firmly planted in cheek,
fingers crossed behind my back) a nontraditional term paper to an

anthropology professor. It is, I tell him, not the failure he perceives but rather a deeply confiding, seriously honoring work by someone who doesn't tell the things in the paper easily. My professor colleague is moved, is effusively grateful. My comrade gets an A in the course. (But she knows what the white professor does not. She tells me one day as we walk along the street, that X. doesn't like her very much, that he avoids her as much as possible and won't even look in her eyes. "He may be an anthropologist," she says, smiling, "but he sure doesn't know anything about Indians.")

And after Shari and I sort out financial aid problems, translating for the white woman in charge, for the black woman at the bursar's office, and then back, into "Indian" for another friend (though this part is mainly whiteman jokes and not really an explanation), I carefully remember to telephone thanks to the first woman. More questions—about tribal traditions, about differences she perceives between this friend and another Native she knows. More exclamations: "Oh it's just all so interesting! I'm just realizing that all you people have different cultures. I've just learned all about Sioux people last week from J.F. and now I see I'll have to go to the library to get some books out about Navajos in order to understand X."

"And," she adds, gathering Shari and me into the same mental fold, "you two will probably want to come to the Indian event we are planning to hold in March. I'll be sure you're on the mailing list." But, I think with despair, how could I not be on the mailing list? *Someone* is going to have to translate.

PAYMENTS (SUBSET: GIFTS—FRANCES PETERS-LITTLE)

"Given" to our talking circle by an anthro professor, Frances is my *carnalita*, instant friend. She recognizes our New York University dilemmas straight away. Even if she hadn't been one of us from the first, she would quickly have learned to see them as we do. First, the directors of the institute, of which she is a 6th-month fellow, made sure that she is terribly cold. Arranging her apartment, they have given her—right off the plane from Sydney's summer, a red desert clan person—one blanket! When she arrives at my door upstairs I hand over several more, seeing shadows of the lost person I was 15 years before, landing from Berkeley's summer in England, freezing. And in both places, not just the weather chills.

Here what shrinks indigenous skins is the extraordinary closeness of the physical and emotional space in which New Yorkers seem to thrive. "They get right up in my face to talk," Frances tells me, surprised. "Do Indians find this as awful as we aboriginal people do? Do you need lots of space?" "Yes," I tell her, "yes! And touching? They keep touching. This drives us *loco*. And you?" "Oh yeah," she says in broad Australian English. "They've been touching me all the time. We don't touch at all, even families. And they do it in public all the time! Just the same as the way they always talk about themselves...stuff we'd never say, even to our closest friends and families. We'd get laughed out of town if we said some of these things!"

And then, despite that fact that it was she who assumed our indigenousness would quickly bind us all together, the anthro is distressed because Frances so quickly and easily joined this family of aliens. After all, it is her acquisitiveness, her desire to collect exotica that has brought Frances thither, and to us. So again she telephones me, insistent, wanting to know: "What do you have in common?" I am briefly dumbstruck so she begins to speculate about a bond she can never understand. "She *is* very intelligent, of course," she reminds herself. ("For an abo..." I add in my mind).

I know the answers, but this time I don't supply information for the thirsty anthro. It is none of her business. But it is, in fact, because Frances doesn't look around the table at all the people and say "Are you all real Indians? Am I spending time with real Indians?" She doesn't ask "What do Indians think about...? How does an Indian man feel about...? What do Indian women think is most....?" She isn't exceptionally thrilled that she can add us to her collection of exotic encounters. She doesn't try to add herself to us by recounting some story that features something she associates with "Indians."

She's a woman of color, too, and knows the male desire that shuns her kind, our kind, first hand. Painful it is, too. And we women talk about it among ourselves. We talk about the power relations that shape the guys' strange desires to own the other, to keep a trophy, to taunt the white guys by holding one of "their" women. Frances tells us that Fanon's truth, Alexie's truth, describe

Australia as they describe our world. There, too, Barbie dolls mean perfection.

Oh.

PAYMENTS (*LISTEN TO THE TALK*)

Anglo professor writes on Indian students' thesis draft: "Read all my comments. go away and pray and meditate until you know what it is you want to say."

Anthropologist asks Dean Curtis Bear Claw: "So how did you people sit down before there were chairs?"

A Euro-American woman friend, an artist, meets Frances. She immediately starts collecting her, recounting a dream, set in Australia, a dream about paintings coming up out of the ground. Fixing her eyes intently on Frances's face she tells her how she's always felt a kinship with that continent...a sense that she knows something about aborigines in her artist's blood. I writhe.

Then finally she concludes: "I need to try to trace my Chippewa ancestors.... No one ever mentioned them when I was growing up, so...." Aboriginal in a former life? Chippewa—though she never knew in 50 years—in this? Why do people do this? A twentieth century form of the historical violence, of the fencing, of the building of borders.

Another friend did it with A. when he visited New York, when she discovered that they had both attended the same Southern California elementary school. Burbling then about how "the Mexicans" at the elementary school they both attended were "never around" as far as she could recall, and funny, she'd been a hall monitor and class president so... She claimed to be charmed to meet A. because, she told him over and over, in all the years of grammar schooling she had never, ever known any of "you." This Euro-American friend, too, was "collecting," at once seeking common ground with something romantic about indigenousness, and erecting a wall, establishing a self different from the exotic other. Though here again, as with the encounter with Frances, this friend was revealing a deep, endemic racism to us, *she* imagined she was bonding.

Frances got it right off. A., usually more perceptive, was initially deaf, though he was in high form and talking and talking as though he felt close to everyone there. Later, he wept.

PAYMENTS (SUBSET: RESISTANCE)

In 1882 Frank Hamilton Cushing, "on a collecting trip for the Smithsonian Institution's Bureau of Ethnology" described in Chapter 3, "reported from the Hopi village of Oraibi that he had encountered implacable resistance from the village elders.... Despite deploying all the kinds of power held by a visiting white man, Curtis Hinsley continues, Cushing was "unable to persuade the people of Oraibi to part with their belongings for deposit in 'Father Washington's' museum of glass boxes in Washington" (Hinsley 1981:11).

FINAL CHARGES

January 31, 1995, 1 A.M. In a San Fernando Valley neighborhood, near my childhood home, beneath a Hollywood freeway overpass, a white man called William Masters pulled out a 9-millimeter pistol and killed 18-year old César Arce. With more shots, this 35-year-old vigilante wounded Arce's friend, David Hillo. Why? The two young men were spray-painting graffiti on the concrete bridge.

Masters claimed he shot the younger men in "self-defense." His victim, Arce, "armed with a screwdriver," was a "murderer" who "this time...died." Masters quickly became a hero to north valley Anglos. Women were particularly charmed. "Diane" telephoned a radio talk show to assure her world "I don't care if he's Looney Toons or what, but we need more guys like him around." Sandi Webb (what do you want to bet she dots her "i's" with little happy faces and wears salmon pink polyester pant suits?) made public a letter she wrote in behalf of the City Council of which she is a member: "Kudos to William Masters for his vigilant anti-graffiti efforts and for his foresight in carrying a gun for self-protection.... If Sun Valley refuses to honor Masters as a crime-fighting hero, then I invite him to relocate to our town. I think he will find Simi Valley to be a much more compatible place to live." (Well, he would. Simi Valley, once a childhood refuge of horned toads, cacti, tumble weeds, manzanita, and shady live oaks, has become a center of paramilitary terror, another place where crosses, imported from the South along with the people, are burned in the dark nights by sheet-covered haters.)

"The police said...he had acted justifiably in self-defense. They set him free after holding him for what he said was six hours. 'In this case...this was not a difficult decision...' said Robert L. Cohen, the Deputy District Attorney.... 'It's clear that what he did came under the law. Would a reasonable person in a like or similar case have reacted int he same way? And I think the answer is yes.'"

"Still," the *New York Times* reported, "the incident is not closed. The city attorney's office is considering filing misdemeanor charges against Mr. Masters for carrying an unlicensed gun. It would not be the first such case against him. In 1985 he was arrested in Texas for carrying two metal martial arts clubs and fought the case for four years until a state appeals court let stand a $1 fine levied against him."

As for Arce's companion, the survivor of this vigilante "justice," "Mr. Garcetti's office is considering bringing charges of attempted robbery against him. If it does, Hillo could face a murder charge, since under California law a person who takes part in a crime that leads to a killing, even of his accomplice, can be charged with murder" (Mydans 1995:20).

ENDINGS: THE FIRST

=============================

WILL BE
EXHIBITED
FOR ONE DAY ONLY!

AT THE STOCKTON HOUSE!
This day, Aug.19, from 9 a.m. until 6 p.m.

THE HEAD
of the renowned Bandit!
JOAQUIN!

—-AND THE—-

HAND OF THE THREE FINGERED JACK!
THE NOTORIOUS ROBBER AND MURDERER

=============================

"Joaquin" and "Three Fingered Jack" were captured by the *State Rangers*, under the command of Capt. Harry Love at the Arroyo Cantina, July 24th. No reasonable doubt can be entertained in regard to the identification of the head now on exhibition as being that of the notorious robber, Joaquin Muriatta, as it has been recognized by hundreds of persons who have formerly seen him (Bancroft Library Collections).

ENDINGS: THE SECOND

Thus the story, like a bad dream, left us stranded suddenly in the island of forgetfulness, prisoners. Not only that, but the genes that guard our culture, the essence of our history, have been left chained up, clogging the arteries that carry the impetus of the blood that animates the voice and soul of our people like rivers. Neither dignity nor education for the slaves, the masters said, only ignominy, prejudice, and death...

RETURN BEYOND THE CROSSROADS. Break the silence of the centuries with the agony of our screams. You will see the fields in bloom where you planted your children and trees that have drunk the sap of the ages, petrified trees without songbirds and without owls, there where the voices of those who have succumbed dwell. Destiny is history, and history is the road stretched out before the footsteps that have not existed. Who has made you believe that you are lambs and beasts of burden?

Tiger knights, eagle knights, fight for the destiny of your children! Know, those who have been immolated, for in this region you will be the dawn and you will also be the river
—Miguel Méndez (1992:178)

Oh my California! Oh my people. Ritchie Valens keeps on dying. *E Pluribus Unum.*

CHAPTER 5

‖HOW THE BORDER LIES:
‖HISTORICAL REFLECTIONS

A sked about the borders that separate Mexico and the United States, Carlos Fuentes replied:

> A big difference, I think, is memory. I have...called the U.S. the United States of Amnesia. They tend to forget their own history. So when I am speaking about a Protestant republic, a republic based on democratic principles of self-government, let me not forget that it is also a republic founded on violence. That it is also a republic founded on the exclusion of important... groups. That in the foundation of the United States, in its Constitution, in the Declaration of Independence, there is no place for...blacks and Indians and Hispanics, and even women are excluded from the body politic" (Szanto 1996:153).

So: "violence" and "exclusion," the unholy twins upon which United States identity rests.

WE, THE PEOPLE

"We, the People," were born in 1623 when the English "Pilgrims" landed and the origin tale began to be written.[1] Violence was in their luggage, wrapped in the Protestant Bible with its language of forgetting. An example: On the night of June 5, 1637, John Mason led English troops to attack a sleeping village of Pequot Indians, purportedly as punishment for the deaths of two English adventurers. As the Pequots awoke inside their wood and straw houses, Mason and his men set everything on fire, shooting or hacking to death those who tried to flee. In one hour, at least 400 people (Cotton Mather estimated 500 or 600) were burnt to death or slaughtered as they ran from their burning homes (Stannard 1992:114).[2] Later, Mason justified the killing: God, he explained, had "laughed his Enemies and the Enemies of his People to scorn, making them as a fiery oven.[...]Thus did the Lord judge among the heathen, filling the place with dead Bodies!" (113-14). William Bradford's account was more colorful: "It was a fearful sight to see them thus frying in the fire and the streams of blood quenching the same, and horrible was the stink and scent thereof, but the victory seemed a sweet sacrifice, and [the Englishmen] gave praise to god who had wrought so wonderfully for them" (quoted in Morison 1952:296).

There *were* dissenters. The Puritans' Narragansett scouts protested. "Our Indians," Roger Underhill wrote, "cried 'Mach it, mach it': that is, 'It is naught, it is naught because it is too furious and slays too many people!'" They were distraught, Underhill explained, because Indians did not fight "to conquer and subdue enemies" but rather "only for sport"(quoted in Jennings 1976:223). But the English themselves were hardly averse to "sport": only a few months later, Capt. Israel Stoughton together with 120 Massachusetts militiamen again crossed the borders of the Pequot nation. Although most Pequots had been exterminated, they still hoped to discover a few refugees. Narragansett scouts again guided the Englishmen. In a swamp near the mouth of the Pequot River, where some 100 survivors had taken refuge after the nighttime massacre of their fellows, the English found their victims. "For sport" Stoughton captured these hapless refugees, then turned them over to John Gallop. Quickly binding the hands and feet of 20 captives, Gallop threw them into the sea, a terrible warning to the rest. He then sent captive women and children to the Massachusetts Bay Colony where most were enslaved (Drinnon 1980:44-45).

The Englishmen's sporting adventure did not end there, however. Joined by John Mason with 40 more militiamen, Stoughton set off after more Pequots, who, Mason later explained smugly, "could make but little hast. by reason of their Children and want of Provision: being forced to dig for clams and to procure such other things as the Wilderness afforded" (Stannard 1992:114-5). Three hundred more Pequots were quickly captured and most were killed, some after what John Winthrop described blandly as "torture." "Hard by a most hideous swamp, so thick with bushes and so quagmirey as men could hardly crowd into it," Winthrop gloated later, "they were all gotten" (Winthrop 1996:220). The survivors provided more "servants" for the colonists. Thomas Endicott wanted both a girl and a boy. Roger Williams wrote Winthrop that he "had fixed mine eye on this little one with the red about his neck" (Drinnon 1980:47).[3] Thus were born two colonial practices, one of which continues to this day. Although the story is lost in most narratives of American slavery, Indians were, in fact, the first slaves in North America, captured by all the invading Europeans and kept either in the colonies or sold into the trans-Atlantic or Caribbean slave trades (Lauber 1969 [1913]; Forbes 1993; Usner 1998; Chap.6 below). The second practice was that of "adopting," or, as Indians say, "adopting out." Of course many of *these* Indian children lived their lives as virtual slaves—though the Puritans preferred other names for their unpaid domestic "servants." This practice of white families adopting Indian children—still the preferred minority—continues today, despite the Indian Child Welfare Act of 1978, created by Native leaders anxious to halt the numbers of children lost from their tribes.

This, then, is the violence out of which our United States was born, resting on the exclusion—by race—of the first in what has become a large group of U.S. "others".

THESES ON BORDERS

I should like next to suggest, via a series of interwoven"theses," that this mirror-making, this building of distances between the "them's" and the "us's," are part of "our" unacknowledged past, part of the total absence of historical memory that has created and maintained "borders." These stand not only as protective fences around "We, the People." Inside the minds of the "others," often unmarked, lie still more borders, built from the detritus of post-colonialist struggles over the tiny pieces of power left when the "we's" vacate their spaces of authority. These contemporary walls are as divisive as the work of fanatical missionaries, or governmental divide-and-conquer policies of earlier eras. Such self-created ethnic mirrors—grounded in essentialist versions of the viewer and the viewed, constructed by one group of othered, colonized people to distort or oppose the activities of another—produce only little images, the kind seen in those warped, tin mirrors handed out so profligately by Anglo invaders as payment for stolen Indian land. Nevertheless, their edges are sharp enough to cut; divided among themselves, people of color cannot challenge the real structures and purveyors of power. In the reflections produced by such tawdry, useless mirrors, moreover, interethnic stereotypes multiply.[4]

Many Chicana/os re-create North America's indigenous peoples in their desired images, Natives whose lands they, like Europeans before them, now inhabit. As Francisco Cacique notes of this kind of appropriation of North American indigenous practices, "it is an attempt to take on a 'subaltern' identity that is somewhat accepted/acknowledged in México (and romanticized in the U.S.) and use it to show how progressive you are that you are identifying with the indigenous community while distancing yourself just enough so as not really to have to deal with the daily hardships and violence that that community goes through." He continues, "Why not appropriate African practices, cosmologies, epistemologies, or, to use Mudimbe, gnosiologies? Is it a subtle whitefication process to deny this part of Xicana/o's identities while embracing a (pseudo) indigenous identity?"[5] Indians, in their turn, fight back, with narratives of nefarious plots in which Chicano/a warriors steal unbidden onto Indian land, occupy its historic centers, build monuments to their conquering heroes, appropriate ceremonies, histories, and spaces with as much avidity as their European precursors. Ironically, all through this Chicano/Indian quarrel, each side claims a particular "Indianness" (usually Aztec or Nahua on the one hand, an unspecified 19th century Plains warrior on the other, both male) each more essentialized than the most nationalistic denizen of an unchallenged Aztlán would take as his or her Chicana/o identity, or any Indian, however influenced by Hollywood's "Indians," would claim when alone among other indigenous people.

La Nueva Edad

At the University of California, Berkeley, in the spring of 1998, a day-long Latina conference, created by seven Latina/India graduate students, was held. A large room was filled with some 200 people, mostly women. Arriving early, I sat near the back of the semicircle of chairs, next to two friends and colleagues, one Chicana, one Puerto Rican.

The day began when a visiting Chicana performance artist, kneeling on a mat in the center of the circle, lit some sage, waving its smoke around her body, her space, the room. She explained that this was a ceremony of purification, learned from Frank LaPena, her professor at Sacramento State University and a well-known Maidu artist. Next she spoke an autobiographical "border" monologue, a life lived in Gloria Anzaldúa's "frontera." This was familiar terrain and my mind wandered. Suddenly, I was startled back to attention: "...*Gerónimo*, our hero of the border wars, our fighter for freedom and independence from the Anglos...." Already a little disconcerted by the *faux* Plains Indian purification ceremony, I was truly stunned by this whimsical rewriting of history, this curious appropriation of a Native hero. Repronouncing his name, I whispered to my friends: "Geronimo?! He hated Mexicans, loathed Mexicans, much more, in fact, than he hated the Americans! Mexicans killed his family. Mexicans drove him to take up war. How can he be a hero of this border? How can this woman appropriate him for her own historical narrative like this?" But my comments elicited no response. My companions, steeped in a postmodern tolerance of historically preposterous inventions, remained unmoved. My historian's sensibilities offended, I tried again: "How can she rename him in the language he most hated—making him into Saint Jerome, patron of Lisbon slavers who bought and sold Indians in a lucrative trade that peopled the world with North American natives? The language of those who slaughtered his wife and children?" Again, bland disinterest. The look both friends turned toward me was mirrored later, by other faculty colleagues, and even by the conference organizers. Amnesia, indeed.

And in recent years, all over the Southwest, tour groups of Chicanos (virtually all of them of indigenous, as well as of African and Spanish heritage) visit the Pueblos, the Navajo Nation, the Apache nations. Everywhere they are carrying their children to view what they describe as "our heritage," despite the fact that both the history of the European and American invasion and conquest of this region and the distinctive histories of the indigenous peoples of Mexico, both before and after the Spanish conquest, should complicate such claims. These visits, while not very different from the Anglo tourism that has afflicted the peoples of the Southwest for a hundred years, remain fairly anodyne, though they aid in the same kind of project of forgetting carried by Anglos in their luggage. Anodyne, too, are the increased assertions of their "Indianness" by Chicana/o undergraduates at the University of California (feelings that bring large numbers of Chicana/o students into Native American Studies courses and draw increasing numbers to Intertribal Student Council events, further complicating, as they should, the selfdestructive "blood purity" identity politics that cut through every Native North American collectivity).

But such shifts in identity assertions, however progressive in a Chicano/a world that once shunned any suggestion of "Indio" heritage, nevertheless both hide the actual indigenous origins of many Chicano/as, whose ancestors were Chol, Purepecha, Maya, Yoemem, and many others, as Francisco Casique reminds me,[6] and disguise the existence of real quarrels grounded in real history, effectively promoting still more of the collective amnesia that maintains the borders and protects power. Moreover, all these behaviors take their part in the capitalist machine—one that will shortly teach others to appropriate and silence the same Chicano/as whose newly created identities depend upon cultural ways taken from indigenous North America. As Deborah Root notes, "Appropriation occurs because cultural difference can be bought and sold in the marketplace." Moreover, "cultural appropriation...signifies not only the taking up of something and making it one's own but also the ability to do so"; and the appropriation of Native North America by those not from this society signals key demographic shifts that place power in new locations. The results are often problematic for those whose worlds are appropriated. "People have always shared ideas and borrowed from one another, but appropriation is entirely different from borrowing or sharing because it involves the taking up and commodification of aesthetic, cultural, and more recently spiritual forms of a society. Culture is neatly packaged for the consumer's convenience" (Root 1996: 68,70).

REMEMBERING

History is the fruit of power, but power itself is never so transparent that its analysis becomes superfluous. The ultimate mark of power may be its invisibility; the ultimate challenge, the exposition of its roots.

—Michel-Rolph Trouillot (1995:xix)

Simon Ortiz: "The most immediate...responsibility that Pueblo and other Native Americans in New Mexico have faced in their struggle for...continuance in 1998 has been to counter the Cuartocentenario,... an audacious celebration of four hundred years of colonization...of Pueblo lands, people, and native culture that began in 1598 (Ortiz, 1999:1).

That year, Juan de Oñate, sent by the governor of New Spain, invaded what is now New Mexico. Shortly thereafter, 31 of his soldiers, led by Oñate's nephew, an officer called Zaldívar, stopped off at Acoma Pueblo to seize provisions for his troops' continued march up the valley of what *they* named the Big River.

Ortiz continues:

> U.S. and New Mexico maps and tourist bureaus do not know the Aacqumeh hanoh's name for the local community. It is Deetseyamah—The North Door. Looking northward from Aacqu and the tall rock monolith on which the mother pueblo sits, there is an opening, like a gateway, between two mesas. Looking northward, too, from Aacqu, one can see Kaweshtima—Snowed Peaked—a dark blue misted mother mountain. Those Aacqumeh names do not appear anywhere except in the people's hearts and souls and history and oral tradition, and in their love. But you will find the easy labels: Mt. Taylor, Elevation 11,950 ft, and Acoma: The Sky City." (Leslie Marmon Silko: "All of creation suddenly had two names: an Indian name and a white name,...And there would be no peace and the people would have no rest until the entanglement had been unwound to the source [1977:53].)

Ortiz again:

> This legacy, and the subsequent translations into a third colonizers' language, scarred the land and the people (Ortiz 1992: 337-8).

In keeping with ancient Pueblo tradition, the people of Acoma welcomed Zaldívar's soldiers with food and clothing. (Ortiz: "They must have felt like kings, even godlike, instead of the mercenaries, errand boys, and mystics that they were" [1992:341].) The Spaniards demanded more and promised to return. When they came back for their booty, some decided to steal some sacred turkeys. Still others raped at least one Acoma girl. Outraged Acoma warriors, women and men together, attacked and killed Zaldívar and 12 of his soldiers, driving the rest to flee, back to Oñate.

Oñate immediately sent a heavily armed expedition to punish the people of Acoma. Very quickly 70 Spanish soldiers killed 800 Indian women, men, and children; 80 men and 500 women and children were captured for trial. The results of the trial, according to Ramón Gutiérrez (1991:54), were these:

> All men and women over 12 were condemned to 20 years of slavery among New Mexico's settlers;[...]

> all men over 25 had one of their feet severed.

> Children under the age of 12 were distributed as servants to monasteries and Spanish households.

> Two Hopi Indians captured at Acoma each lost their right hands and were dispatched home as testaments of the Christians' wrath.

LEGACIES

Ortiz comments further:

> When I was a boy...on the Acoma Pueblo reservation, I...never heard a specific...account of the destruction of Acoma in January of 1599. I've racked my memory trying to recall if there was any mention of it among many other stories told about "the old days" of Acoma..., but no, there were no oral stories about this terrible knowledge. And it was not until I was in college that

> I came across...references to it in one or two books....
> For years I wondered why Acoma people never talked
> openly about the destruction...almost as if it had never
> happened, almost as if the people felt it was their fault,
> almost as if they were burdened by an immense guilt.
> Now, I realize, it is because this historical truth was
> purposely and deliberately dismissed...and better left
> unheard and forgotten. Sadly, the result is that we do
> not have a truthful, honest account of ourselves as a
> Pueblo Indian people. And as a further result, we are
> diminished as an indigenous people (1999:1).

Others know these silences, hybrids born of the shame of survivors, the horror of the truth, the fear of the personal and collective consequences of acknowledging the enormity of human cruelty, of the collective tragedy. Primo Levi (1988) has limned these borders in his terrible memoirs of the German camps. More recently, at the dedication of the Angel Island Immigration Station as a National Monument, its founder, Paul Chow, noted that at last "the stories of Angel Island could be told without fear, without shame." Angel Island Immigration Station, San Francisco's Ellis Island, marked the year 200 with an exhibit by Flo Ow Wong. She called her work, "made in USA: Angel Island Shhh."

Ortiz reclaims Acoma history for all Southwestern Native people: "It is our responsibility, to dedicat[e]...ourselves to... acknowledging the historical background of the 1998 Cuartocentenario...to...realize ourselves in terms of our struggle, hope, and continuance as First Nations, First Peoples, First Voices"(1999:1). But it isn't easy. First the Spaniards rewrote the story of their invasion. Then came the Anglos. The narrative of their conquest of the U.S. Southwest, bolstered by the English-invented "Black Legend," which demonized their Spanish predecessors, created yet another cast of characters. In Anglo stories, the violent, angry Pueblo peoples were transformed yet again, their "savage" resistance forgotten. In Anglo eyes, they were ancient, peaceable, nonviolent people, tillers of the soil, gentle potters, architects of quaint little hillside cities. Their image contrasted sharply with that circulated about their still-unconquered neighbors, the Apaches and Navajos.

The Anglos did not stop at rewriting their narrative of rescue of helpless people from the horrors of Spanish (and Mexican) occupiers. As time passed and as the remaining "dangerous" Indians were conquered, the Southwest began to assume yet another image. This desert land, "opened" by the coming of the railroads, began to attract rapacious Eastern tourists, led, as always, by artifact-collecting, career-pursuing anthropologists. Tour brochures and anthropological freak shows, the results of dozens of "expeditions" into the desert, not only circulated the stereotypes launched by the first Anglos, offered them an even wider audience. The image of a peaceable, slightly stupid, even "feminine" Pueblo people spread.

HEADLINES

"Cowed by a Woman"
March 6, 1886: *The Illustrated Police News*:
A Craven Red Devil Weakens in the Face of a Resolute White Heroine—Exciting Adventure in an Indian Village in Arizona.

The story: At Oraibi, an ancient Hopi town, an anthropologist, Mathilda Coxe Stevenson, together with her husband, Col. James Stevenson and eight Indians (four "friendly Moquis" and four Navajos), decided to investigate Hopi religious practices by climbing into a ceremonial space. With the arrogance she and her sister anthropologists carried in their vast, artifact-hiding handbags, Mathilda Stevenson asked no permission. Indeed, none of her party so much as acknowledged the watching Hopis, gathered in their distress at the whites' sudden appearance. Instead, she simply invaded the sacred space. As more people became aware of the Stevensons' activities, they gathered, circling the Anglos threateningly. When Mrs. Stevenson persisted, some demanded that all the whites be captured and, in the police reporter's words, taken to "the underground chapel of the village, and there summarily dealt with.[...] The friendly Moquis [in keeping with their stereotype] stood their ground only a few minutes and then disappeared, but the Navajos, who are made of firmer material, remained. Col. Stevenson," the reporter assured his Eastern readers,

> says that while the situation was highly interesting, it
> was probably less alarming than it would have been

> to people unacquainted with the *natural timidity of the Pueblos*. Mrs. Stevenson, who has sojourned with her husband among many wild tribes and knows the Indian character well, created an opportune diversion by shaking her fist in the face of a hunchbacked savage, whose vindictive eloquence seemed to exert a most mischievous influence over his fellows, addressing to him at the same time several brief, but vigorous remarks in English and Spanish, which he was, of course, quite unable to understand. Before the man had recovered his self-possession, the strangers had backed down the ladder, and then slowly made their way, with the whole howling pack—men and women, children and dogs—at their heels, to their ponies, mounted and rode down to camp (Babcock and Parezo 1988:11, emphasis added).

This sordid tale—written to disguise the ignorance, the cowardice and the avarice of the whites in the face of organized Hopi hostility—is quoted by Barbara Babcock and Nancy J. Parezo in a catalogue celebrating an exhibition, "Daughters of the Desert: Women Anthropologists and the Native American Southwest, 1880-1980" held at the Arizona State Museum on the campus of the University of Arizona. Their comment on this newspaper story, reads: "Stevenson's crusading zeal in collecting data occasionally offended her subjects. In the late 19th century, however, her field methods were unfortunately the accepted practice" (10).

Zuni artist Phil Hughte strikes back: *A Zuni Artist Looks at Frank Hamilton Cushing* satirizes Cushing's stay among the Zuni people, where his depredations on behalf of The Smithsonian Institution were many and terrible and often very funny. Hughte's work includes one telling portrait of Mathilda Stevenson, here trying to "invade" Zuni, the pueblo Cushing considered his own. One drawing is captioned: "Yes, I *can* take a picture!" The text explains, "Cushing is telling Mathilda Coxe Stevenson not to take photographs of the Kachinas, but Mathilda was so stubborn that she had to have everything her way. Here she takes her umbrella and hits him over the head while the little Kachina Dancer is wondering what the heck this box is and is shaking his rattle at the camera" (Hughte 1994:92-93).[7]

The Stevensons and others from the East worked their artifact-collecting myth-making more than a hundred years ago. But the tales they told, of brave and clever whites outwitting dumb Indians (who could not speak "civilized" languages but could, instead, only "howl" with their dogs) or "protecting" stupid, passive Puebloans from the incursions of other whites continue to find voice. Both anthropologists and historians still retell a whitewashed past; Pueblo people still resist. But over time, the clarity of the pre-World War I anthropologists' "us" and "them"—Yankee anthropologists, Southwestern Indians—muddled, assuming shapes more representative of the region's messy ethnicity.

One of the most influential (though by no means the first) to repaint the pre-war Southern Pacific Railroad's tourist brochure version of the Southwest was Walter Prescott Webb, professor at the University of Texas and president of the American Historical Association. His 1935 hymn to male-bonding, *The Texas Rangers*, divided the Southwest into three distinct groups: Indians (hopelessly savage, hopelessly warlike), Mexicans (cruel, addicted to horses, to "gay attire," and Catholic "superstitions") and Anglos (Protestant, straight-shooting, brave, honest). His triumphalist portrait, although focused on Texas, left no doubts in Southwestern Anglo hearts: The conquest, from the Gulf of Mexico to the Pacific, was right, was just, was inevitable, and the best possible outcome for all the parties concerned. Although Webb's viciously racist characterizations of Indians prompted no criticism, his view of Mexicans was quickly challenged, most publicly in the works of a progressive journalist from Los Angeles, Carey McWilliams.

McWilliams's first work, *Factories in the Field* (1939), denounced the exploitation of Mexican migrant farmworkers.[8] A decade later, he published the first history of Chicanos in the United States, *North From Mexico: The Spanish-Speaking People of the United States* (1948). This work, frequently republished (including in a Spanish version, in 1968), immediately prompted warm and on-going praise from an early generation of Chicano scholars. The book jacket of the 1990 edition carries these accolades from George I. Sanchez: "Since its first appearance in 1950, I have placed a heavy reliance on this book—in my university classes, in my lectures, and in my counsel to those who would know my people...

North from Mexico is a persistent cry in a wilderness of neglect, mistreatment, and ignorance on the part of those who became dominant after the American occupation of the Southwest..." "*North from Mexico,*" Tony Calderon adds in the same space, "is my bible on knowing about my heritage."

But Pueblo Indian peoples—or any of the indigenous peoples of the Americas—cannot feel any more sanguine about McWilliams than they did about Walter Prescott Webb. To Indian eyes, McWilliams's 1949 book is little more than an extended apologia for the Spanish invasion. In McWilliams's narrative, in fact, the Spaniards hardly invaded at all. Instead, like Webb's manifestly destined Anglos, McWilliams's conquistadores merely hastened a mysterious historical process already well under way when Oñate mounted his horse to ride north in 1598. "Prior to [the Spaniards'] appearance in the Southwest," McWilliams assures readers,

> a great drama had been enacted of which they knew nothing and concerning which not too much is known today. It would seem, however, that the Pueblo Indians had for many years been fighting a losing battle against their hereditary enemies, the nomadic tribes. Driven out of the river bottoms and valleys, they had finally sought shelter in the nooks and crevices of the mountainous portions of the Southwest. Here, in cliff-dwellings, terraced adobes, and mountain villages, they were able to survive although in constant peril. As a result of protracted defensive warfare, their culture had begun to disintegrate and showed a marked decline in vigor at about the time the Spaniards arrived. *In fact, it is altogether probable that the Spaniards rescued and to a degree revitalized the culture of the Pueblo Indians*"
> ([1949]1990:38-39, emphasis added).

I should have hoped that this effort by an Anglo writer to mute the facts of the Spanish conquest is so patently outrageous, so ridiculous, that it would have elicited some criticism from George Sanchez or Tony Calderon, or at least a reluctance to "blurb" the reprint of the work, however heroic the book's revisionist portrait of their Mexican forebears. But alas, it did not. More problematic still, with the advent of the Chicano movement of the 1960s the distortion and erasure of the history of the Southwest's indigenous populations have increased as many Chicanos site their origin story in that same Southwest, their Aztlán, a place completely devoid of indigenous occupiers when their forebears came north from Mexico. Both in words and deeds, many Chicano activists have located *their* struggle for liberation from Anglo oppression in the land won by a brutal Spanish conquest of Native American peoples, thereby setting the stage for Indian-Chicano conflict.

Intellectuals, most infamously Ramón Gutiérrez, have enthusiastically joined this recuperative project. In the process, Gutiérrez has outraged contemporary Indians everywhere. His brilliantly written *When Jesus Came, the Corn Mothers Went Away* (1991), published to loud acclaim from intellectuals in both Spain and the United States, offers a more nuanced apology for the invasion than that of McWilliams, but one that nevertheless echoes those of the earlier writer. Gutiérrez, too, blames the victims while at the same time minimizing the Spaniards' evil. His main focus in his apologetic version of the Spaniards' invasion is Pueblo women. According to Gutiérrez, "traditional" Pueblo women lived out their lives as passive, heavily sexualized servants of men. In their ancient, idyllic world women's lives unfolded naturally: "Rain fertilized seeds as men fertilized their women....In the household, women gave men their love and their bodies." Indeed, "after feeding, the activity of greatest cultural import to Pueblo women was sexual intercourse." Thus was their biology their destiny. Gutiérrez concludes, "women were empowered through their sexuality" (14, 15, 17). Gutiérrez's sources for such curious observations are not Pueblo people or their histories. Rather, they are those same prewar anthropologists, praised by the screamer press, satirized by Phil Hughte. Gutiérrez's footnotes cite a notorious crew: Elsie Clews Parsons, Frank Hamilton Cushing, Mathilda Coxe Stevenson, Jesse Fewkes. Still more evidence comes from the self-serving contemporary narratives of Spanish soldiers and priests, whose admitted treatment of Pueblo women and girls (as well as men and boys) would not render them particularly reliable sources in the eyes of most historians.[9]

When Gutiérrez reports that Spanish friars killed men in order to steal their wives for sexual slavery, he not only removes agency from women whose participation in resistance to the Spaniards was violent and on-going, but he also adds an excuse, again blaming the victims:

> As we saw in Chapter 1, successful men who became caciques, as the friars in essence had done, were surrounded by secondary wives and concubines who offered their love and bodies in return for gifts and benefits for their children....The Puebloans always transformed that which they deemed potently dangerous and malevolent into a beneficial force by offering it food and sexual intercourse. Just as the Spanish soldiers *had fallen into the loving arms of Indian women,* so too eventually did the friars, though undoubtedly nagged by pangs of guilt. (123, emphasis added)

Reading these words, I am reminded of those Hollywood films of the postWorld War II era that featured U.S. soldiers or occupation officials "falling into the loving arms" of Japanese women. The sacrificial female, charged with a distinctly non-Protestant sexuality, wears many racial masks, it seems.

Indigenous North American readers of *When Jesus Came, the Corn Mothers Went Away* not only protested the title's implication—that Pueblo religion disappeared in the face of Christianity—but they also winced at the portrait of Puebloans, especially women Puebloans, as highly sexualized people, whose every act, before or after the invasion, bore an intense sexual charge. This is, as many have noted, not only a bizarre misreading of the Pueblo world, but it is also a version of the invasion in which anything the Spaniards did—whether they were murderous *conquistadors,* fanatical priests, or thieving "settlers"—was overdetermined, mere adjustments of the social structures of the preconquest world.

Even the 1680 Pueblo Revolt undergoes "hispanization" in Gutiérrez's hands. He describes the Spanish "colonists'" retreat. As they hastened south, driven by enraged Pueblo warriors, their journey was

> filled with horrors. In every village they found piles of mutilated bodies strewn amid ashes of still smoking fires. At Sandia Pueblo the mission's statues were covered with excrement. Two chalices had been discarded in a basket of manure and the paint on the

altar's crucifix had been stripped off with a whip. Feces
covered the holy communion table and the arms of
a statue of Saint Francis had been hacked off with an
ax. At every mission along their route they reported
the most unspeakable profanations of Christian sacra
(134).

(Rudy Giuliani could not be more outraged.) Still, Gutiérrez nods
in the direction of fairness though with an equivocal gesture that
equates the Pueblo resistance and the Spanish invasion of their
homes:

Though the Christians were aghast at how the Pueblo
Indians manifested their anger, one only has to recall
the massive desecration of katsina masks, kivas, and
other native sacra that occurred during the Spanish
conquest to understand why the Indians retaliated
so exactly during the Pueblo Revolt. The tables were
now turned in this contest of cultures. The Indians
had learned well from their overlords the function of
iconoclasm in political spectacle (135).

"Contest of cultures?" "Iconoclasm in political spectacle?" What of
murder, rape, torture, enslavement, theft? The Spaniards' destruction of the Pueblos, their mutilation and murder of Pueblo people
fall well behind these racing abstractions, running toward an
entirely metaphysical finish line.

Many among the "peaceable" Puebloans, angered by Gutiérrez's work, articulated their concerns. Of Gutiérrez's claims that
his work "gives vision to the blind and gives voice to the mute and
silent," that it demonstrates that "the conquest of America was
not a monologue but a dialogue between cultures," Evelina Zuni
Lucero (from Isleta and San Juan Pueblos) replied:

How can citations of a few Pueblo stories and reliance
on data recorded by non-Pueblos possessing a vastly
different worldview constitute a Pueblo view, a Pueblo
voice? I find an unexplainable contradiction between
Gutiérrez's claim that there was a historical dialogue
that included the Pueblos and his statement that he
could find "no way around" using what he admits is
European-biased information because "there are no

Pueblo Indian records of the seventeenth, eighteenth, and nineteenth century...." A dialogue between cultures, at least one that includes Pueblos, cannot occur if Pueblos continue to be spoken for by 'others' but are not heard from 1993:175).

Gutiérrez seemed surprised that Pueblo people were not among his many fans. Responding to criticism, he claimed on several websites and in public lectures that he had received a letter from the "All Pueblo Council" thanking him "for writing about the history of the Pueblo Indians and for bringing attention to their historical plight." At this, Simon Ortiz, who had been involved in the New Mexico conference, again weighed in on the same websites:

> Because Gutiérrez pointedly says that the All Indian Pueblo Council "wrote" to "thank" him "for writing about the history of the Pueblo Indians," I asked Herman Agoyo about it. Mr. Agoyo's reply was that it was "highly unlikely that AIPC would write such a letter." As an Acoma Pueblo citizen, I have to say that scholars and academics cannot dismiss our orally transmitted historical knowledge which is carried from the past to the present. (Gutiérrez, Ortiz 2000).

Still, Gutiérrez's book pleases many people. And it is certainly true that he has succeeded in his goal: to generate "a sustained discussion of the painful history of race relations in New Mexico that goes beyond the silly romanticism of harmonious pluralism" (Ibid.).

There are other indications—perhaps too subtle for most outsiders to see—of the differences maintained between "Hispanic" and "Indian" communities in contemporary New Mexico. Peter Nabokov (2002) comments on the annual Matachines Dance, which "is a featured Christmas offering among a number of Rio Grande Pueblo Indian villages as well as in neighboring Hispanic hamlets." He describes the dance: "lines of mitre-wearing male dancers skip to the polka-like melodies of scratchy violins and strummed guitars, and weave around a 'monarch' and little girl wearing her all-white communion attire." What is going on? Nabokov notes that these dances are celebrated quite differently in the two communities.

> Unlike its adaptation in Hispanic mountain hamlets of New Mexico, among the Pueblos it is better known as "Montezuma's dance," and scholar Sylvia Rodriguez argues that the Matachines provided Pueblo Indians with theatrical release for their sense of historical injustice, emphasizing "an oppositional contrast or juxtaposition between symbols of Indian religion and symbols of Christianity"....Introducing such characters as the "Malinche," the Indian mistress of Cortez, allows the Pueblos a rare opportunity to reflect on the "illicit, bittersweet miscegenation" that remains one of the touchier aspects of the Hispanic-Pueblo heritage (184).

Commemoration of the Spaniards' sexual conquest of Pueblo women provides evidence of "biting historical awareness," as Nabokov reminds readers.

> When the Hopi kachina named *Yo-we* appears on Third Mesa during the Midwinter Powamu ritual cycle, older Indians readily identify him as the killer of the priest at Old Oraibi during the 1680 all-Pueblo Revolt, and their children internalize the sobering lesson behind the fact that the earring in his hand was torn from the ear of the priest's Indian mistress. (184)

TELLING OUR (HIS)STORIES IN POEMS

Simon Ortiz tells a very different Pueblo history in his poems. "Our Homeland, a National Sacrifice Area" is his epic of the invasion. I shall quote at length. It begins:

It was only the second day,
and I was on my way home
from being with Srhakaiya.
It is the mountain west
of Aacqu.
  I was sick,
feeling a sense of "otherness."
How can I describe it?
An electric current
coursing in ghost waves through me?

"Otherness."

> Otherness: inflicted by the overculture's re-creation of a Pueblo Indian man; prompted by the alienation of this land of the Aacqumeh hanoh, Ortiz's land, now a trash dump, a poisoned well, a [radioactive] tourist attraction.

> "Otherness."/I can't describe it/and perhaps there is/such a sensation./I had drunk some water the evening before/ on the northside of Srhakaiya./The spring was scummed over./A Garden Deluxe wine empty lay nearby.

> Years ago, in the 1950s,/when I was a boy of 9 or 10,/ I'd come with my father/and the sheep we herded.../... we drank from the spring./The clear cold water was covered/with heavy plank boards/and the pool was fed by the seep/from the shale rock./The pool had a stone lining.

> ...../

> Pueblo Bonito in Chaco Canyon/is maintained by the U.S. Park Service./Northwards, 65 miles away,/is Aztec National Monument./To the northwest, another 85 miles,/is Mesa Verde National Park./The park service has guided tours,/printed brochures, clean rest rooms,/ and the staff is friendly, polite,/and very helpful./You couldn't find a better example/of Americanhood any-where./the monuments, or ruins/as they are called, are very well kept/by the latest technology/in preserving antiquity./....

> At Mesa Verde, not long ago,/they had Esther in a glass case./She was a child, born/from a woman/1000 years ago./The U.S. Park Service/was reluctant to let her go/ when some Indian people/demanded her freedom./ Government bureaucrats/said Indians were insensi-tive/to U.S. heritage/For years they sold/postcards of Esther./Maybe they still do./By pushing buttons, thousands of yearly tourists to these places can get an audio-taped narration./....

See Museum for More Information.

....

By 1980, there were 43 uranium mines operating in the Grants Uranium Belt and 5 mills....There were 31 companies exploring for and developing uranium in New Mexico. Kerr-McGee, Conoco, Gulf, Mobil, Phillips, TVA, Pioneer Nuclear and United Nuclear are all energy corporations; they were all there. Mobil and TVA were planning *in situ* mining in which chemicals are pumped into drill holes, interacting with uranium ore bodies deep in the earth, and the solution is pumped out and processed....

by the early 1980's uranium ore extracting and processing was drastically reduced, and there was almost none going on by the 1990's. The market for uranium had dropped, some of it due to concerns and protests about radiation hazards and pollution.

This much is certain now however: the people of Deetseyamah and Deechuna and Kahwaikah downstream from the Grants Uranium Belt do not have enough water any more for their few remaining cultivated fields and gardens and the water they drink is contaminated by Grants and the past processing mills. The hanoh anxiously watch the springs at Ghoomi and Gaanipah. Their struggle will go on; there is no question about that (1992:337-63).

FIRST PEOPLES' FIRST STRUGGLE: COLONIZATION

I read from the Anglo newspaper: *The New York Times*, Monday, February 9, 1998:

"Conquistador Statue Stirs Hispanic Pride and Indian Rage"

by James Brooke

Espanola, New Mexico.—One moonless night in early January, just as Hispanic New Mexicans were starting to celebrate the 400th anniversary of the first Spanish settlement in the American West, an Indian commando group stealthily approached a bronze statue...of the first conquistador, Don Juan de Oñate. With an electric saw, the group slowly severed his right foot— boot, stirrup, star-shaped spur and all.

So: Who stole Oñate's foot?

Michael Lacapa:

> My grandmothers and grandfathers stole the foot. For it was Oñate himself who ordered hands and feet to be cut off Native Americans after defeating the Acoma Pueblo in 1599. It was our grandmas and grandpas that had to go through life without hands to touch and feel the future. Yes, my grandparents stole his foot.
>
> ....
>
> We the Native American people took his foot and ground it up into a powder and threw it into the wind. Then we took our sacred cornmeal and made four lines on the ground, so this foot will not be able to return and harm us again. We did this so we can claim our right to be as every person, a human being.
>
> Because now you see, today Oñate, he is defeated (1999:32).

The New York Times article, together with its large photograph, writes a different scenario, one seen from the Anglo center, written in the voice of white, male privilege. Here, in the Southwest, site of generations of Anglo tourist dreams, two U.S. subjugated "others" are quaintly at each other's throats. Brooke explains, "below the bland, homogenized landscape of franchise motels and restaurants, ancient history [sic!] is exerting a powerful, subterranean pull."[10] Like some mysterious ophiolatrous sea creatures, Brooke continues, "Hispanic residents are clinging to Oñate out of insecurities over losing their language, culture and political...dominance.... Spanish," Brooke claims, "no longer echoes around Santa Fe as the 10th generation of Spanish descendants has assimilated to the point of losing its ancestral language."

Such ignorant observations of Santa Fe's recent Anglo-ization position Brooke firmly in his all-white world, where the language spoken by those who cleaned his hotel rooms, cooked the food he ate, ran the tourist offices and guide services, was a silent one, although the same silent language spoken all across *The Times's* home city. Still, Brooke's dubious portrait relegates Santa Fe's Latino population to Euro-America's standard location for Others, that historical reservation long-occupied by the ever-vanishing Indians. There, behind the barbed wire of white ignorance, the ethnics quarrel among themselves. But the quarrel is very real. Commemorating Juan de Oñate 400 years after his ride north was an act sure to awaken every latent tension between Chicanos and Indians. The midnight theft of Oñate's foot from the 1992 statue erected in Alcalde, New Mexico, was the first shot in what grew into a vigorous, three-pronged battle. When Albuquerque officials proposed their own statue for the Cuarto Centenario, war broke out in earnest. Unlike Anglos, Indians and Chicanos remember:

> Conroy Chino, TV newsman from Acoma Pueblo: "He inflicted tremendous pain and suffering, death and destruction, especially among the Acoma people."

> John Kessell, Spanish colonial historian: "Consider that something happened and it brought people together and that's something to examine."

> Herman Agoyo, San Juan Pueblo Tribal Council: "From our viewpoint, we would prefer that it never did happen."

> Renaldo "Sonny" Rivera, sculptor of mutilated statue: "He is the father of New Mexico. I think he was a hell of a man" (all quoted in Rolwing, 1998. see also Linthiuim, Jan. 9, 17, 18, 1998).

Recounting a dispute between one Acoma woman and Hispanic supporters of another Cuartocentenario Oñate statue in Albuquerque, Brooke quotes Darva Chino's plea to the City Council: "Don't dishonor those Acoma families who have chosen to live in this city." But her plea fell on hostile ears: "Millie Santillanes, a Hispanic organizer of the Oñate festivities *shot back*, 'Acoma has no place in *our* memorial.'"

In Albuquerque, the more numerous "Hispanic" citizens won, though it was not all a matter of numbers, nor did they gain a heroic, unmediated hero figure such as the one in Alcalde that "lost" its foot.[11] Their memorial, representing

Spain's contribution to New Mexico—representing
Oñate and the Indians before and after the colonization, will be designed by three local artists, one
Chicano, one Puebloan, and one Anglo. Together, they
will attempt to bridge the distance yawning between
supporters of Oñate and those who decry the invasion,
who agree with Adres Lauriano, a former governor
of Sandia Pueblo: "Oñate was a ruthless killer, a man
motivated by greed" (Associated Press Archive 1998:
n.p.) .

Moreover, this collectively produced memorial is to be joined by
an uncontroversial Holocaust memorial sponsored by the 1% of
the Albuquerque population that is Jewish.

Why memorialize the Holocaust that is *not* ours rather than
the one that *is* ours? Surely the answer here has less to do with the
Spanish descendants' local dominance and more to do with how
the United States racializes its exclusions. A Nazi Holocaust memorial in virtually every major city of the United States (some cities
have two or more) while history books whisper nothing about the
violent histories of the United States? Amnesia, indeed.

That James Brooke's article offers *Times* readers a view from
the center to the touristy non-Anglo peripheries is underscored by
its conclusion. In their behalf, Brooke has located an authoritative
voice to mediate among the fractious ethnics. It is that of Marc
Simmons, Anglo biographer of Oñate, who offers both Indians
and Latinos satisfyingly American reasons why the conquistador
should be honored by "us": "In what is now the Western U.S.,"
Simmons tells Brooke, "he was the founder of the livestock industry, the mining industry, and he opened the first major road....He
brought Christianity and Western Culture" (quoted in ibid.).

Oh good: cattle have eaten the plains and are in the process
of destroying the desert. Mining and roads have poisoned both
the Indians who have dug the coal and uranium and copper and
the air they breathe. And as for the "civilization" brought to the
savages, well, I can only think of Gandhi's [possibly apocryphal]
reply when he was asked what he thought of Western Civilization.
"I think it would be a good idea," he said.

So *The New York Times* judges: Oñate is to be honored. But the story's photograph tells an additional story. Oñate is the noble— *but* vanished—past of the "Hispanic" population of the Southwest, a glorious past to be sure, one that will provide the stooped and bowed living figure, as well as other parents and grandparents of assimilated English-speaking children, *some* pride, because Anglos have honored their entrepreneurial ancestor, if not them. In a process all-too-familiar to Natives, the conquistador's statue freezes Chicanos' positive images in the past, here cloaked in what are recognizably European *and military* regalia.

IT'S ALL ABOUT LAND

Joke: In the 1960s, NASA set up a moon-landing practice area in the Arizona desert. One day the astronauts and NASA officials noticed two Diné sheep herders, watching intently. Curious, one of the NASA men approached the two men to explain that this was practice for a landing on the moon. The older Navajo regarded him silently for a few seconds, then he turned to his companion and said, in Navajo, "Ask them if I can send a message to the moon." When the younger man translated the request, the NASA official was quick in his enthusiasm. "Of course we will carry a Navajo message to the moon," he told them, handing the old man a paper and pen. The old man wrote only one line. Then he handed the paper solemnly to the white man. "What does it say?" the NASA man asked. "Oh, I can't tell you that," the younger Navajo said. Frustrated, NASA tried for several days to find a willing translator in the Navajo Nation. Everyone approached took the paper, read the message, laughed, and handed it back without telling them what it said. Only later, in Phoenix, did the frustrated officials find a translator. "Watch out for these guys," the message read, "they come to steal your land."

And they did. In a process many Native people call "Trick or Treaty," the invaders from Europe, together with their descendants, mapped the borders between the hundreds of Native nations in North America. Then they eliminated them one by one, shrinking Indian land into smaller and smaller parcels. Finally, when reservations still held land whites desired, they sold it out from under Native feet. It was quite blatant. Posters plastered all across the Eastern United States trumpeted the possibilities:

INDIAN LAND FOR SALE

Get a Home	Perfect Title
Of	*
Your own (photograph of a Plains chief)	
*	Possession
EASY PAYMENTS	Within 30 Days

FINE LANDS IN THE WEST

IRRIGATED	GRAZING	AGRICULTURAL
IRRIGABLE		DRY FARMING

IN 1910 THE DEPARTMENT OF THE INTERIOR SOLD
UNDER SEALED BIDS ALLOTTED INDIAN LAND AS
FOLLOWS:

Location   Acres   Average price per acre
(Library of Congress)[12]

which brings me to:

BUILDING BORDERS

How does exclusion work? Where are borders built? How are they are maintained? There are many languages of amnesia, all of which shape discourses that themselves become borders. First, the pioneer's tale. Here is Thomas J. Farnham, who carefully recorded the manifestation of his destiny in *An 1839 Wagon Train Journal* (1977). His text employs several of the mechanisms of historical forgetting. Here is the male Yankee pioneer map of North America. Its axis moves from East to West. Behind lies civilization, ahead, untamed wilderness. Farnham and his companions reached the "border of the Indian domains...anxious...to...linger over every object that reminded us we were still on the confines of that civilization which we had inherited from a thousand generations: a vast and imperishable legacy of civil and social happiness. It was painful to approach the *last* frontier enclosure—the *last* habitation of the white man—the *last* semblance of home....We drank at the well and traveled on. It was now behind us" (6, emphasis added).

Still, that "civilization's" discontents had driven Farnham and his companions to seek relief. They found it immediately. [Though] indeed beyond the sanctuaries of society...the spirit of the Red Man, wild and careless as the storms he buffets, began to come over us: and we shouldered our rifles and galloped away for a deer in the lines of timber that threaded the western horizon. Our first hunt in the depths of the beautiful and dreadful wilderness! (Ibid).

Like today's New Agers, these invaders wanted only spirit, not reality. *Real* Indians, flesh and blood Indians, were to be dispossessed, killed. Thus they deserved the white man's conquest. "The savages" in Farnham's text, are only semihuman, nearly inarticulate: "Our savage visitors seized...[a pair of discarded boots] with the greatest eagerness, and in their pantomimic language, aided by harsh, guttural grunts, congratulated themselves upon becoming the possessors of so much wealth" (7). But how did Farnham know what the grunts and signs meant? No matter: his blithe assumption of authority to speak for others marked that vast sense of privilege, carried in the saddlebags, tucked into covered wagons, that marched West across countless Indian borders, taking, renaming, "taming," the "dreadful wilderness."[13]

Pioneer arrogance included excuses for the massive dislocation of Indian peoples across North America that made way for white conquest. Here is how Farnham explained the dozens of infamous "removals," all those "trails of tears," which forced so many Native nations from their homes to the "Indian Territory" designated for them:

> And various and numerous were the efforts [whites] made to raise and ameliorate [the Indians'] condition in their old haunts within the precincts of the States. But total or partial failure followed them all.... All experience tended to prove that [the Indians'] proximity to the whites induced among them more vice than virtue;... both the welfare of the Indians and the duty of the Government [thus] urged their colonization in a portion of the western domain where, freed from all questions of conflicting sovereignties, and under the

protection of the Union...,they might find a refuge from those influences which threatened the annihilation of their race (7).

Such a self-servingly false tale demanded obfuscation. In this—and other invaders'—texts, writers employed both abstractions as agents—here "influences"—and the passive voice to hide white responsibility.

That was 1839. Lest we imagine that the amnesia has lifted, here is part of the entry called "Sioux Indians" from the recent *New Encyclopedia of the American West.* Note the obfuscatory passive voice here, too: "By the 1880s, increasing pressure for Sioux lands led to the division of the Great Sioux Reservation into five reservations. This policy of allotment and assimilation was accompanied by an all-out program of *cultural modification*"(Lamar 1998:304).[14]

"Who-Whose-Whom?" cries Lenin's ghost.

Note, too, the accompanying illustration chosen by *The New York Times* to illustrate its review of this book. It is an Indian version of Oñate's statue, a familiar photograph of the vanishing, but still noble, savage. There he stands, still proud in his ragged blanket, Sitting Bull, great Lakota leader, vanquished. This is a memorial photograph, celebrating white victory, remembering an opponent once worthy of white conquest. This is Kevin Costner's Sioux chief, just after the white lieutenant abandons him to the cavalry.

CARING FOR BORDERS

It's tough. Here's Newt Gingrich: "From the Jamestown Colony and the Pilgrims, through de Tocqueville's 'Democracy in America,' up to the Norman Rockwell paintings of the 1940s and 1950s, there was a clear sense of what it meant to be an American....Go and look at *The Saturday Evening Post* from around 1955," he commanded (quoted in Lind 1995:3).

I did: Countless clever freckled white kids, grinning white-maned, whistle-whittling granddads, turkey-toting, rosy-cheeked grandmothers, side by side with their brave pioneer forebears who, week after week, in the magazine's serialized novels, battled war-whooping, grunting, painted savages. *The Saturday Evening Post's*

1950s version of the conquest soon spread as John Ford and others brought these heroic fictions to the silver screen.

The many mechanisms that continue to maintain racial and gender hegemonies are many and complicated. But I'd like to suggest that perspective—the location of "us" and "them"—is inculcated early on until dozens of little-questioned assumptions veil both practice and theorizing about the quotidian acts of exclusion.

Two Opposing Views, or, "Woody Guthrie vs Los Tigres del Norte"

First, Guthrie: "Deportees," written in the 1930s to condemn the forced expulsion of Mexican farm workers, captures the song writer's indignation in the farm laborers' loss of name—though here the names are only first names, and of course it is only the whites, the deporters, who "lose" the farmworkers' names. (Like Bartleby, they know who they are.)

The refrain:

> Goodbye to my Juan/Goodbye Rosalita./Adios, mis amigos/Jésus y Maria./You won't have a name/When you ride the big airplane/All they will call you will be.... deportees.

The song's effects—anger at the government for kicking people out of the U.S., pity for the deportees—depend upon a familiar U.S. assumption, one that became increasingly dominant as the Cold War wore on. Everyone in the whole world (all those tired and poor, we learned in school) wants more than anything else to live in this golden (money *and* sunshine) land, to become "one of us," or, and this is rarely said, to become "white."

(George Sanchez offers some gringology: A Tejano, working for the Border Patrol as a translator in the 1920s, recalled an incident involving an Anglo officer "who thought his Spanish was fluent. This man walked up to one fellow and asked, '¿Como se llama yo?' ("What would you call me?") [The Mexican replied] 'Pues quien sabe, señor' (Who knows, señor) then he turned to the Tejano translator and said, '¡Qué tan estúpido puede ser esta gente que ni siquiera sabe su proprio nombre!'" (How stupid is this guy who doesn't seem to know his own name!) (1993:55).

But no *corridos*—sung by "'my' Juan," or "Rosalita"—sing of this desire to become (North) American, to become white. Instead, countless songs describe terrible loss, of home, of place, of family, of community, of the values that differentiate a Mexican world from "ours." Yet like Farnham in the presence of Kaw Indians, few Norteamericanos listen. They see instead only thousands of poor inhabitants of dusty pueblos, heading north, dreaming of the day when they will hop into a big new Jeep Cherokee, drive three blocks to a giant Wal-mart and spend an hour deciding which of the 43 different brands of shampoo is just right for *their* hair.[15]

It is a rather different view of "us" provided in dozens of *corridos*. Here is a bit of Los Tigres del Norte's 1988 "Jaula de Oro," or "The Gilded Cage," cited (and translated) by Timothy Brennan:

> In order to earn some money I am like a prisoner in
> this huge country./When I remember Mexico I'm at
> the point of tears/And although this is a cage of gold,/it
> hasn't stopped being a prison[16] (1997:193).

(Of course the situation is more complicated than that. Brennan does not note that the song does not stop with these sentiments but instead continues into an exchange between the singer and his U.S.-born son, who makes it quite clear—in English—that he does not want to "return" to Mexico.)

There is other testimony to the sorrows of leaving home for the north. José Juárez, a Honduran on his way to the U.S., interviewed as he road a freight train over the Mexican border heading for work in the U.S., told Ginger Thompson, a *New York Times* reporter, "This has to be the most sad experience a person could live, leaving your children. There are no words to describe that kind of pain" (*The New York Times* Jan.18,1999:1).

MELTING THE POT, OR "SO YOU WANT TO CROSS THE BORDER?"

1896 Plessy v. Ferguson—The Supreme Court tries to close one route of crossing over:

Petitioner was a citizen of the U.S. and a resident of...Louisiana of mixed descent, in the proportion of seven eighths Caucasian and one eighth African blood; [because] the mixture of colored blood was not discernible in him,....he [argued that he] was entitled to every recognition, right, privilege and immunity secured to the citizens of the United States of the white race by its Constitution and laws....Thereupon [he had] entered a passenger train and [taken] possession of a vacant seat in a coach where passengers of the white race were accommodated (Harris 1995:276).

Plessy's one-eighth was too much for the Court, as you all know. The Court decided that he had to ride with other people of color though their coaches were supposed to be as "equal" as they were "separate."

Nevertheless, some did slip across the border. The key was a sufficient quantity of the privilege granting whiteness that gained citizenship. But they paid a high price. Cheryl Harris describes her grandmother's "passing" in order to get a job as a clerk in a Chicago department store:

> Every day my grandmother rose from her bed in her house in a black enclave on the southside..., sent her children off to a black school, boarded a bus full of black passengers, and rode to work. No one at her job ever asked if she was black; the question was unthinkable.... Each evening, my grandmother, tired and worn, retraced her steps home, laid aside her mask, and reentered herself. Day in and day out, she made herself invisible, then visible again (1995:276).

The belief that all people *want* to "pass" is, of course, another form of the universalist assumption that "we-ness" is something everyone desires. It is not, of course. Hinmató`wyalahtqinm, the man whites renamed Chief Joseph, put it differently: "Let me be a free man—free to travel, free to stop, free to work, free to trade where I choose, free to choose my own teachers, free to follow the religion of my fathers, free to think and talk and act for myself" (1995:44).

CONCLUSIONS

Chief Joseph, again: "That All People May Be One People, Send Rain to Wash the Face of the Earth" (44).

In February, 1999, I was invited to address a conference held at the University of Oregon. Titled "Where the Border Lies: Race and Citizenship in Theory and Practice," the conference intended to explore issues related to these subjects. After I had looked at the list of speakers, I decided to end my talk with the following:

> Borders, then, are sticky and long-lasting, much less permeable than California's recent governor [Pete Wilson], who tried to exclude "illegal aliens" or "undocumented Mexicans" from the state, would have us believe. They are everywhere, even here, in this conference. In a spirit of provocation, I should like to suggest a new title for this conference: "Academic Women of Color: An Exhibition." This re-naming is an effort to point out the unstated assumptions of today's program. We, the speakers, are all inhabitants of bordered worlds—born into zones constructed for us by others. We know the fences; we recognize the border patrols. What is missing from this program are representatives of these latter, the people born across the border, the people with the privileges protected by border patrols of all kinds. The conference has selected us to "introduce the theoretical constructs around highly contested matters of race and identity in the academy and race and citizenship in the political realm." But I'd like to ask, instead, and once again, "Who/Whom?" *Who* contests "matters of race and identity in the academy?" *Who* contests "race and citizenship in the political realm?"

Again I refer you to "We, the people," all white, all male.[17]

MORE CLEANSING RAIN

In the early 1990s, the Maryland Historical Society invited Fred Wilson, an African American artist, to create an exhibition about the state's "other" history, the story of those displaced by the founding of Maryland. Wilson agreed to choose rarely seen objects held in the Society's storerooms. Interviewed later, he explained

> All this denial. All this history of America, all this history of Europe and the relationship between people is not being talked about. Museums just pretend that we can overlook it, that we can experience "culture" without having those feelings [of oppression]. In short,

I am trying to root out that kind of denial. Museums are afraid of what they will bring up to the surface and how people will feel about certain issues that are long buried. They keep it buried, as if it doesn't exist, as though people aren't feeling these things anyway, instead of opening that sore and cleaning it out so it can heal. Museums just pretend that we can overlook it, that we can experience "culture" without having those feelings [of oppression].....In short, I am trying to root out that kind of denial. Museums are afraid of what they will bring up to the surface and how people will feel about certain issues that are long buried. They keep it buried, as it doesn't exist, as though people aren't feeling these things anyway, instead of opening that sore and cleaning it out so it can heal" (quoted in Corrin 1994:29, 34).

Wilson's exhibit, "Mining the Museum," offered visitors a radical shift in perspective. Two examples. Wilson hung an 1826 family portrait by Robert Street, called "The Children of Commodore John Daniel Danels," on one wall. Next to it, he hung reproductions of two of the picture's faces, both black, both hidden in the shadows behind the three Danels children. He captioned these isolated faces: "Where did I come from? Where did I go? Where do I sleep? What are my dreams? Who washes my face? Who combs my hair? Who calms me when I'm afraid?"

A second picture came from the early 18th century. Painted by Justus Engelhardt Kuhn, it features a colonial child, "Henry Darnall III." From this portrait, Wilson isolated another black face, this of the boy's servant, standing beside and just behind him. The caption here asks, "Am I your brother? Am I your friend? Am I your pet?"

The exhibition's catalogue included lengthy interviews with a group of Maryland women museum volunteers, the docents who guided people through the various installations. Docent 9 recalled, "One fourth-grader asked me about the painting of Henry Darnall, 'Why does he have the silver band around his neck?' I said (because that's the way *we* used to say it), 'That's his little friend.' He said, 'You don't put a collar around your friend's neck'" (51).

That's all.

CHAPTER 6

‖"'TIL INDIAN VOICES WAKE US..."

This is a love story. It is about two kinds of love: the love we share, Kamau Brathwaite and I, of a home place, though our homes are so distant, so different; and the love of a person, a man, who, fifteen years ago, on a rainy night in Canterbury, handed this exile a light, a map of the path back home, and a lexicon with the words I needed to speak about the journey and the arrival. Like so many of us, I, too, followed Brathwaite, became an arrivant.

———————

Home at last, I wrote, I taught, I continued to read. Then I visited Kamau Brathwaite in Barbados. Interested in my trajectory homeward, Kamau took me to look for Indians:

> "Now, final, Bathsheba. But we must include the whole wild Maroon coast from RiverBay right round to Pico & the miracle of Cove the ancien (T) Amerindian religious settlement, through Cattlewash to Martin's Bay and congoRock & Consetts in the distance..." (Brathwaite 1994: 228).

We drove around most of one morning, Kamau driving the little yellow moke, Beverley beside him, Tim and I in the backseat, my Indian straight hair blowing wildly into my face, sticking to my eyelids, my mouth, my ears, and we could not get to that holy site where those Arawaks (and, I dream, those Pequots and Wampanoags, those Natchez and proud Powhatans) prayed to the sun and the sea and sent their canoes (or their dreams) skimming out over the reef into that wild wild sea (turning North, toward home).

Figure 6.1. The Bay at Pico

I did learn then and on a later trip when we, Tim and I, found Pico, found that place, lingered there and took its picture (Fig 6.2), that most such "Amerindian sites" (like those all over North America) are the focus of archaeological excavations, the results of which end up in the new, post-independence Barbados National Museum in the "Prehistory" section. Here they are assuming another familiar role: "our (Barbadian) heritage," a role that differs little (except in its scope) from that played by North American Indian artifacts in U.S. museums.

[And so the naming - *pre*-history - once again highlights who is "us", and who lives only as "them." Michel-Rolph Trouillot: "Contact with the West is seen as the foundation of historicity of different cultures. Once discovered by Europeans, the Other finally enters the human world" (1995:144).]

I wondered about this, about the spread to its empire of European prejudices that assign the lives of indigenous peoples to a static, ahistorical world. I wondered, too, at the evident ease of their erasure. I knew, from teaching Native American history, from reading Caroline Foreman (1943) and Jack Forbes (1993), as well

Figure 6.2. The Village above the Sea at Pico

as from tantalizing references in many colonial history books—about those enslaved North American tribal people who were sold into colonial-era slave markets. I had heard, too, about boatloads of restive African slaves traded from the West Indies for cargoes of similarly locally troublesome North American Indian slaves. Was Barbados involved in such exchanges? Did some North American Natives, captured by the English or their Indian allies, find themselves working in Bajan cane fields? Especially after ambitious, land hungry planters from the island founded the South Carolina city of Charles Town where they took an enthusiastic role in the trans-Atlantic and Caribbean slave trades?

Despite doubts fostered by both histories and historians of Barbados, my curiosity drove me to seek a familiar refuge. Following a tiny wooden sign, spotted along the highway just north of Bridgetown, I turned a corner and drove up a narrow road to the National Archives, Barbados. I didn't have much time: This trip was not planned for this kind of research. But aided by a skeptical but willing archivist, I started in on the records of the Barbados Assembly, beginning in the middle of the 17th century when the first of North America's Indian slaves were captured and sold south.

Several hours of fascinating reading provided many hints. All slave regulations, for example, referred to "African and other slaves." Still, I knew that Indian slaves had also been brought from Guyana and from Venezuela, so perhaps *these* were the "others"? Then I came across the following act, dated June 1676:

Act to Prohibit the Bringing of Indian Slaves to this Island

> This act is passed to prevent the bringing of Indian slaves and as well to send away and transport those already brought to this island from New England and the adjacent colonies, being thought a people of too subtle, bloody and dangerous inclination to be and remain here.

So there it was: clear evidence that North American Indian peoples had worked in Barbados's sugar plantations. I next took up Richard Hall's *Acts Passed in the Island of Barbados from 1643-1762* (1764). Inside lay several tantalizing titles:

October 27, 1692.

"An Act for the encouragement of all Negroes and other slaves that shall discovery any conspiracy..."

"An Act for prohibiting sale of rum or other strong liquor to any Negro or other Slave...."

"An Act for the encouragement of such Negroes and other slaves that shall behave themselves courageously against the enemy in time of invasion (manumitted if two white men proved that they killed an enemy)."

6 January 1708.

"An Act to prevent the vessels that trade here, to and from Martinico or elsewhere, from carryingoff any Negro, Indian, or Mulattoe slaves or persons indebted or contracted servants...."

August 8, 1727.

"An Act for the punishment of runaway slaves and of slaves who shall wilfully entertain, harbour, and conceal any runaway slaves. Whereas divers Negroes and other slaves do often run away and absent themselves from the service of their owners and are willfully entertained, harboured, and concealed by other slaves....

[The punishments? Running away or concealing a runaway '21 lashes on the bare back for the first offense; 39 for the second offense; 39 plus branding "R" on right cheek, then for any further offenses, "any punishment the owner sees fit save execution."]

11 November 1731.
"Act for amending an Act...entitled 'Act for the Governing of Negroes and for providing a propermaintenance and support for such Negroes, Indians, or Mulattoes as hereafter shall be manumitted or set free....'"

I left Barbados then and began a journey. This then, is the narrative of my going from that day to this.

————————

A diversion:

Had I known (as Kamau knew—why didn't I ask him?) that Jerome Handler had been in those archives before me, I should have discovered that law much sooner. In 1968, in *Caribbean Studies*, Handler had quoted the Assembly's record of the act (1968:57). Still, had I accepted Handler's conclusions about that act, or about the origins of Indians enslaved in Barbados, I should not, perhaps, have undertaken this research. For Jerome Handler (as for many other historians), North American Natives formed only a minuscule and insignificant number of Barbadian slaves. In Handler's mind, all references to "Indians," any Indian placenames in Barbados records, indicated Native peoples brought either from the coast of South America or from other islands. In both cases these Indians were primarily, in Handler's view, either Caribs or Arawaks. His work, then, altered only slightly the "prehistoric" portrait of Barbados's indigenous people, adding Caribs and Arawaks from neighboring islands and relocating both groups from "prehistory" to Euro-historical time. When North American Natives *were* sold to Barbados, he argued, they were too few to matter. Even those Arawaks and Caribs from elsewhere in the Caribbean, in Handler's mind, called for no further study. As he put it, "Indian slaves always formed a very insignificant minority of Barbados' population and by the end of the first few decades of the 18th century there are few traces of them existing as a distinctive subcultural group" (39).[1]

————————

TRACES

Stubbornly ignoring Handler and the others, I continued collecting my fragments, piecing together the little stories that make up this chapter.

There were words. At the beginning of the 18th century, when Native slaves provided South Carolina with some one-third of its slave population, "mustee" meant people born of Indian, African, and European parents. And then there was the word "mulatto." In 1771, a Society of Gentlemen in Scotland produced an *Encyclopedia Britannica: or a Dictionary of Arts and Sciences*. Here is their version: "Mulatto: a name given in the Indies to those who are begotten by a Negro man on an Indian woman, or an Indian man on a Negro woman" (1771:314).

There were facts: James Axtell, writing of 17th and early 18th century North American colonies, noted that there was profit to be made in trading in Indian slaves. "The English," he wrote, "incited 'civil' war between the tribes" and then "rewarded one side for producing Indian slaves who were then sold to the West Indies, often for more biddable black slaves" (1981:239). Axtell's assertion that "black slaves" were more desirable because more tractable reflects a view, born in the practice of African slavery, with many echoes. Here is Yasuhide Kawashima, writing of the Pequot warriors captured after escaping the Puritans' genocidal attempt to exterminate their people in the 1630s. After capture they were "sold to the West Indies in exchange for more docile Blacks who became the first Negro slaves in New England" (1988:404). Peter Wood agrees: "before 1640, colonists in Massachusetts and Virginia...bartered captive Indians for Blacks in the West Indies" (1974:43). Wilcomb Washburn, once "dean" of US historians of Native America adds a subtler version: "The use of Indian slaves was rarely successful and in most instances was soon supplanted by black slavery" (Washburn and Sturtevant 1988:61). How did this stereotype of willing black slaves and rebellious Indian slaves arise? Mason Wade offers this clue: "The French...at Biloxi and New Orleans attempted to use Indian slaves to work the tobacco plantations but these ran away and it was decided to import Blacks from the French West Indies"(ibid. 1988:4).

Of course Indians *could* run away—to their own tribes, to other Indians, to escaped black slaves in the many maroon communities that grew up wherever there was African slavery. So long as they were *home*, Indians knew where they were—much better than any European, as the records of Indian rescues of witless Europeans attest. Rather than trading boatloads of rebellious Indians for cargoes of "biddable" Africans, it is surely more likely that the English—in New England, Virginia, Barbados, and elsewhere—rounded up and exported *any* leaders or fomenters of rebellions, whether African or Indian. Removed from whatever place and community they knew, they were perhaps more easily subdued, more easily reduced to a state of hopeless exhaustion characteristic of any dislocated, enslaved peoples. (But, it should be reiterated, the laws of the Barbados Assembly testify to the extent that enslaved peoples still rebelled, still ran.)

This stereotype also justified the importation of vast numbers of Africans to "replace" the "disappearing" Indians. But however "troublesome," or increasingly scarce these Indians, their enslavement, and their sale to Barbados, continued. After the 1670 founding of Charles Town by Sir John Colleton and his fellows, dozens more landless Barbadians quickly flocked to the area, eventually settling what became South Carolina. That these new invaders would quickly replicate Barbados economic and social practices was soon apparent. Anthony McFarlane tells us, "there was...an ominous sign that [Carolina] would eventually follow this path [of Barbados's social and economic structure], in that the settlers took Indians as slaves, both for their own use and for export to the West Indies" (quoted in Alleyne and Fraser 1989:10). As commodities on the slave market, they were quite valuable. In neighboring Virginia, "a child was worth more than her weight in deerskins; a single adult slave was equal in value to the leather produced in 2 years of hunting...By the latter half of the 17th century, if not before," Joel Martin reports, "slavery was big business in Virginia, an important part of the English trading regime" (quoted in Hudson and Tesser 1994:308).

Marking the historical moments when the British sold captive Indians into the slave trade is possible. Every single rebellion against the invaders, beginning with the first organized resistence to the Virginians at the beginning of the 17th century and continuing through the Pequot genocide (1630s), Metacom's Rebellion (1675-76), the Tuscarora Revolt (1711), the Yamassee war against their former English allies (1715-28), Pontiac's Rebellion (1763-66), sent still more Indians on their way to the Caribbean cane fields. From other invaded regions of North America came more rebellions, more slaves. The Carolinians' conquest of Spain's Florida Indian missions in the five years beginning in 1702 garnered hundreds for the Caribbean slave markets, these "missionized" Indians, already trained to serve and readily captured.

And all the years between these markers, and all over North America, slave raids and violent conflict produced humans for sale. The "Plantation Records" of the Barbados Museum and Historical Society carried these fragments: In 1630, John Winthrop sold an Indian to John Mainford of Barbados; in the 1660s, Narragansetts from Connecticut (once the Puritans' loyal allies in their war of extermination against the Pequots) were sold to Barbados; in 1668, an Indian slave was sent from Boston to the island; in 1700, a "big sale" of Indians from North America to the West Indies occurred; and, in 1701, Acolapissa Indian captives were sold by Virginians into the Caribbean. But the early 18th century did not see a gradual end to the Indian slave trade as Handler and others have claimed. In 1729, the French, together with their Choctaw allies, put an end to constant Natchez Indian revolts, capturing "hundreds" and selling them to the West Indies. These captures and sales to the islands continued until, one historian notes bleakly, by 1742 "the Natchez tribe had virtually disappeared" (Usner 1989:109).

Small additional markers, perhaps, but markers nonetheless of a vast dislocation, a terrible colonial "trail of tears" as later forced removals came to be known. Indian slaves were useful; Indian slaves were profitable; Indian slaves left behind land for the English to steal.

————————

More recently, colonial Indians—including slaves—have become an important aspect of the career-making trajectories of younger colonial-era historians. These "new" US historians, according to Gordon Wood, are paying "new attention...to the Indians.... A century ago, historians of early America scarcely acknowledged their existence...Through the efforts of a squadron of scholars, the Indians have now made their presence felt in early America" (G.Wood 1998:48). One of this "squadron" noticing Indians is Jill Lepore, who has studied the massive 1675 rebellion of Northeastern Natives led by Metacom (who, together with his war, was renamed "King Philip" by the colonizing English) (1998:173-75). As was customary in those colonial days, the victorious English slaughtered the captives they considered dangerous. They then beheaded Metacom and put his head on extended public display, a grisly warning to all other would-be Indian rebels. Those captives deemed less dangerous faced another fate, this shared by Metacom's wife and children. Ever in pursuit of profit, the English sold some 1,000 Natives into the West Indian slave trade (Axtell 1981:148).

At least Lepore *mentions* Indians. But do they "make their presence felt" in her text? Alas, in her work Indians merely add background color, despite the book's claim to explore "King Philip's War." What matters to this historian are not the indigenous people or their reasons for taking up arms against the Puritan invaders, but rather the English and their motives for barbarous acts. Seeking explanation for what most would-be descendants of these same Puritans would find a startling revision of their national origin myths, Lepore argues away the most appalling behaviors: selling Metacom's wife and children into Caribbean slavery was driven, she argues, not by material greed or even by vengeance, but rather by Biblical imperatives which taught that sons should be punished for fathers' transgressions. (Wives and daughters were evidently accidental inclusions.) Lepore further cites Cotton Mather's 1703 Bible-supported approval for selling other Indians into the African slave trade (his justification beginning "tis a Prophesy in Deuteronomy 28:68. The Lord shall bring thee into Egypt again with ships...") and concludes that what happened to the thousands of Indians sold after "King Philip's War" might also have elicited such citations as this one from Jeremiah 22:12: "But he shall die in the place whither they have led him captive and shall see this land no more." Even absent any biblical justification, the Puritan clergy, in Lepore's view, considered "slavery...to be just this kind of compassionate compromise: notorious Indians, like Philip himself, were executed; harmless enemies, mainly women and young children, were forced into servitude for a period of years; and those who were neither notorious enough to be hanged nor harmless enough to remain in New England were routinely sold into foreign slavery" (Lepore 1998:153).

What then happened to these transported Indian slaves? Lepore shows little interest. "Of...the hundreds of other Algonquians shipped out of the colonies, including Philip's son," she assures her readers blandly, "*we* know precious little. By the time Philip's son left the colonies, Barbados and Jamaica had both passed legislation preventing the importation of Indians from New England" (170). Without any further research, she assumes that these laws were completely effective. This assumption justifies a flight of fancy:

> Turned away at port after port it is possible that slave ships from New England simply dumped their now valueless cargo somewhere in the Caribbean Sea, or abandoned groups of New England Indians on uninhabited islands. Perhaps some number of them were illegally smuggled into English colonies in the West Indies. Yet one small piece of evidence, a letter from John Elliot to Robert Boyle written in 1683, suggests that at least some New England Indians, after being bounced from port to port, were shipped all the way to Africa (170).

This young and much-celebrated denizen of the "new, Indian-noticing U.S. historians" concludes her portrait of the Puritans by asserting that colonial era Indian slavery was not as bad as African slavery, resulting solely from the Puritans' and other Europeans' inability to understand the nature of Indian societies (which neither worshipped the Puritans' god nor possessed other human beings as property) rather than from more material factors, such as lust for Indian land or greed for the money to be made in the slave trade.

Despite its shortcomings, her book offers some material of interest. She notes that Nathaniel Saltonstall's *Continuation of the State of New-England, together with an Account of the Intended Rebellion of the Negroes in the Barbados* was published in London in 1676 and thus linked—for "readers in London" at least—the revolt of African slaves in Barbados to the revolt of New England Indians. She creates the following links among events: "Terrified English colonists in Barbadoes [sic] believed that the Africans had 'intended to murther all the white people there,' just as panicked English colonists in New England feared that the Indians had 'risen almost round the countrey.'" And so, she concludes, "the parallels between the two uprisings were uncanny and profoundly disquieting"(167-8). (She notes further that Virginia also experienced Indian revolts in 1676 when Governor Berkeley complained that the "New England Indian infection" had spread. And so Barbados's governor, Jonathan Atkins, had earlier warned London: "the ships from New England still bring advice of burning, killing, and destroying daily done by the Indians and the infection extends as far as Maryland and Virginia" [168].)

That her linkages among rebellions of enslaved peoples might have been real—not grounded in "disquieting" coincidences but rather in plans shared among enslaved Africans and Indians—does not occur to her. Like most historians writing from the "outside"—from a European-American perspective—she simply cannot imagine a world in which enslaved and conquered peoples communicated among themselves, plotting the overthrow of *all* Europeans, wherever they enslaved others. But of course it is clear from dozens of sources that the indigenous peoples of the Americas, together with enslaved Africans, communicated constantly and in sometimes wildly imaginative ways: through songs that encoded routes to freedom, through messages carried by captives sold into exile, through weapons and intelligence (sometimes stitched into fabric or decorated onto objects) shared by boatloads of slaves exchanged between Barbados and Virginia or the Carolinas, through conversations between the personal attendants who accompanied white men wherever they traveled between the West Indies and the North American coast. As the whites always feared (as their laws and restrictions and punishments attest), enslaved peoples of color worked exhaustively and collectively to end their servitude, to expel the invaders, to go home.[2]

Had Lepore actually been interested in Indians, and not in painting a colorful background against which to set the struggles of her fearful English colonists, she might have explored more deeply, delving into archives that, as the above shows, record numbers of North American Indian arrivals before, during, and after the outbreak of King Philip's War in 1675. Moreover, she might have concluded that the laws she'd heard about—including that 1676 law I came across at Cave Hill—were direct results of the arrival of "infected" war captive slaves as well as the "diseased" news carried by ship's officers. Looking still deeper, she might quickly have seen that far from halting the lucrative trade in Indian slaves, the law did nothing to prevent its spread well into the next century.

———————

Indian voices, then, however muted, however mixed in the "Negroe, Indian, and Mulattoe" slave worlds of the 17th and 18th centuries, formed an as yet little heard chorus mixed into the complicated sounds of Barbados that Kamau Brathwaite has given that nation and the world. Even as I listened to Kamau sing us the drumming sounds of Mile and a Quarter that drizzly night in Canterbury, I heard, too the softer sounds, audible nearby at "Indian Groun(d)," (now a Seventh Day Adventist Church—Fig. 6.3) the sounds of the houmfort, the tonelle, the music of his Great Uncle Bob'ob, the Ogoun, (and the sounds of the prejudice: "white man better than red man better than black man" [Brathwaite 1994: 129]) even as I thought: but I am hearing our Indian sounds, too, the drumming, the sounds of moccasined feet dancing the earth. (An Indian voice, speaking English so slooowly, asks "Hey, why wud they call Esse's father 'Red Man' if he wuzn un Indi'n?") I wondered: how to track their notes, map their footsteps, record their voices mingled with those many others from Africa, from South America, the Caribbean, and Europe?

Figure 6.3. Church at Indian Ground

And even here some suggestive fragments, more links. Here is Duke Ellington's sister, Ruth, telling Modoc Indian jazz musician Dave Brubeck, "All the credit's gone to the African for the wonderful rhythm in jazz, but I think a lot of it should go to the American Indian." And it is true. Carl Fischer, called a "full-blooded Indian" by one jazz historian, wrote "an orchestral suite called "Reflections on an Indian Boy," while Brubeck himself began and ended "They All Sang Yankee Doodle" with Indian songs he had learned from other Native jazz musicians. And here are more jazz artists whose heritage was Indian as well as European and African: Kay Starr, John Lewis, Joe Williams, Bobby Scott, Art Farmer, Lena Horne, Benny Golson, Ed Thigpen, Ben Thigpen, Earle Warren, Jim Hall, Doc Cheatham, Kid Ory, Big Chief Russell Moore, Joe Mondragon, Oscar Pettiford, Trummy Young, Mildred Bailey, Lee Wiley, Horace Silver, Sweets Edison, Frank Trumbauer, and Duke Ellington himself. There are hundreds of other players known mostly only to other Indians: Jim Pepper—whose life is the subject of my friend Sandy Osawa's documentary, *Pepper's Powwow,* and the "Nez Perceans" who featured the guitarist grandfather of another friend, Beth Piatote. Connecting again to Africa, Dave Brubeck's son Darius (named after Brubeck's teacher, Darius Milhaud) has for many years been teaching jazz at the University of Natal in Durban (Lees 1994:40, 57, 39).

––––––––

In Barbados again, a few years later, this time in May. A guide-book told the existence of "Yarico's Pond" where an "Amerindian woman" had either drowned herself in despair or given birth. The despair scenario had her lover, the Englishman Inkle whom she had rescued from her tribe's killing of his fellows, taking her to Bar-bados where he callously sold her into slavery. The birth occured during her time working as a slave on an island plantation. This was the tale we found, a few words, a crude map. This, we soon discovered, pointed only to a patch of bare ground, stripped by developers building holiday homes for Europeans who come to Barbados now not for the profit in sugar and slaves but to find sun in what is touted as the "safest" of the Caribbean nations, the most like "home," Kamau's loved/despised "L'il England."

But my Yarico was not this guidebooked figure. Standing then by the empty ground the map had designated "Yarico's Pond" I paused "for them...for those who have gone before...'once you were here...hoed the earth...and left it for me........that I may attempt here...that may I have strength to attempt here...strength enough to attempt here..." (Brathwaite 1994).

––––––––

And Kamau's words once again sent me questing. I wanted—still want—to find Yarico—to hear her voice, or, failing that, to walk in her moccasins—off the ship, along the Bridgetown wharf, up the road (Fig. 6.4), seeing the colors of the earth: white (from the coral she wouldn't know grounded the island, gave it its white white sands, held its fresh water, fed its long strands of sea grapes running down the beaches to the sea), mahogany red (though if she came from the Southern North American coast she would know this color, red Georgia clay), deep brown, almost black (the fertile home of the cane) and, here and there, a strange mauve, soft tone, almost of the desert (the earth dug now by archaeologists, the homes of the Arawaks), ending in the dark closed road leading into the plantation's slave quarters (Fig. 6.5).

Figure 6.4. The Road to the Plantation

I wanted to look behind me at the vanishing sea: home. I wanted to smell the island, heavy with sweet strangeness, to see with dread the dark little house where I—used to the air, used to my body's freedom, used to the open sky—would live. (Fig. 6.6)

I wanted to watch the tiny hungry finches who chased crumbs then as they do now, the losers gesturing their anger with spread and lowered wings and tails, hissing at their fellows. And I wanted to find the real pond, Yarico's Pond, where she worked, washed, drew water for the household and its foreign guests and perhaps died..

A little narrative of Yarico:

(Kamau knows all this story, knew it before I did. But he never told. I never asked.) Richard Ligon traveled to Barbados in the

Figure 6.5. The Road to the Slave Quarters

middle of the 17th century. Back in England, he wrote his *True and Exact History* of the island (1657). He recorded his many encounters with Indian slaves who worked in the houses of his hosts. One nameless woman taught him how to make corn pone by "searing it very fine (and it will fall out as fine as the finest wheat-flower in England) if not finer" (29-30). Other Indian men made "Perino," a drink "for their own drinking and is made of Cassavy root, which I told you is a strong poyson; and this they cause their old wives, who have a small remainder of teeth, to chaw and spit out into water (for the better breaking and macerating of the root). This juyce in three or four hours will work, and pure it self of the poysonous quality" (32).

Ligon liked these Indians:

> As for the Indians, we have but few, and those fetcht from other Countries; some from the neighboring islands, some from the Main, which we make slaves; the women who are better vers'd in ordering the Cassavie and making bread, then the Negroes, we imploy for that purpose, as also for making Mobbie: the men we use for footmen and killing of fish, which they are good at; with their own bowes and arrows they will go

Figure 6.6. A House in the Quarters

> out; and in a dayes time, kill as much fish as will serve
> a family of a dozen persons two or three dyes...They
> are very active men, and apt to learn any thing sooner
> than the Negroes...they are much craftier and sutiler
> then the Negroes; and in their nature falser; but in
> their bodies more active: their women have very small
> breasts and have more of the shape of the Europeans
> than the Negroes (55).

Having approved the Indians and disapproved the Africans,
Ligon then offered the first of the references others would shape
into dozens of later narratives of Yarico:

> We had an Indian woman, a slave in the house, who was
> of excellent shape and colour, for it was a pure bright
> bay;...This woman would not be woo'd by any means to
> wear Cloaths. She chanc'd to be with Child, by a Chris-
> tian servant, and lodging in the Indian house, amongst
> other women of her own country, where the Christian
> servants, both men and women cam; and being very
> great, and that her time was come to be delivered, loath
> to fall in labour before the men, walk'd down to a Wood
> in which was a pond of water, and there by the side of

the pond, brought her self abed; and presently washing her child in some of the water of the pond, wrapped it up in such rags as she had begg'd of the Christians; and in three hours time came home, with her child in her arms, a lusty Boy, frolick and lively (55).

And then *the* narrative:

This Indian dwelling near the Sea-coast, upon the Main, an English ship put in to a Bay and sent some of her men to shoar, to try wat victuals or water they could find, for in some distress they were: But the Indians perceiving them to go up so far into the country as they were sure they could not make a safe retreat, intercepted them in their return and fell upon them, chafing them into a wood and being dispersed there, some were taken and some kill'd: but a young man amongst them stragling from the rest was met by this Indian Maid, who upon the first sight fell in love with him and hid him close from her Country-men (the Indians) in a cave, and there fed him till they could safely go down to the shoar, where the ship lay at anchor expecting the return of their friends. But at last, seeing them upon the shoar, sent the long-boat for them, took them aboard, and brought them away. But the youth, when he came ashoar in the Barbadoes, forgot the kindness of the poor maid, that had venture her life for his safty, and sold her for a slave, who was a free born as he: and so poor Yarico for her love, lost her liberty (55).

———————

Where did he find this curious tale, so strangely familiar to English readers of American stories, so appealing to English men who wanted to believe that their rape of indigenous women and girls was desired by their victims? It was Ligon's countryman, John Smith, who had fabricated the first story of male desire and rescue, this the story cooked up in 1624, decades after his departure from Virginia in 1609. Evidently unhappy with the first published version of his time in North America, a long letter to a friend printed in London in 1608 as *The True Relation...*, John Smith decided to embroider his story. In *The General Historie of*

Virginia, New-England, and the Summer Isles, Smith added one of the most re-told scenes of early American history, that of his capture by Powhatan and subsequent rescue from death by Powhatan's beautiful daughter, Pocahontas. Just as Yarico's embellished story would prompt hundreds of echoes among European commentators narrating the history of their Caribbean empires, so Pocahontas's tale quickly stimulated North American poets, playwrights, and fiction writers into action. Most recently, her story has achieved the American apotheosis: Walt Disney Company's myriad animators have given us the movie-length cartoon version, suitably complete with cunning hummingbirds and talking trees. Although Yarico has yet to find herself luring audiences into her Pocahontas's universalizing (animated) "colors of the wind," she has elicited dozens of portraits, each retelling an increasingly lurid and romantic story.

Like Yarico's first appearance in print 30 years after, Pocahontas's emergence in Smith's 1624 tale was quite brief. Writing in the second person, Smith described a bound captive, brought before Powhatan, the king of the Powhatans. After "two great stones" had been placed before the King, "as many as could laid hands on him, dragged him to them, and thereon laid his head, and being ready with their clubs to beat out his brains, Pocahontas, the King's dearest daughter, when no entreaty could prevail, got his head in her arms and laid her own upon his to save him from death: whereat the Emperor was contented he should (1624:18).

It seems likely that Richard Ligon had read these words before he wrote his similarly abbreviated story. Even if he had not, however, his short tale of a Caribbean John Smith and Pocahontas clearly resonated in English breasts, ready to imagine a "New World" peopled with beautiful, naked young women anxious to rescue from their fellow Natives these invading blond, blue-eyed European men.

So popular was Ligon's little story of his Englishman and Indian that Richard Steele re-told it in the *Spectator,* no. 11, Tuesday, March 13, 1711. Here the tale took on the details that have clung to it through the centuries: one Thomas Inkle of London, 20, left for the West Indies on "the 16th of June, 1647, in order to improve his Fortune by Trade and Merchandize." He was "a Person every way agreeable, a ruddy Vigour in his Countenance, Strength in his Limbs, with Ringlets of fair Hair loosely flowing on his Shoulders." When he and some comrades put ashore "on the Main of America" seeking provisions, they were attacked by Indians who killed all but Inkle. Fleeing into the forest, "he threw himself, tired and breathless, on a little Hillock." Here "an Indian Maid rushed from a Thicket behind him." They discovered the requisite mutual attraction: "If the European was highly Charmed with the Limbs, Features, and wild Graces of the Naked American; the American was no less taken with the Dress, Complexion, and Shape of an European, covered from Head to Foot." Of course this naked, wild being reacted more primitively, untroubled by "civilization's" racial and sexual constraints. "The Indian," Steele assures readers, "grew immediately enamoured of him and consequently solicitous for his preservation." In the cave to which they repaired, Yarico produced all kinds of "New World" wonders for her lover—and in odd moments, charmed him still more by playing with his golden hair and wondering at the contrast between her darkness and his whiteness. Moreover, like Pocahontas, whose royal pedigree helped mitigate the consequences of her inferior race, Yarico soon showed Inkle that she, too, was "A Person of Distinction."

Steele's early 18th-century Yarico and Inkle spent some considerable time together, she caring for him, he promising her a home with him and the all-important share in his worldly goods. "In this manner did the Lovers pass away their Time, till they had learn'd a Language of their own.... In this tender Correspondence these Lovers lived for several Months." Yarico then discovered a ship on the coast and together, they set out for Barbados. Once there, however, Inkle reverted to his English mercantile self, beginning "to reflect upon his loss of Time and to weigh with himself how many Days Interest of his Money he had lost during his Stay with Yarico.... Upon which Considerations, the prudent and frugal young Man sold Yarico to a Barbadian Merchant; notwithstanding that the poor Girl, to incline him to commiserate her Condition, told him that she was with Child by him: But he only made use of that Information to Rise in his Demands upon the Purchaser" (Addison, Steele 11:38-39). From this point it was but a short distance to the version in which Yarico, now enslaved, either bore

Inkle's child beside her pond or, in more romantically satisfying terms, drowned herself, despairing.

Steele's version, however, already remote from Ligon's simpler tale, presaged what was to come. From that moment any echo—however slight—of Yarico's own voice vanished as she was turned first this way and then that—first into an embodiment of antimercantile sentiment, then into an icon of the antislavery movement (when she moved through racial stages from "Amerindian" to "Mulatto" to "Nubian" to "African"), then into a romantic, "wild," and noble heroine. Recently, Beryl Gilroy's England-written retelling, her 1996 novel, *Inkle and Yarico*, abandons Yarico again in favor of the tale of the immoral Inkle, forced by his poverty and natural indolence to sell his Carib wife, Yarico, once his many years of exile among the Indians ended with his rescue by his countrymen. Except to act the stoic Indian princess and wife, silently pained by Inkle's passion for a child captive from another tribe but protesting only in a sullen, passive-aggressive stereotype of a 1950s television sitcom housewife, Yarico hardly exists at all in this text. Only her cover picture suggests a corporeal presence and this shows only a naked, bow and arrow carrying Diana, holding a parrot aloft to site her in the exotic western hemisphere. Her world inside the novel is nothing but stereotypes, these racial. Gilroy's Inkle relates, "She was pure instinct, for to survive in her world, to be at one with Nature's rhythms and to heed its customs, there was no place for thought and reason." Later, "I called her by name but never would she address me as Tommy because she said, 'Spirits would call you away to their land of death.'" In fact in this indigenous world, "All activities were surrounded by superstition and ritual, and many times I was scolded by Paiuda, the irascible priest, for violating some rule which they had absorbed into their spongelike natures from birth" (Gilroy 20, 28, 29).

(One cannot help wondering if some of this stereotype, of the nasty-tempered, unpredictable evil Indian shaman did not stem from Gilroy's viewing of the awful film, *Black Robe*, based on the deeply racist account of the French invasion of Canada written by the English novelist, Brian Moore—and based, by his account, on the notorious *Jesuit Relations*.)

Figure 6.7. A Contemporary Inkle and Yarico

The women in Gilroy's Carib world are a disgrace: will-less, they serve the Carib men, already enslaved. So no Yarico here. Rather this novel—like its European predecessors—is Inkle's tale, the narrative of his collapse from a youthful a-morality into an adulthood of hot proslavery passions.

But the story has not ended. Just two years ago Yarico played again, this time on a Caribbean stage, here the beautiful, (white) befeathered protagonist of a musical, performed for white Barbadians and their tourist cousins, featured—together with a "Caribbeanized" *Tempest*—in the annual Season held at Holders Plantation House in March, 1999 (Fig. 6.7).

Then, in 1999, Yarico entered yet another realm, this one almost as absurd as Disney's. With Inkle, she has become the object of heavy, postmodern academic analysis. Frank Felsenstein has introduced and edited *English Trader, Indian Maid: Representing Gender, Race, and Slavery in the New World*, published in 1999.

While the Barbados-produced musical version of the story was titled, simply, "Yarico," Felsenstein returns matters to their earlier state: Inkle is first, described by occupation. Yarico comes second, described only by a sexualized body. Together they "represent" a world "new" only to Inkle.

> (Michel-Rolph Trouillot notes: "The lexical opposition Man-versus-Native...titled the European literature on the Américas from 1492 to the Haitian Revolution and beyond. Even the radical duo Diderot-Raynal did not escape it. Recounting an early Spanish exploration, they write, 'Was not this handful of *men* surrounded by an innumerable multitude of *natives*...seized with alarm and terror, well or ill-founded?'"[Trouillot 1995:82].)

Here is Felsenstein explaining:

> Current critical interest in the tale reflects a growing awareness of the value of studying the often intangible points of contact between oral traditions and written or printed cultures. Described by David Brion Davis as one of the great folk epics of its age, "Inkle and Yarico" provides just such a site of mediation between the oral and the literate (2).

But: who "studies," producing "value" to whom?

Thanks to Richard Steele, one oral Indian assumed a privileged place. Felsenstein tells us that Steele's Yarico is special. "As a festishized native, a Noble Savage, reduced to a mere possession, Yarico is perhaps unique among such figures in being given [by Steele] the opportunity to answer back."(5) Answer back? Pleading with Inkle to keep his promises to marry her? Confessing to a pregnancy that raised her price? Or is it simply that she has a name and a story that Europeans could read, remember, retell, reimagine, represent, albeit entirely in their own terms?

Despite his dubious assertion that Yarico speaks, Felsenstein elsewhere unknowingly gives readers an Indian woman who actually does answer back, more insistently, more stridently than Yarico managed with her soft, impotent pleading. *This* Indian woman—nameless—reminded me of those the old people meant when they warned us "Never mess with Indian women."

This Indian woman lives in a French text, an early 17th century travel narrative by Jean Moquet who recounted the story of one English pilot, lost on the shores of Newfoundland.

> He had found an Indian woman, of whom he was enamoured, making her fine promises by signs, that he would marry her; which she believed and conducted him through these desarts; where she shewed him the fruit and roots good to eat and served him for an interpreter amongst the Indians....They had a child together; and found there an English ship....He was very glad to see himself escaped from so many dangers and gave these English an account of all his adventures,...but being ashamed to take along with him this Indian-woman thus naked, he left her on land, without regarding her any more....But she seeing herself thus forsaken by him, whom she had so dearly loved, and for whose sake she had abandoned her country and friends, and had so well guided and accompanied him through such places, where he would, without her, have been dead a thousand times. After having made some lamentation, full of rage and anger, she took her child, and tearing it into two pieces, she cast the one half toward him into the sea, as if she would say, that belonged to him, and was his part of it; and the other she carried away with her, returning back to the mercy of fortune and full of mourning and discontent[3] (quoted in Felsenstein 1999:214-15).

(And thus this "New World" Medea wreaks vengeance!)

Reading without the European male ego-commentary—the promise of European marriage so meaningless to any indigenous woman, the selfless passion this man believed she must have felt, the abandonment of him she "so dearly loved"—there stands an angry woman. She replies—rejecting the rape, the theft, the conquest. Saying no

> that children above all others would be like the sun.

> rise (Brathwaite 1992:46).

————————

Edward Said:

> *European geographical centrality...is buttressed by a cultural discourse relegating or confining the non-European to a secondary, racial, cultural, ontological status. Yet this secondariness is, paradoxically, essential to the primariness of the European....For natives to want to lay claim to that terrain is, for many Westerners, an intolerable effrontery, for them actually to repossess it unthinkable* (quoted in Felsenstein 1999:42).

So let us "affront," offend; let us lay claim to this terrain.

Gordon Wood, still praising Lepore's book, worries a little that "we" shall take too seriously the young historian's implied condemnation of Indian and African slavery. "She never mentions the fact that during the English Civil War the English likewise sold Scottish and Irish prisoners into bondage in the West Indies. It was a cruel and brutal age, and human life was a good deal cheaper than it is for *us* today" (G. Wood 1998:43 emphasis added).

I'll leave aside his implication that if white people were sold into "bondage" (*not* slavery) then the enslavement of North American Indians (or Africans) was not so bad. I'll also ignore his "two-other-wrongs-make-the-first-wrong-less-wrong" argument. I cannot overlook his entire dismissal of those whose lives "we"—U.S.ers—continue to "take cheaply," those millions, some so close by, just across the (barricaded) U.S. southern border, who labor for "our" wealth, "our" greed for an endless supply of ostentatious commodities, to fill the shopping malls where we satisfy "our" lusts—and *for our time and money to travel to "their" world*, albeit a world protected, sanitized for "our" protection by the Hilton Hotel Corporation.

> "[In order to construct the Hilton Hotel at Needham's Point in 1960, Nature itself, it seems, had to be altered....]" (Brathwaite 1994:115)

What also cries out for reply is Wood's evident inability to imagine what slavery—ownership of body, your life—meant to Indian people. Wilbur Jacobs, another white man, another eminent historian of the United States whose work is discussed in Chapter 1, at least worked hard to move his inborn Euro-imaginary closer to that of the Indians he wrote about. Noting that hundreds, maybe thousands of Native peoples killed themselves (throwing themselves from departing ships and so on) rather than endure slavery, Jacobs asked himself: "Why would the average woodland tribesman [women did it too - and in the face of impending rape as well as enslavement] choose death as an alternate to being a white man's slave?" His reply? "Freedom was the Indian's element: freedom of movement, freedom of speech, freedom of action, freedom to do whatever he pleased whenever he chose to do it" (G. Wood 1998:43; Jacobs 1972:167).

———————

if yu cyaan beat prospero
Whistle (Brathwaite 1992:77)

They have always wanted to possess the women of the Americas, these Europeans. But not every woman proved as willing as Pocahontas or Yarico. In 1524, Giovanni da Verrazzano "attempted to capture an Indian family consisting of an old woman, a young girl, and six children on the northeast coast of North America. But the girl proved so intractable that the soldiers were forced to give up the attempt to take the whole family to the ship, and finally carried away but one small boy who was too young to make any resistance" (Lauber 1913:71). You know what they say: Don't mess with Indian women! And so, when Verrazzano and his brother landed at a Caribbean island—probably Guadaloupe—in 1528, "the fierce cannibal Caribs killed and ate Captain Verrazzano" (Olexer 1982:18).

———————

Again, Yarico:

Fig. 6.8. The walk

Fig. 6.9. The glimpse

Fig. 6.10. The home place

Escape: Richard Ligon gives us a picture:

> But there is a Bird they call a Man of War and he is
> much bigger than a Heron and flies out to Sea upon
> discoveries (for they never light upon the Sea) to see
> what ships are coming to the island; and when they
> return, the Islanders look out and say, a ship is coming
> and find it true (1857:61).

Did Yarico watch these great birds? Did she follow her eyes
seaward? Home? Did she watch the new ships unload their captives and weep?

Yarico was a "house slave" and as such the keeper of male visitors. Here was one of her tasks, performed on this occasion for Richard Ligon, afflicted with the chiggers (called "chegoes") that buried themselves in the soft European skin:

> This vermine will get thorough your stocken and in a pore of your skin in somepart of your feet, commonly under the nail of your toes and there make a habitation to lay his offspring, as big as a small Tare, or a bag of a Bee, which will cause you to go very lame, and put you to much smarting pain. The Indian women have the best skill to take them out, which they do by putting in a small pointed pin or needles, at the hold where he came in, and winding the point about the bag, loosen him from the flesh and so take him out....some of these Chegoes are poysonous and after they are taken out, the Orifice in which they lay will fester and rankel for a fortnight after they are gone. I have had ten taken out of my feet in a morning by the most unfortunate Yarico, an Indian woman (1657:65).

Daily Yarico went to her pond—to wash (Indians startled the dirty Europeans when they insisted on bathing every day) to get water for the household, to wash the household's laundry, to dream (Fig. 6.11).

Her pond:

Water, its sounds and its silences....in this place of still water... Did she hear, too, Kamau's coral springs? The silvery fall of fresh island water coming up from underground? Did she gather with the others at Indian Spring? Still there, beside the plantation great house but down the hill from Indian Town...

And did she run?

There are the caves—all along the wilder Atlantic Coast (looking toward Africa, Kamau says as he looks East). Tim and Kamau climbed down and around and through a labyrinth of caves while Beverly and I waited, watching, up on the cliffs above. If she did run to these caves, Ligon gives us the consequences of her certain capture:

> These caves are very frequent in the island and of several dimensions, some small, others extremeley

Fig. 6.11. Yarico's Pond

large and capacious: the runaway Negroes, often
shelter themselves in these coverts for a long time
and in the night range abroad the countrey and steale
pigs, platins, potatoes, and pulling and bring it there;
and feast all day upon what they stole the night before
and the nights being dark and their bodies black they
escape undiscerned'd... (1657:98).

Or did Yarico find that bay—the little Arawak settlement
among the tall palms, shivering and clattering in the strong winds
blowing from Africa? The smooth flat rocks climbing down in flat
wide terraces to the bay where they had once launched their canoes
into the Atlantic beyond? Did she walk on that shore and long...?

Silences.

Fig. 6.12. The Bay at Pico

———————

What can Yarico tell us—herself—now?

Perhaps these words will give a small voice to all the Yaricos, all the war-captive women, all the children who walked the earth of Barbados, who ran away to the Arawaks' caves, who died in the tiny dark slave houses set back from the main plantation roads. Perhaps too the story still to be told will complicate all our understanding of origins. Now the stories begin in Africa, cultural manners and modes traced to present-day African worlds. It will not be easy to uncover the connections between the North American Native cultural worlds and those of Africa. There exist now only traces of North America-Caribbean ties: the use in Santería ceremonies (in New York *and* in Latin America) of a North American Plains Indian plaster bust, weirdly pink, and a "gold dust Indian spray," available in every Washington Heights *bodega*. Plains Indian costumes appear in Crop Over parades—and coloring books—in Barbados (Fig. 6.13).

Neighboring Trinidad's carnival celebrates North American Indians—as does the all-"black" "Indian Crewe," parading through the streets of New Orleans, every year (Bellour and Kinser 1998:147-69). There are all those stories still to be found in the

Figure 6.13. Crop-Over Colouring Book

law books, the plantation sales and tax records, the parish lists of deaths and baptisms, and in the archives of colonial South Caro- lina, Massachusetts, Connecticut, in those of Bridgetown and Cave Hill. And then there is Yarico.

NOTES

NOTES TO INTRODUCTION

1. Timothy J. Reiss, *Against Autonomy: Global Dialectics of Cultural Exchange* (Stanford, CA: Stanford University Press, 2002)1.

2. One example is Mary Rogin's lurid "Please Take Our Children Away," in *The New York Times Magazine*, Sunday, March 4, 2001. Beneath this horrifying headline, Rogin narrates the story of two native villages in Labrador where addiction to gas sniffing is endemic among the children and where one village leader, Paul Rich, asked the Newfoundland government to remove the worst addicted children to detox facilities away from Sheshatshiu, their home village. Sympathetic to Innu problems, Rogin takes pains to describe the terrible conditions in which these Innu people are living. She writes, "The Innu trace their problems with poverty and substance abuse to government relocations that forced them to give up their nomadic way of life..." and "to the chronic physical and sexual abuse their children suffered when they were forced to attend Christian residential schools from the 1950s to the 1970s." Present conditions feature alcoholism, domestic and child abuse, suicide, grinding poverty, hopelessness. The conclusion Rogin reaches is familiar: for the best interests of the poor children, they must be seized from their home communities and sent to urban centers far away. Of course they can never return, since conditions at home are hopeless. Reading this story, I was certain that there was another story behind this. We are all familiar with Indians' "plights": as Vine Deloria noted some years ago, where other peoples have various attributes, Indians have "plights." So I called Shari Huhndorf, Cook Inlet Yup'ik, scholar of Native North America, and my frequent collaborator, to ask her

what was missing from the story. She told me what only a handful of readers—these mostly indigenous people themselves—would know: that what underlies the poverty of these Innu villages is the fact that the land to which they were removed has long been a major weapons testing ground for Canada's armed forces. After decades of constant heavy bombardment, the land is virtually dead, useless for any of the activities Innu people might pursue, including hunting (the animals are gone), fishing (the fish are gone), gathering (the land is poisoned) or....The story says nothing whatever about these ugly facts, all of which are the responsibility of the government, and all of which would have been available to a more skeptical reporter, someone less willing to assume that native people, once forced to change some timeless, "premodern" way of life, cannot possibly survive.

3. The most impressive of these is a new book cited above, no.1, so erudite that it may not get the wide reading it deserves, Timothy J. Reiss's *Against Autonomy*. See also Peter Nabokov, *A Forest of Time: American Indian Ways of History* (Cambridge: Cambridge University Press, 2002) for a refreshingly unarrogant non-Native's exploration of American Indian epistemologies.

4. As such encounters continued through our session, Sonia Saldívar-Hull, who was sitting next to me and who was similarly dismayed by the reactions to our words, wrote me a note: "They are not listening to a single word we are saying!" She was right.

5. That a British writer uses a Japanese car manufacturer as her ideal product speaks powerfully to the decline and ultimate disappearance of the British Empire, where once Rovers and Rolls Royces, all made in England of products drained from the colonies and sent back as transport for rulers and their minions, would have been a *TLS* writer's choice.

6. Kunuk has made two earlier films, both aimed exclusively at his own community and exhibited there, or in private venues. I am grateful (again) to Shari Huhndorf for sharing this information.

7. There are many critiques of this common practice. Among the most incisive recent critiques is found in Peter Nabokov's *A Forest of Time*, cited above in n 3.

8. Again, there are many scholars who have articulated these matters, including both Simon Ortiz, who has been talking about stories for a very long time, and Craig Womack. I have learned everything I know about Nez Perce stories from Haruo Aoki, and I am grateful.

9. Many young scholars are contesting this simple-minded view, including, for example, Dulcinea Lara, Delberto Ruiz, and others.

10. Moya defines identities as "socially significant and context-specific ideological constructs that nevertheless refer in non-arbitrary (if partial) ways to verifiable aspects of the social world," p. 13. As she acknowledges, she joined the "post-positivist realist" school of thought founded by Satya Mohanty at Cornell.

11. Of course there was American literacy long before Europeans came to burn all the books and documents they found.

12. These events occurred during the first meetings of two of the required "core" courses in August, 2001 and January 2004. They were reported to me by the students involved. Although the two Native American students were from the same nation, the two Pacific Islanders were from two quite distinct nations, with distinct histories, languages, and cultures. Nevertheless, they were instantly lumped together and assigned all the stereotypes associated with them, mainly an inordinate love of both football and food.

13. The main building of this museum has just opened on the National Mall in Washington D.C. Like all other materials from these museums, my charter members' invitations to special receptions both for the Heye Center and for the museum on the Mall are replete with the kinds of expected "Indian" motifs used for the interior of the Heye Center and both interior and exterior of the National Museum. One major addition to the Heye Center's presentation of "Indianness" is the bigger museum's use of "Native smells" (cedar, sage, and so on) that machines send wafting over visitors as they walk—through successive "native ecology zones," planted with plants indigenous to the various regions, toward the building's entrance.

NOTES TO CHAPTER 1

1. Needless to say, I hope all such formulations stem from Ngugi wa Thiong'o's seminal rereading of Frantz Fanon. See, inter alia, Ngugi's *Decolonising the Mind* (1986) and *Moving the Center* (1993).

2. These ideas were taken from a work that, for lack of a publisher, has been abandoned. It was titled *Fry Bread and Wild West Shows: Museums and American Indians* and written with two co-authors: Shari Huhndorf and Carol Kalafatic.

3. George Gustav Heye was the tycoon who, during the first half of this century, collected the more than 4 million artifacts that made up the displays in the semi-public Museum of the American Indian,

on 155th Street in New York City. Fraud and theft decimated the collection, reducing it to its present size. This museum merged with the Smithsonian in 1989.

4. I am indebted for this formulation to Beth Piatote, now a PhD candidate at Stanford University and a member of the Nez Perce nation, enrolled at the Colville Reservation, Washington.

5. Contrary to stereotype, there *are* Native American Rush Limbaughs. Some, not surprisingly, are anthropologists.

6. Westerman, a Lakota singer/songwriter, wrote "Here Come the Anthros" to condemn the whole profession of anthropology. Vine Deloria Jr. is the most vociferous critic of anthropology and its practitioners but there are dozens of others. At the same time, there are Native anthropologists, including the late Alfonso Ortiz and Wendy Rose.

7. Of course such hidden burials, such "as if" gestures, carry another charge: centuries of grave robbing by "collectors" of Indian material culture sharpens Indian wits. Too, they would not be possible in some places such as the Southwest, where the material culture of Native burials carries so much monetary value for the kinds of collectors whose artifacts form some of the subject of the books under review here.

8. Short sufficient labor in the burgeoning cities of post-War America, the federal government instituted a policy that offered reservation Indians bus tickets, housing, and job training and referrals if they moved from reservations to various cities. Typical of most Bureau of Indian Affairs programs, relocation was inefficiently run, stranding thousands of Native people on the streets of Minneapolis, Chicago, Los Angeles, Oakland, and so on.

9. This is the title of a recent exhibit, "Shooting Back from the Reservation: A Photographic View of Life by Native American Youth." Beth Piatote wrote a strikingly original commentary on the exhibit (1996).

10. Gerald McMaster is a Canadian art curator and artist, at present working at the National Museum of the American Indian. James Luna is a performance artist who, among other things, "exhibits" himself and records the comments of museum visitors. Nora Naranjo-Morse exhibits her pots and small pottery sculptures very widely. Ortiz is the prize-winning author of many collections of poetry, stories, and critical work.

11. I want to acknowledge Matt Dirkes's contributions here: in the spring semester of 1997 the two of us read widely in the broad area of museum and exhibition studies and our conversations have enriched my own thinking considerably.

12. Although his information is a bit different, James Faris, interestingly, shares the opinion that Puebloans and Navajos have received different treatment by outsiders. In his version, "the West is prepared to accept in rough outline the antiquity of the Pueblo peoples to the region and thereby at least some of their claims to aboriginality and to the land on which they are found.... Quite the contrary is true of photography of Navajo, which denies their status as aboriginals, as claimants, as indicators of their own social relations.... Anthropological orthodox and conventional wisdom deny them...indigenous status...[and see] Navajo as adapter"(Faris 1996:18).

13. It should be noted here that there are many in Martin's generation and in the one following who have been more successful at bringing Native voices together with those of non-Natives in revisions of U.S. master narratives. None has adopted Martin's essentialist Native in order to do so. They include, among many others, Colin Calloway, Ronald Wright, Charles Hudson, Gordon Brotherston—all worthy heirs of the legacy of Jennings, Jacobs, and others. Understandably, Native historians have had much less difficulty with this project.

14. Like almost everything Native people did, Ghost Dancing, too, has been interpreted to highlight Indians' primitive difference from "us." Most texts—still!—describe Ghost Dancing as an atavistic ritual, aimed at comforting Indians with superstition. Thus Indians are said to have ghost danced because they believed (ho, ho) that if they danced with sufficient frenzy, bullets would not kill them and their enemies, white people, would eventually disappear. (The slaughter at Wounded Knee in 1890 thus becomes merely another lesson to these savages that white ways were better.) That this movement represented organized political resistance was, and remains, quite beyond the imaginations of inhabitants of the West.

NOTES TO CHAPTER 2

1. The phrase "decolonizing the mind" is the title of an earlier book by Ngugi wa Thiong'o (1986).

2. Of course such an aestheticizing of African art came in reaction to its earlier rendering as object of anthropological study, artifact of "primitiveness" and "otherness." Nevertheless, though a move "forward" the move remains fraught with "first world" difficulties.

3. Some of these were mainly traditional in form and conception, some were among the museum world's most critical exhibitions. Among the former were "Africa and the Renaissance: Art in Ivory" (1988), "Yoruba: Nine Centuries of African Art and Thought" (1989), "Likeness and Beyond: Portraits from Africa and the World" (1990), "Africa Explores: 20th Century African Art" (1991). The latter included "ART/artifact: African Art in Anthropological Collections" (1988), "Secrecy: African Art That Conceals and Reveals" (1991), and "Face of the Gods: Art and Altars of Africa and the African Americas" (1991).

4. Vogel is particularly addicted to this grammatical form. See Baldwin et. al. (1987:11).

5. Timothy Reiss commented on this: "Were there no *African* architects who could design this space for the display of *African* art?" Mary Nooter Roberts answers: "Lin is not African, and has never been to Africa. But her previous works, notably the Vietnam Veterans Memorial, demonstrate a sensitivity to space, and an interest in a performative, journey-like experience of it, that seemed conducive to the presentation of African art in regularly changing exhibitions. [...] She accents color, lighting, pattern, and materials, and hers is a handcrafted space, its asymmetry and human scale suggestive—though not imitative—of African uses of line, space, and design" (Nooter Roberts and Vogel 1994:65). Presumably, an African architect would only have succeeded in "imitating" African uses of asymmetry, color, lighting, and so on?

6. The Malcolms were lenders of many of the objects chosen for the "Perspectives" exhibit, including a Fang Reliquary Guardian, chosen by William Rubin (a curator at the Museum of Modern Art), a Kongo Female Figure of ivory, chosen by Ivan Karp, a Mumuye figure, chosen by Nancy Graves (a New York artist), and Kongo mother and child, chosen by Robert Farris Thompson (professor of African and African American art history at Yale University). Thompson explains that he became "taken" by African art by his exposure to the "diaspora," the "mambo music of Mexico in the 1950s." He adds,"Cuba was my entrée. Cuba gave me a kind of intellectual head start in Kongo, Yoruba, Dahomean and especially Cross River—Ejagham—art"(quoted in Baldwin, et.al. 1987:179).

7. The National Museum of the American Indian's officials are deeply concerned with maintaining a particular image for visitors. Those Native artists featured in the talking circle are restricted to that space or to larger spaces carefully organized by the Museum. When I have

begun reading through the stacks of questionnaires left behind by tourists each day I have been challenged by "volunteers". When three of us annotated the visitors book (now replaced by question-naires), "writing back" to those whose comments were offensive to us, our annotations quickly disappeared—along with the pages with the offending remarks. So carefully were the pages excised from the book that we had trouble locating where they had been when we returned to the Museum two weeks later. I and others have had many similar experiences with the Museum's officials (mostly non-Native) who keep a tight control over every aspect of the Muse-um's functioning. In other words, despite all the rhetoric about the NMAI "belonging" to "us," it only belongs to "some of us" and only if we behave ourselves while within its marble precincts.

8. Armand Arman was a regular lender to exhibits at the Center and later the Museum. He loaned a Shona neckrest (selected by Ivan Karp) for the 1987 "Perspectives" show. A photograph of Arman's home (Nooter Roberts and Vogel 1994:47) shows a large floor-to-ceiling bookcase along one wall. A small, very modern sofa sits before it. Two end tables and what appears to be a coffee table hold vases, lamps, papers, and books. The caption reads, "This interior shows African art alongside various sorts of contemporary art, found objects [two Tiffany lamps? or the mounted conch shell in one of the case's cubicles?] and ordinary household items [books, stereo speakers]."

9. Franz Kafka's short story, "In the Penal Settlement," includes a punishment machine that inscribes its illegible, incomprehensi-ble message on the body of the "prisoner", selected, like most of Kafka's protagonists, at random. Only the author of the story—or the executioner—understands the meaning of the marks.

10. It is important to note that the Museum has since altered this, and many other, exhibits so that now the link between the diorama and the Ghost Dance movement is much less visible. Only one caption makes reference to the Ghost Dance, here in reference to one of the dresses.

11. The White Mountain Apaches followed another prophet who preached a similar message of resistance to white invasion and colonization. One of the Museum's original selectors, Edgar Perry, spent a good portion of his video taped interview talking about this movement and its importance both to him and to the Apache people living in the early years of the 20th century. The Museum, however, has effectively silenced his message by fragmenting his

comments into little short films, each of which can be viewed by tourists who choose to press the categories on a screen. There is also one placard describing the movement, though it does it in deadly "anthro-speak"—a language that always and everywhere reduces politics to quaint and hopeless cultural manifestations.

12. The government, represented by its corps of corrupt, Washington-appointed "Indian agents," each responsible for one reservation or a group of reservations in one region, was well aware of the political dangers posed by Ghost Dancing and other resistance practices. Each was outlawed by the federal government, beginning with the Ghost Dance in 1890. It was its illegality that justified the massacre of unarmed people at Wounded Knee in 1890, as well as the arrest and murder of dozens of other Indian resistors. Still, the anthropologists, led by James Mooney (who published what remains the most-read version of the Ghost Dance shortly after the event when, as the official government ethnographer, he visited the site), shifted the historical landscape entirely, portraying Ghost Dancing as I have described it. Thus was yet another Native movement effectively dehistoricized so that it need not be taught in US history courses but could rather be assigned to the historical and a-political oblivion of anthropology departments.

13. The Native American Graves Protection and Repatriation Act (NAGPRA) was passed in 1990, implementing the return of "funerary and sacred objects and objects of cultural patrimony," though the Smithsonian was specifically excluded from the act. With the merger of the Smithsonian with the old Museum of the American Indian, bones and other remains were to be returned for reburial. Other items were not mentioned, however, although the Museum's many discussions of this issue insist that it will comply with demands for objects covered by NAGPRA (Greenfield 1995:179). Richard West Jr. does add Masayesva's name to a long list of people who "helped" with the inaugural exhibits at the Museum. See West, in Hill and Hill (1994:12).

14. Playing Afri*can* is, in the contemporary U.S., an option usually reserved for people identified as possessing African descent, though playing African-American is increasingly common among European American kids, as Robin Kelley (1996, 1998) and Tricia Rose (1994) and many others have remarked.

15. This echoes the Museum for African Art's decision to choose Maya Lin as architect of the interior of the SoHo site. Culture, and seemingly constructions of race, have become completely interchange-

able in this global world, *unless, of course, the culture is Western and the race is white.*

NOTES TO CHAPTER 3

1. The "we" of the text refers both to the authors and Carol Kalafatic, who made the tour of the museum together, and—at times—to two other indigenous people: Dean Curtis Bear Claw, and Chris Eyre.

2. Significantly, the *NMAI Runner*, published since 1994, first announced itself as "A Newsletter for Native Americans from The Smithsonian Institution, Washington, D.C." In 1995 the subheading changed to read, "A Newsletter *About* Native American Activities at the Smithsonian, From The Smithsonian Institution, Washington, D.C." (emphasis added). The language then shifted again, to a more accurate statement of the Museum's real power structure: "The Newsletter for The Smithsonian's National Museum of the American Indian."

3. Chris Eyre was then a film student at New York University's Tisch School of the Arts. He has subsequently launched a successful career as a film director, most recently of the films *Smoke Signals*, *Bringing It All Back Home*, *Skins*, and two PBS "Mystery" specials, *Skin Walkers*, and *A Thief of Time*, both adaptations of books of the same title by Tony Hillerman.

4. A tape of the original interview is in our possession. Excerpts from the interview were included in a "Night Waves" program, "Culture in New York," which aired on the British Broadcasting Corporation's Radio 4 on November 17, 1994.

5. In the early moments of our contact, the interviewer demonstrated his immersion in Hollywood stereotypes, joking while waiting for a cab "Here I am, a white man surrounded by savages. Should I be afraid?" Later, as we sat waiting for our drinks order in an uptown restaurant he wondered aloud if the delay was "because the waitress thinks you're all drunken Indians." We reacted politely to both sallies. His post-interview change of heart, his efforts to tie his ethnicity to ours, signaled, we thought, his amazement that we didn't fit his stereotypes but were, instead, articulate, educated, and "modern." Of course, as one reader of this text noted, the interviewer's awkward attempts to connect the Irish experience to that of Native Americans were not entirely without foundation. As Francis Jennings and many others have shown, many of the genocidal practices that accompanied the British invasion of North America were created during the invasion and conquest of Ireland in the

16th century (see Jennings 1976). Connections between Ireland and Native America have continued. During the Irish famine of the 1840s, Native Americans, including both tribal governments and groups of Quaker-schooled Native children, collected funds which they sent to Ireland for the relief effort.

6. "Ishi" was the name given a Northern California Native who alone survived the decimation of his Yana nation by white settlers' massacres and diseases. Generations of California schoolchildren— including one of the authors—learned about Ishi when one of their 9th grade "set texts" was the self-congratulatory and stereotype-ridden *Ishi in Two Worlds*, a best-seller by Theodora Kroeber, wife of one of Ishi's original "keepers." This California Native man, found wandering near Oroville, California, in 1904, was housed in the University's anthropology museum, then in San Francisco. He was immediately popular with tourists until his untimely death in 1911 (See also Heizer and Kroeber 1979). In death, and doubtless because of the success of Theodora Kroeber's and others' books, Ishi remains popular, one of the most visited exhibits at the present-day Phoebe Apperson Hearst Museum of Anthropology at the University of California, Berkeley, where a permanent Ishi display disappoints only because there is so little evidence of the "Stone Age Man" on display—and no dioramas! (A Visitors' Book solicits comments from tourists, and this disappointment is quickly obvious to anyone reading through the pages.) For many decades, Native people at the University of California told each other that his pickled brain—removed despite Kroeber's supposed protection of his "friend's" body from desecration—was stored in the Hearst Museum on the Berkeley campus. Recently, however, the brain was located: it had been sent immediately—by Kroeber and his Berkeley colleagues—to The Smithsonian Institution, where it remained until recently when vehement tribal claims grounded in NAGPRA's laws, forced its repatriation and reburial near Ishi's California homeland.

7. We are not suggesting, here, that those employed as guides or as demonstrators—or indeed in any of the other jobs the Museum offers Native people—are *necessarily* themselves complicit in this museum's obfuscatory project. Nor do all suffer from "colonized minds." There are some Native people working in the Museum who are genuinely concerned to do what one reader of this text suggested, that is, "address misconceptions about Indians at the site itself." Moreover, there is the practical fact of life in New York that, as more than one of the interpreters told us, drives them to accept

the Museum's employment. The interpreters who were willing to talk to us (and not all were) were in fact quite aware of their role and the criticism it evoked from other Natives. Most had spent much time anguishing about their jobs. None wanted his/her names used in our article and all assured us that he/she was not "colonized" or "apple Indian" (red on the outside, white on the inside).

8. The current fashion in bus station "bodice rippers" features a much less "cowed" male Indian who, in splendidly muscled nakedness seduces a blonde, blue-eyed, and fully clothed heroine. When the Custom House was built, however, despite the "taming" of Sitting Bull, Geronimo, Chief Joseph, and other famous war chiefs (subjugations performed in dozens of traveling Wild West Shows), the western Indian wars were still a living memory and fears that some noble savages still rode a "war path" against the United States remained. Ellen Fernandez-Sacco, speaking with the authors about a draft of the chapter, asked a cogent question here: "Why hasn't this 'recycled colonial fantasy' been used as a point of iconographic and ideological deconstruction by the museum itself"? Our essay provides some of the answer: the NMAI is not *about* "deconstructing" anything.

9. This visitors' book has been removed from the NMAI, replaced by single questionnaires, with carefully orchestrated inquiries about tourists' experiences of the Museum. In the first months, the book stood open on a pedestal in the Rotunda, a pen chained nearby. On several visits the authors copied all the remarks that went beyond the expected "Wow! Really great!"

10. Much of it was borrowed from another local "ethnic" museum, the Museum for African Art, discussed in Chapter 2, and from its museologist and founding director, Susan Vogel (see Nooter Roberts and Vogel 1994 and Vogel in Karp and Lavine 1991:191-204).

11. Most of the millions of artifacts and "remains" collected by Heye and his field agents were stored where they remain, in vast warehouses in the Bronx where they await their move to Washington, D.C. Much information about the sorry past of this museum's care for this collection forms the dissertation research project of Dean Curtis Bear Claw.

12. Stephen Greenblatt writes that "wonder" is evoked by "the power of the displayed object to stop the viewer in his or her tracks, to convey an arresting sense of uniqueness" and assures viewers of the timeless universality of the objects they are seeing (quoted in Karp and Lavine 1991).

13. This speech was first "collected" by Paul-Émile Victor, in *Poèmes Eskimo* (Paris 1958). It was then translated from the French (not from Inuit, though the Museum's caption here suggests this) by Armand Schwerner and published by Jerome Rothenberg (1986:124).

14. For example the avant-garde theatre director, Richard Schechner, was invited to visit a Pascua Yaqui Waehma in the 1980s. That the Yaquis' confidence was well-placed is reflected in Schechner's unusually respectful and perceptive story of his experience, published in *The Future of Ritual* (1993).

15. Of course the Spaniards came first, in the mid-16th century.

16. The extensive trading practices indigenous to the Américas before the European invasions meant that the production of all kinds of artifacts—as well as food, tools, and so on—was always affected by the demands of consumers. Too, the sudden availability of new dyestuffs or new materials or new design patterns or new tools continually transformed these same processes. Ironically, the arrival of European and Euro-American collectors halted such change, fixing—forever, it sometimes seems to contemporary Native artists—the markers of authenticity and thus of value and effectively stifling the constant innovation and change that has marked both modernist and postmodernist Western art.

17. Considerably more research has been done on such life-figures by Ellen Fernandez-Sacco (1998) who has traced their use to the late 18th century.

18. Some shopping malls, including the Riverwalk mall in San Antonio, Texas, include a chain store called "Reservation" which sells all kinds of *faux*-Indian artifacts and New Age objects.

19. How unthinking are the consumers of such "educational toys" is reflected in the ubiquity of these "discovery" kits in the money-making gift catalogues of public television stations from San Francisco to New York, Miami to Minneapolis. As the popularity of countless savage-despising children's books testifies (see Laura Ingalls Wilder's *Little House* series for examples), Indians are meant to educate and entertain America's (white) young. Still, the irony of connecting "our" museum to this deleterious trade in racial stereotypes has evidently quite escaped the Museum's Native participants.

NOTES TO CHAPTER 4

1. The ideas in this chapter owe a lot to repeated conversations with Timothy J. Reiss, though of course the conclusions are not necessarily his. In addition, Arturo Aldama generously engaged with much of the text. Rainier Spencer, Shari Huhndorf, and W.S. Penn also read the chapter and offered many helpful suggestions, and I am grateful to them all.

2. Francis Jennings and others have expressed surprise at the absence of technologically sophisticated weapons or tools among the indigenous peoples of the Americas. Although they had knowledge of wheels, for example, they restricted their use to children's toys, just as the ancient Greeks used their knowledge of steam engines only to power children's toys.

3. Is it necessary to say that Disney's version bears little, if any, resemblance to history? Perhaps so: Russell Means, the voice of Powhaton, has, after all, declared that this cartoon of singing rodents and talking plants "is the most authentic film ever made about Native America." Perhaps so when a bankrupt Wayne Newton suddenly "comes out" as an Indian, declaring himself a "direct descendant of Pocahontas," who, prompted by Disney, stands ready to disinter his ancestor's remains in order to bring them home from their uneasy rest in England. But alert viewers will surely note that the invaders' ship flies the Union Jack, flag of a kingdom not united for a further 200 years. Or should one suppose that the American public is just as ignorant as Disney's animators?

4. Although the ideas and evidence for what follows comes from several months of reading in the archives of the Bancroft Library at the University of California, Berkeley, I have been aware that many of my choices of themes, quotes and incidents concerning the history of Mexicans, Chicanos, *vaqueros*, and Texas Rangers were also choices made by my colleague, José David Saldívar in his wonderful 1991 book, *The Dialectics of Our America*. Thus, although I wrote this before reading his book (to the likely poverty of the ideas herein), I feel I should note that these similarities, though enormously pleasing, are coincidental.

5. By 1860, when the new state held 379,994 inhabitants (a dream population for today's whining counteraffirmative actioneers, it was 70% male and 60% white male), Indians, together with "coloreds"—who may have been Mexicans and those of Mexican origins as well as those of African descent—and "Asians" in the language of the census, formed but a small fraction of California's people.

6. This was, and remains, a common pejorative for young Indian men.

7. The women's feeling were not recorded. In 19th century Euro-American eyes, females were possessions of men—like gold, like land. It is interesting—and horrible—to note that today's "paramilitaries," the armed, war-playing loonies, live primarily in areas where their vigilante forebears once flourished, killing, raping, and stealing from Natives and "Mexicans" with impunity and even—as in the case of the killers and beheaders of Joaquin Murieta in the 1850s—rewarded (in that case by a grateful state legislature).

8. The settlement was permitted by the Mexican governor, Juan Alvarado, who hoped that the presence of Anglo settlers would discourage the constant Indian raids against rich Mexican landowners. Too, as Hurtado points out, Alvarado hoped to stem the ambitions of his uncle, Mariano Guadalupe Vallejo, then commander of the northern frontier. Vallejo was in large part responsible for native restiveness as he had long been capturing natives from rancherias and sending them to work for Mexican ranchos. In Hurtado's words, "Thus, Vallejo kept Indian society in turmoil and built a loyal following among rancheros who needed Indian labor" (1988:48).

9. This reputation for horsemanship accompanied *vaqueros* through the decades, though clearly-defined Mexican nationals were preferred for the dozens of wild west shows that toured the U.S. and the world at the turn of the century. In the 1940s and 50s, schools in Chicano neighborhoods, such as ours in the north San Fernando Valley, frequently invited a movie *vaquero*, Monte Montana, who regaled us with his roping skills. All of us, "honoring" those of Mexican descent among us, thus learned to do rope tricks with a lasso. One of the results of this curious effort at multiculturalism *avant la lettre* (as well as the bleak and nasty history of the Texas Rangers, as Arturo Aldama pointed out) is that most of my Chicano friends from those days loathe and despise anything that has to do with "cowboys."

10. *Out West* was edited by a mugwump immigrant from the East, Charles F. Lummis, Indian collector, *L.A.Times* journalist, and director of that city's Southwest Museum.

11. Until they, too, were needed, either to fight United States wars—in Europe, in Korea, in Vietnam—or to make up a reserve army of cheap and malleable labor in America's urban centers. Then they found themselves recruited for "relocation" to city sweat shops.

12. The beautiful little Chinese town of Locke, California, which lies along the Sacramento River delta, remained a thriving community when I first visited it in the early 1970s. Then the only language heard in its streets was Chinese. Tourists have since discovered Locke, though it is still a predominantly Chinese community.

13. In a wash of more hypocrisy than I have seen in a long time, California growers once again plead for the importation of Mexicans, "urging Congress to pass a new temporary guest worker program," according to a story in the *San Francisco Chronicle* (December 20, 1995): "Virtually all major grower organizations in California are backing a program that will allow them to bring workers legally from Mexico and elsewhere to temporarily work [sic] in the fields." Although everyone remembers the so-called *bracero* program that recruited Mexicans to labor at starvation wages and in awesomely horrible conditions—documented in a 1960 CBS television report narrated by Edward R. Murrow, *Harvest of Shame* and so critical of Americans' exploitation of agricultural workers that it was quickly banned from USIA libraries all over the world. That program brought some 2 million Mexican workers to California between 1942 and 1964, many of whom stayed to raise families despite the harsh conditions of their lives. (Charley Trujillo's 1994 *Dogs From Illusion* tells some of the story of these people, thousands of whose children were drafted for the frontlines in Vietnam. Of course hypocrisy has no limits.

    "The program that is being discussed has about as much similarity with the 'bracero' programs as the Kitty Hawk has to the space shuttle," said Russell Williams, president of Agricultural Producers, Inc., in Valencia...." As a practical matter, farmers will be responsible to see that workers are properly housed." But that is not what happened before, as all of us who were there remember vividly. Why should it happen this time? And what about those who stay? Only another draftee-needing war will discover their numbers.

14. This was reported as part of the debate about the constitutional amendment to prohibit flag burning that had just been passed (again!) by the House on June 28, 1995.

15. With an utter absence of irony—suitable to accompany the blithe indifference with which he airbrushes the genocide that lies at the heart of this nation stolen by his immigrant ancestors—Wilentz fails to note the fact that the United States was very directly responsible for at least one of the heinous "other peoples' wickednesses" he cites, that in Indonesia. But this Princeton history professor here wants

only to do two things: remind an historically ignorant populace that violence is nothing new in America (though he rejects mentioning the real violence at the heart of this nation) and soothe every European American with the assurance that "we" never do or have done things that are as bad as what "they" do or have done.

16. As these authors demonstrate, there is much dispute about all the early figures. It serves the myth to believe that the Americas were mostly uninhabited when Europeans arrived. But recent demographic studies show a much, much larger population than anthropologists and myth-makers had previously described. Such figures also underscore the problem most non-Latinos encounter when they think of Indians. For most writers, including native scholars, "Indians" live north of the U.S. border with Mexico.

17. Such renaming was by then a familiar colonialist tactic. Native American children were given "white" first names to go with their translated Indian surnames on the first day they entered boarding school. Biblical names were common. Thus a child whose translated last name was "Standing Shield" was dubbed "Mary Standing Shield" and so on. Ngugi wa Thiong'o tells of a similar practice at his boarding school in British Kenya. There he was assigned the name "James" which the school officials added to Ngugi, making a nonsense of Kikuyu naming practices but a strong statement of power.

18. These and subsequent quotations come from Governor Pete Wilson's Second Inaugural Address, "California: Forging America's Future," January 7, 1995. Desolate? Frozen? Why did whites want them badly enough to kill thousands who loved those lands?

19. The reference to Asians is Wilson's cynical recognition of the Asian American community's economic prosperity and thus respectability. The Great Depression was, of course, one of the many eras of xenophobic hatred in California, when the "we" of Wilson's discourse were busily throwing poor Mexicans, and those of Mexican heritage, out of the state.

20. This, like much else in this chapter, comes from Alfred Arteaga (1994).

NOTES TO CHAPTER 5

1. Let me assure the more literal readers (including one surprisingly blunt-minded, self-styled European American "expert" in Native American history who complained to another University of Pennsylvania literature professor that these comments suggested to him that I was ignorant of other European invaders before this date) that

I am fully aware that there were European would-be settlers (as well as "explorers") in North America before 1623: both the arrival of the English at Jamestown and the Spanish in the South and Southwest predate this event. Let me explain to him and to others who evidently have some difficulty reading texts that I refer here to the origin story's mythical birthplace as well as to the religious proclivities of "We, the People"'s forebears, keeping in mind Homi Bhabha's comments on the historical forgetting that underpins Ernest Renan's definitions of nation. To Renan's argument that the existence of nations depends upon the collective will of participants, Bhabha adds, "Renan's will is itself the site of a strange forgetting of the history of the nation's past: the violence involved in establishing the nation's writ. It is this forgetting—a minus in the origin—that constitutes the *beginning* of the nation's narrative." Bhabha commands us to hear Renan: "Listen to the complexity of this form of forgetting which is the moment in which the national will is articulated: yet every French citizen has to have forgotten [*is obliged to have forgotten*] Saint Bartholomew's Night's Massacre, or the massacres that took place in the Midi in the thirteenth century." Thus, Bhabha argues, "it is through this syntax of forgetting—or being obliged to forget—that the problematic identification of a national people becomes visible" (Bhabha 1990: 310).

2. How effective their ruthless surprise attack, their superior weapons, was obvious: only two Englishmen died. Twenty more went home wounded.

3. Winthrop's journals for the period from 1630 to1649 document the constant theft of Indian crops and goods—all supported by arms, every episode accompanied by the murder of one or more Indians, the burning of their homes, the destruction of their boats, and so on. He writes of all this with bland self-assurance, as though the Native peoples deserved only to serve the English by allowing them to steal everything they had and kill any Indians they wanted to kill. They also tortured any Indians they captured (and "kept" any "squaws" they wanted). Paying bounties for Pequot body parts, they managed to collect up dozens of hands and heads from other Indians and from whites who killed Indians for sport. (How it was decided that the hands and other body parts offered for pay were those of Pequot Indians one doesn't know from reading Winthrop's smug accounts.) If read from a Native perspective, the journals are terrifying and angering reading. It is also quite telling that Winthrop's status as a "founding father" is certified by Harvard University, which published these scary journals under its rare book imprint, edited by three

prominent scholars, none of whom, judging from the footnotes and other text, has the least sympathy for the Native peoples invaded and killed by the Puritans. Instead, they see the whole history as that written by whites, and as that narrating a "cultural conflict" or "encounter" or merely "difference"—which made the armed and greedy English unable to understand the Native peoples whose land and goods and human beings they were stealing, enslaving, torturing and so on.

4. Vijay Prashad's *The Karma of Brown Folk* (2001) is one of the first extended attempts to work through the conflicts that often arise between African American and South Asian American communities. Many of the problems—usually created or encouraged by an Anglo overculture, wise to the usefulness of dividing and thus conquering—are similar to those between Chicana/os and Native Americans.

5. Francisco Casique, who is a PhD candidate in the Department of Ethnic Studies at the University of California, Berkeley, wrote a long E-mail to me after reading this chapter. I am grateful to him for his smart and useful criticisms and for permission to quote him here, as well as for our many conversations about these, and related, matters.

6. Casique has noted that many ceremonies of his own Mexican Purepecha indigenous people might look, to skeptical North American Indian eyes, so like North American Indian practices that they would be understood as acts of appropriation. Yet of course they are not. So care must be taken by North American Native scholars not to blur the edges of this very complicated debate.

7. Cushing's most (in)famous act was to dress up as an Indian and have himself photographed. Although this picture is funny enough, his portrait, painted by Thomas Eakins in 1895, which hangs in the Gilcrease Museum in Tulsa, shows him dressed as a mixture of mountain man and Indian. Together with bow and arrows, fringed leather and feathers, he sports a rifle and the aggressive attitude of a white man.

8. The second-printing copy I own, which was first owned by one Mrs C. W. Rapson of San Diego, has some annotations that suggest the work's reception among some Anglo readers. On the frontispiece, Mrs. Rapson has written the date "6/1/39" and the comment "mostly lies." Pasted inside the front cover is a newspaper clipping headlined "A Vicious Volume, But One To Read." The story begins "Recommended as Exhibit A to end all Exhibit A's insofar as inaccuracy,

slander, bias, and onesidedness are concerned is Carey McWilliams' blast at California's agricultural situation." The story is signed "JBS" though no newspaper is named.

9. There is a separate analysis to be written of the discursive regimes into which Gutiérrez places his portraits of Pueblo women. It is that created by the contemporary women's movement, which, beginning in the late 1960s, undertook countless revisions of women's history and the history of the Western family. Many of these sources, particularly those produced by feminist historians of the European Middle Ages and Renaissance (Caroline Bynum, Judith Brown, Marina Warner), lie in the footnotes, evidence of the behavior and attitudes of women a world away from their subjects. The second discourse that bolsters this work is that of contemporary anthropology. Evidence for all kinds of Pueblo activity was located by the author in works by anthropologists researching the South Pacific (Marshall Sahlins), women in general (Rayna Rapp and Sherry Ortner), rural France (Martine Segalen) and so on. Although historians might readily borrow techniques and concepts from anthropologists, evidence for behavior must surely at least emerge from documents relating to the people and place and time under investigation. Gutiérrez's work is creative, but that creativity, in the eyes of this historian, at least, ought not to include only this kind of dubious evidence.

10. The forces of Nature often provide the metaphors in this Anglo-centered discourse about American Indians—who, of course, are usually represented as nearer the "natural world" than are Westerners.

11. The use of Hispanic, rather than "Chicana/o" or the more-inclusive "Latina/o," carries some heavy freight, though Brooke is doubtless unaware of any nuances. Used here, it brings to mind El Vez's wonderful "Never Been to Spain," on the album of the same name (recorded in "Graciasland"). It contains the words "Well I've never been to Spain/So don't call me a Hispanic...." Madrid, Munster Records, n.d. José Davíd Saldívar first introduced me to El Vez.

12. I am grateful to Gerald Johnson for bringing this advertisement to me.

13. Here was expressed, again, what Edouard Glissant describes as "the hierarchical division into written and oral languages....The latter were crude, unsuited to conceptualization and the acquisition of learning" (1989:104).

14. Such grammatical passivity is *de rigueur* when speaking of things Native: A recent *New York Times* article, brought to me by a student (without the paper's date) explained how L.A.'s Southwest Museum was virtually forced to collect thousands of Native artifacts and ceremonial objects (and bodies): "Many of these items were acquired near the turn of the century when experts realized that Indian tribes *were moving inexorably to reservations*, and that this was the opportunity for preserving artifacts from the old way of life" (emphasis added).

15. There are other views. In 1922, the U.S. Secretary of Labor complained that "the psychology of the average Mexican alien unskilled worker...is that when he enters in any manner into the U.S...he is only on a visit to an unknown portion of his own country. He is independent and does not consider he is an immigrant alien, but rather in what is termed the U.S. by right of birth and possession, the country of his forebears....To him, there is no real or imaginary line" (quoted in Sanchez 1993:15). Shortly thereafter, a merchant in Mexico, interviewed by a North American sociologist, insisted ("with intense emotion") that the U.S. "will be Mexico again, not now, but in hundreds, or a thousand years" (ibid.:35-36).

16. One anonymous reader of this chapter was concerned that these words allowed readers to imagine that the song held only this message. As noted above, however, the next stanza records the response of the homesick narrator's Americanized child who is adamant about his distaste for going back to Mexico. That this is the case, however, does not mitigate the homesickness for Mexico expressed in this song and in many others, including some written and performed by Los Lobos, a more contemporary Chicano band from Los Angeles.

17. Unfortunately, the following views are shared by much of the group at present representing (itself?) as "We, the People." It is articulated by Robert Patterson, a columnist for the paper of Trent Lott's and Bob Barr's and Jesse Helms's Council of Conservative Citizens. Echoing John Winthrop and his colleagues, Patterson told *The New York Times*: "Western civilization, with all its might and glory, would never have achieved its greatness without the directing hand of God and the creative genius of the white race. Any effort to destroy the race by a mixture of black blood is an effort to destroy western civilization itself" (quoted in *The New York Times*, Friday, January 15, 1999).

NOTES TO CHAPTER 6

1. Perhaps I should note that Jerome Handler is himself extremely miffed that I did not accept his conclusions, or, indeed, his right to exclusive ownership of all knowledge relevant to this discussion (though he knows nothing whatever of the North American documents or materials). In fact, he wrote a lengthy and rather abusive E-mail to me two years ago, complaining vociferously about this. I did not reply, though that E-mail is an excellent example of the perpetual gate-keeping of knowledge and knowledge production (not to mention consumption) by white males.

2. This kind of Euro-ignorance is well-known among historians of color who invariably find themselves confronted by those who simply cannot imagine real agency amongst those who are not white. That the indigenous peoples of the world communicated with each other—across vast distances—about the awful, stinking, and hairy Europeans, long before many had encountered those creatures, is well-known to indigenous intellectuals. It still seems impossible, however, to many white people. Recently, I heard a Samoan historian, Toeutu Fa'aleava, describe the extensive knowledge of whites that had spread across the Pacific decades before Samoans first encountered the invaders. Several white anthropologists present, all self-described "authorities" on the Pacific, denied the possibility of such sharing of information across such vast distances, despite both Fa'aleava's evidence and the histories of the vast trading networks, thousands of years old, that these scholars knew existed across the Pacific's vastnesses, drawing thousands of Pacific Island sailors into their routes. They did not wonder why they believed that people might trade goods and so on but not information. Apparently, knowledge (especially, to these anthropologists, knowledge of "other people") is a European phenomenon.

SELECT BIBLIOGRAPHY

Abley Mark. "Review." *Times Literary Supplement* 21 Feb. 2003:6.

Achebe, Chinua. *Arrow of God.* Garden City, NY: Anchor Books, 1969.

Addison, Joseph, Richard Steele et al. *The Spectator.* 4 vols. Ed. Gregory Smith. 1909; reprinted London: Dent; New York: Dutton, 1979.

Albuquerque Journal. Jan. 17, 1998.

Alexie, Sherman. "13/16" *The Business of Fancydancing.* Brooklyn: Hanging Loose Press, 1992.

Ames, Michael. *Cannibal Tours and Glass Boxes: the Anthropology of Museums.* Vancouver: University of British Columbia Press, 1992.

Appiah, Anthony. *In My Father's House: Africa in the Philosophy of Culture.* New York: Oxford University Press, 1992.

Arteaga, Alfred. *An Other Tongue.* Durham: Duke University Press, 1994.

Axtell, James. *The European and the Indian: Essays in the Ethnohistory of Colonial North America.* New York: Oxford University Press, 1981.

Babcock, Barbara and Nancy Parezo. *Daughters of the Desert: Women Anthropologists and the Native American Southwest, 1880-1980: an Illustrated Catalogue.* Albuquerque: University of New Mexico Press, 1988.

Baldwin, James, et al. *Perspectives: Angles on African Art.* New York: Center for African Art, 1987.

Bellour, Helene and Samuel Kinser. "Amerindian Masking in Trinidad Carnival: the House of Black Elk in San Fernando." In *TDR: The Drama Review* 42 (Fall 1998):147-69.

Benjamin, Walter. *Illuminations.* New York: Schocken Books, 1985.

Bennett, Tony. *The Birth of the Museum: History, Theory, Politics.* London: Routledge, 1995.

Berkhofer, Robert. *The White Man's Indian: Images of the American Indian from Columbus to the Present.* New York: Vintage Books, 1999 c.1998.

Bhabha, Homi. "Introduction." In *Nation and Narration,* edited by Homi Bhabha. New York: Routledge, 1990.

Bourdieu, Pierre. *Distinction: A Social Critique of the Judgement of Taste.* Translated by R. Nice. Cambridge, MA: Harvard University Press, 1984.

Bourke, John G. *The Snake-Dance of the Moquis of Arizona: Being a Narrative of a Journey from Santa Fe, New Mexico, to the Villages of the Moqui Indians of Arizona.* London: Sampson Low, Marston, Searle & Rivington, 1884.

Brennan, Timothy. *At Home in the World: Cosmopolitanism Now.* Cambridge, Mass.: Harvard University Press, 1997.

Calloway, Colin, ed. *The World Turned Upside Down: Indian Voices from Early America.* New York: St. Martin's Press, 1994.

Castillo, Edward. "The Impact of Euro-American Exploration and Settlement." In *Handbook of North American Indians: California.* Vol. 8. Washington, DC: The Smithsonian Institution Press, 1978: 104.

Césaire, Aimé. *Discourse on Colonialism.* Translated by Joan Pinkham. New York: Monthly Review Press, 1972.

Chavez, Ernesto. *"Mi Raza Primero!": Nationalism, Identity, and Insurgency in the Chicano Movement in Los Angeles.* Berkeley: University of California Press, 2002.

Christopher, Robert J. "Robert J. Flaherty: the Autobiography of an Arctic Photographer, 1906-21." In *Imagining the Arctic.* Edited by J.C.H. King and Henrietta Lidchi. London: The British Museum Press, 1998:181.

Ciabattari, M. "Animal Kingdom: Step Into the African World." *Parade Magazine* (month and day lost, 1990):11.

"Commentary: *When Jesus Came, the Corn Mothers Went Away.*" *American Indian Culture and Research Journal* 17 No.3 (1993):141-178.

Corrin, Lisa G., ed. *Mining the Museum: An Installation by Fred Wilson.* New York: The New Press, 1994.

De Certeau, Michel. *The Practice of Everyday Life.* Translated by Stephen Rendell. Berkeley: University of California Press, 1984.

Select Bibliography

Deloria, Philip. *Playing Indian*. New Haven: Yale University Press, 1998.

Deloria, Vine. *Custer Died for Your Sins: An Indian Manifesto*. New York: MacMillan, 1969.

Dent, Gina. "Black Pleasure, Black Joy." In *Black Popular Culture*. Edited by Gina Dent. 1-33. Seattle: Bay Press, 1992.

Diawara, Manthia. "Afro-Kitsch," In *Black Popular Culture*, edited by Gina Dent. 285-91. Seattle: Bay Press, 1992.

Dilworth, Leah. *Imagining Indians in the Southwest: Persisten Visions of a Primitive Past*. Washington DC: The Smithsonian Institution Press, 1996.

Douglas, F. and René d'Harnoncourt. *Indian Art of the United States*. New York: Museum of Modern Art, 1941.

Drinnon, Richard. *Facing West: the Metaphysics of Indian-hating and Empire-Building*. New York: Schocken Books, 1980.

Encyclopedia Britannica. Vol III. Edinburgh, 1771.

Fabian, Johannes. *Time and the Other: How Anthropology Makes Its Object*. New York: Columbia University Press, 1983.

Fanon, Frantz. *Black Skin, White Masks*. Translated by Charles Markmann. New York: Grove, Weidenfeld, 1967.

Farnham, Thomas J. *Travels in the Great Western Prairies, the Anahuac and Rocky Mountains, and in the Oregon Territory, an 1839 Wagon Train Journal*. Monroe, OR: R.R. McCallum, 1977.

Faris, James C. *Navajo and Photography: a Critical History of the Representation of an American People*. Albuquerque: University of New Mexico Press, 1996.

Felsenstein, Frank. *English Trader, Indian Maid: Representing Gender, Race, and Slavery in the New World: An Inkle and Yarico Reader*. Baltimore: The Johns Hopkins University Press, 1999.

Fienup-Riordan, Ann. *Freeze Frame: Alaska Eskimos in the Movies*. Seattle: University of Washington Press, 1995.

Forbes, Jack. *Africans and Native Americans: the Language of Race and the Evolution of Red-Black Peoples*. Urbana: University of Illinois Press, 1993.

Foreman, Caroline. *Indians Abroad, 1493-1938*. Norman: University of Oklahoma Press, 1943.

Foucault, Michel. *Les Mots et les Choses*. Paris: Gallimard, 1966.

Freedberg, Louis. "Growers Push for 'Guest' Field Hands." *San Francisco Chronicle*, June 30, 1995: 1, A23.

Gallo, Bill. "Review." *East Bay Express*, July 3, 2002: 41.

Gilroy, Beryl. *Inkle and Yarico: Being the Narrative of Thomas Inkle Concerning His Shipwreck and Long Sojourn Among the Caribs and His Marriage to Yarico, a Carib Woman.* Leeds: Peepal Tree Press, 1996.

Glissant, Edouard. *Caribbean Discourse: Selected Essays.* Trans. J. Michael Dash. Charlottesville: University Press of Virginia, 1989.

Gomez-Peña, Guillermo. *The New World Border.* San Francisco: City Lights Books, 1996.

Greenblatt, Stephen. "Romance and Wonder." In I. Karp and S. Lavine, *Exhibiting Cultures: the Poetics and Politics of Museum Display.* Washington, DC: The Smithsonian Institution Press, 1991.

Greenhalgh, Paul. *Ephemeral Vistas: the Expositions Universelles, Great Exhibitions, and World's Fairs, 1851-1939.* Manchester, UK: Manchester University Press, 1988.

Gutiérrez, Ramón. *When Jesus Came, the Corn Mothers Went Away: Marriage, Sexuality, and Power in New Mexico, 1500-1846.* Stanford: Stanford University Press, 1991.

Hall, Richard. *Acts, passed in the Island of Barbados. From 1643-1762.* London: For R. Hall, 1764.

Hall, Stuart, ed. *Representations: Cultural Representations and Signifying Practices.* London: Sage, 1997.

Handler, Jerome. "The Amerindian Slave Population of Barbados in the Seventeenth and Early Eighteenth Centuries." *Caribbean Studies* Vol. 8 (1968):38-64.

Haraway, Donna. *Primate Visions: Gender, Race, and Nature in the World of Modern Science.* New York: Routledge, 1989.

Heizer, Robert and Theodora Kroeber, eds. *Ishi, the Last Yahi: a Documentary History.* Berkeley, University of California Press, 1979.

Hilden, Patricia Penn. *When Nickels Were Indians.* Washington DC: The Smithsonian Institution Press, 1994 (paperback 1995).

Hill, Tom and Richard Hill Sr. *Creation's Journey: Native American Identity and Belief.* Washington, DC: The Smithsonian Institution Press, 1994.

Hinsley, Curtis. *The Smithsonian and the American Indian: Making a Moral Anthropology in Victorian America.* Washington, DC: The Smithsonian Institution Press, 1981.

Hogan, Linda. *Mean Spirit.* New York: Atheneum Press, 1990.

Horsecapture, George P. "An American Indian Perspective." In *Seeds of Change.* Edited by Herman Viola and Carolyn Margolis. 32-34.Washington DC, Smithsonian Institution Press, 1991.

Hudson, Charles and Carmen Chaves Tesser, eds. *The Forgotten Centuries: Indians and Europeans in the American South, 1521-1704.* Athens: University of Georgia Press, 1994.

Hughes, Marie M. and Reuben R. Palm, eds. *Proceedings: Los Angeles County Schools Workshop in Education of Mexican and Spanish-Speaking Pupils.* Los Angeles: Office of the County Superintendent of Schools, 1942.

Hughtie, Phil *A Zuni Artist Looks at Frank Hamilton Cushing.* Pueblo of Zuni: A'shiwi a'wan Museum and Heritage Center, 1994.

Huhndorf, Shari. Personal Communication. November 22, 1994.

---. *Going Native: Figuring the Indian in Modern American Culture.* Ithaca, NY: Cornell University Press, 2001.

Hurtado, Albert. *Indian Survival on the California Frontier.* New Haven: Yale University Press, 1988.

Jacknes, Ira. "Franz Boas and Exhibits: On the Limitations of the Museum Method of Anthropology." In *Objects and Others: Essays on Museums and Material Culture.* Edited by George Stocking Jr. 99-113. Madison: University of Wisconsin Press, 1985.

Jacobs, Wilbur. *Wilderness Politics and Indian Gifts: the Northern Colonial Frontier, 1748-1763.* Lincoln: University of Nebraska Press, 1966.

---. *Dispossessing the American Indian.* Norman: University of Oklahoma Press, 1972.

---. *The Fatal Confrontation: Historical Studies of American Indians, Environment, and Historians.* Albuquerque: University of New Mexico Press, 1996.

Jara, René and Nicolas Spadaccini, eds. *Amerindian Images and the Legacy of Columbus.* Minneapolis: University of Minnesota Press, 1992.

Jennings, Francis. *The Invasion of America: Indians, Colonialism, and the Cant of Conquest.* New York: Norton, 1995 [1975].

---. *The Founders of America.* New York: W.W. Norton, 1993.

"Jones' Pantoscope of California." In *Quarterley of the California Historical Society* (1927):240-41; 242.

Karp, Ivan and Steven Lavine, eds. *Exhibiting Cultures: The Poetics and Politics of Museum Display.* Washington, DC: The Smithsonian Institution Press, 1991.

Kawashima, Yasuhide, "Indian Servitude in the Northeast." In *Handbook of North American Indians: Vol. IV: The History of Indian-White Relations*, edited by Wilcomb Washburn, Washington, DC: The Smithsonian Institution Press, 1988:404-6.

Kelley, Robin D.G., Personal Correspondence, November 11, 2003.

---. *Race Rebels: Culture, Politics, and the Black Working Class*. New York: Free Press, 1996.

---. *Yo Mama's DisFunktional*. Boston: Beacon Press, 1998.

Klanwatch IntelligenceSupport. no.78 (June 1995):7.

Konare, Alpha Oumar. "The Creation and Survival of Local Museums." in *Museums and the Community in West Africa*, edited by Claude Daniel Ardouin and Emmanuel Arinze. Washington, DC: The Smithsonian Institution Press, 1995.5-9.

Kundera, Milan. *The Book of Laughter and Forgetting*. New York: Alfred A. Knopf, 1980.

Kupperman, Karen. *North America and the Beginnings of European Colonization*. Washington, DC: The American Historical Association, 1992.

Lacapa, Michael. "Who Stole Onate's Foot?" *First Nations, First Peoples* (1998):32

Lamar, Howard, ed. *Reader's Encyclopedia of the American West*. New York: Harpercollins, 1987.

Lauber, Almon. *Indian Slavery in Colonial Times Within the Present Limits of the United States*. New York: AMS Press, 1969 [orig. 1913].

Lawton, Henry. *Willie Boy: a Desert Manhunt*. Balboa Island, CA: privately printed, 1960.

Lees, Gene, *Cats of Any Color*. New York: Oxford University Press, 1994.

Lefebvre, Henri, *The Production of Space*. Translated by Donald Nickelson-Smith. Oxford, Blackwell, 1994 [1974].

Leone, M. and B. Little, "Artifacts as Expressions of Society and Culture: Subversive Genealogy and the Value of History." In *History from Things: Essays on Material Culture*. Edited by S. Lubar and W.D. Kingery. 160ff. Washington, DC: The Smithsonian Institution Press, 1993.

Lepore, Jill, *The Name of War: King Philip's War and the Origins of American Identity*. New York: Alfred A. Knopf, 1998.

Lidchi, Henrietta, "Filmic Fantasies in Arctic Lands: Photographing the Inuit of North-West Greenland in 1932." In *Imaging the Arctic*.

Edited by J.C.H. King and Henrietta Lidchi. 197-206. London: The British Museum Press, 1998.

Ligon, Richard. *A True and Exact History of the Island of Barbadoes: Illustrated with a Map of the Island and Also the Principal Trees and Plants There, Set Forth in their Proportions and Shapes, Drawn Out by their Several and Respective Scales.* London: Frank Cass and Co Ltd., 1673 [orig. 1657].

Lindfors, B., ed. *Conversations with Chinua Achebe.* Oxford: University of Mississippi Press, 1997.

Lucero, Evelina Zuni. "Commentary." *American Indian Culture and Research Journal* 17 No.3 (1993):141-178.

McFarlane, Anthony. *The British in the Americas, 1480-1815.* London: Longman, 1994.

McWilliams, Carey. *Factories in the Field: The Story of Migratory Farm Labor in California.* New York: Anchor Books, 1969 [orig. 1939].

---. *North from Mexico: The Spanish-Speaking Peoples of the United States.* New edition by Matt S. Meier. Westport, CT: Praeger Publishers, 1990 [orig. 1948].

Manuel, Frances and Deborah Neff. *Desert Indian Woman: Stories and Dreams.* Tucson: University of Arizona Press, 2002.

Martin, Calvin, ed. *The American Indian and the Problem of History.* New York: Oxford University Press, 1987.

Mathews, John Joseph. *Sundown.* Norman, OK: University of Oklahoma Press, 1988 [orig. 1934].

Melville, Herman. *The Confidence Man: His Masquerade.* New York: Dix, Edwards, and Co., 1987 [orig. 1857].

Mendez, Miguel. *Pilgrims in Aztlán.* Translated by David William Foster. Tempe, AZ: Bilingual Press/Editorial Bilingue, 1992.

Ménil, René. "Concerning Colonial Exoticism." In *Refusal of the Shadow: Surrealism in the Caribbean.* Edited by Michael Richardson. Translated by K.Fija»kowski and M. Richardson. 176. London: Verso, 1996.

Mereweather, Charles. "Signs of a Transnational Fable." In *American Visions/Visiones de las Américas: Artistic and Cultural Identity in the Western Hemisphere.* Edited by N. Tomassi, M.J. Jacob, and I. Mesquita. 46ff. New York: American Council for the Arts, 1994.

Mignolo, Walter. *The Darker Side of the Renaissance: Literacy, Territoriality, and Colonization.* Ann Arbor: University of Michigan Press, 1995.

Moquet, John. *Travels and Voyages into Africa, Asia, America and the East and West Indies; Syria, Jerusalem, and the Holy Land.* Translated by Nathaniel Pullen. London: 1676.

Morison, Samuel Eliot. *Story of the Old Colony of New Plymouth, 1620-1692.* New York: Random Library, 1952.

Morse, Edwin Franklin. "The Story of a Gold Miner: Reminiscences of Edwin Franklin Morse." *Quarterly of the California Historical Society.* No 3 (September 1927):234.

Moses, Lawrence. *Wild West Shows and the Images of American Indians, 1883-1993.* Alburquerque: University of New Mexico Press, 1996.

Moya, Paula. *Learning from Experience: Minority Identities/Multicultural Struggles.* Berkeley: University of California Press, 2002.

Mydans, Seth. "A Shooter as Vigilante and Avenging Angel." *The New York Times,* February 12, 1995:20.

Nabokov, Peter. *A Forest of Time: American Indian Ways of History.* New York, Cambridge University Press, 2002.

Naranjo-Morse, Nora. *Mud Woman.* Tucson: University of Arizona Press, 1992.

Ngugi wa Thiong'o. *Decolonising the Mind: The Politics of Language in African Literature.* Harare: Zimbabwe Publishing House, 1987.

---. *.Moving the Center: The Struggle for Cultural Freedoms.* London, Nairobi: Heinemann: 1993

Nooter Roberts, Mary and Susan Vogel. *Exhibition*-ism: *Museums and African Art.* New York: Museum for African Art, 1994.

Olexer, Barbara. *The Enslavement of the American Indian.* New York: Library Resources Associates, 1982.

Ortiz, Simon. *Woven Stone.* Tucson: University of Arizona Press, 1992.

---."Telling About Coyote" In W.S. Penn, ed. *The Telling of the World: Native American Stories and Art.* New York: Stewart, Tabori, and Chang, 1996: 231-2.

---. "The Cuartocentenario" *First Nations, First Peoples* (1998):1.

Ostler, Jeffrey. "Rethinking Ghost Dance Categories." Paper presented to the American Society for Ethnohistory, Kalamazoo, Michigan, 1995.

Owens, Louis. *Other Destinies: Understanding the American Indian Novel.* Norman: University of Oklahoma Press, 1992.

Penn, W.S. ed. *The Telling of the World: Native American Stories and Art.* New York: Stewart, Tabori, and Chang, 1996.

Select Bibliography

Piatote, Beth. "An Indian Considers Shooting Back in Six Parts." *The Register Guard*. Eugene, OR: Jan. 21, 1996. 1,8c.

Prashad, Vijay. *The Karma of Brown Folk*. Minneapolis: University of Minnesota Press, 2001.

Quinney, Josiah. "July 4 Speech, 1854." In *The World Turned Upside Down: Indian Voices from Early America*. Edited by Colin Calloway. 40. New York: Bedford Books, 1994.

Raftery, Judith Rosenberg. *Land of Fair Promise: Politics and Reform in Los Angeles Schools, 1885-1941*. Stanford: Stanford University Press, 1992.

Reddish, Jennifer Gray. "Pocahontas." *Tribal College* no. 4 (Spring 1995): 22.

Reiss, Timothy. *Against Autonomy: Global Dialectics of Cultural Exchange*. Stanford: Stanford University Press, 2002.

Rogin, Mary. "Please Take Our Children Away." *The New York Times Magazine*. March 4, 2001:22.

Rolwing, Rebecca. "Native Americans *Object* to Celebration of Spanish Conqueror." www.worldfreeinternet/news [reprinted from *Los Angeles Times: Orange Country Edition*. May 17, 1998].

Root, Deborah. *Cannibal Culture: Art, Appropriation, and the Commodification of Difference*. Boulder, CO: Westview Press, 1996.

Rosaldo, Renato. *Culture and Truth: the Re-making of Social Analysis*. London: Routledge, 1993.

Rose, Wendy. *Going to War With All My Relations*. Flagstaff, AZ: Entrada Books, 1993.

---. *Bone Dance: New and Selected Poems, 1965-1993*. Tucson: University of Arizona Press, 1994.

Rothenberg, Jerome. *Shaking the Pumpkin: Traditional Poetry of the Indian North Americas*. New York: Alfred Van Der March, 1986.

Rushing, W. Jackson. *Native American Art and the New York Avant-Garde: A History of Cultural Primitivism*. Austin, TX: University of Texas Press, 1995.

---. "Marketing the Affinity of the Primitive and the Modern: René d'Harnoncourt and 'Indian Art of the United States.'" In *The Early Years of Native American Art History: the Politics of Scholarship and Collecting*. Edited by Janet Berlo. 3ff. Seattle: University of Washington Press, 1992.

Rydell, Robert. *All the World's a Fair: Visions of Empire at America's International Expositions, 1876-1916.* Chicago: University of Chicago Press, 1984.

---. *World of Fairs.* Chicago: University of Chicago Press, 1993.

Sadashige, Jacqui. "Film Review." *American Historical Review.* (June, 2002):989-90.

Said, Edward. *Culture and Imperialism.* New York: Alfred A. Knopf, 1993.

Saldívar, José Davíd. *The Dialectics of Our America: Genealogy, Cultural Critique, and Literary History.* Durham: Duke University Press, 1991.

Sanchez, George I. *Becoming Mexican American: Ethnicity, Culture, and Identity in Chicano Los Angeles, 1900-1945.* New York: Oxford University Press, 1993.

Sanchez, Joseph P. "Hispanic American Heritage." In *Seeds of Change.* Edited by Herman Viola and Carolyn Margolis. 43. Washington DC: The Smithsonian Institution Press, 1991.

Sandos, James A. and Larry Burgess. *The Hunt for Willy Boy: Indian Hating and Popular Culture.* Norman: University of Oklahoma Press, 1994.

Schechner, Richard. *The Future of Ritual: Writings on Culture and Performance.* London and New York: Routledge, 1993.

Sherman, Daniel and Iris Rogoff, eds. *Museum Culture: History, Discourses, Spectacles.* Minneapolis: University of Minnesota Press, 1994.

Silko, Leslie Marmon. *Ceremony.* New York: Viking, 1977.

Smith, John. *John Smith's True Relation 1608.* New York: A. Lovell, 1896.

---. *The Capture and Release of Captain John Smith. Including his rescue from death by Pocahontas. In his own Words from the Generall Historie of Virginia as published at London in 1924.* New York: the Clements Library Associates, 1960.

Sontag, Susan. *On Photography.* New York: Farrar, Straus, and Giroux, 1977.

Stannard, David. *American Holocaust: Columbus and the Conquest of the New World.* New York: Oxford University Press, 1992.

Stewart, S. "Death and Life in that Order in the Works of Charles Willson Peale." In *Visual Display: Culture Beyond Appearance.* Edited by L. Cooke and Peter Wollen. 56-62. Seattle: Bay Press, 1995.

Stiffarm, Lenore, with Phil Lane Jr. "The Demography of Native North America: A Question of American Indian Survival." In *The State of Native America: Genocide, Colonization and Resistance*. Edited by M. Annette Jaimes. 22-31. Boston: South End Press, 1992.

Szanto, George. *Inside the Statues of Saints: Mexican Writers on Culture and Corruption, Politics and Daily Life*. Montréal: Véhicule Press, 1996.

Thornton, Russell. *We Shall Live Again: the 1870 and 1890 Ghost Dance Movements as Demographic Revitalization*. New York: Cambridge University Press, 1986.

Tomassi, Noreen, Mary Jane Jacob, and Ivo Mequita, eds. *American Visions/Visiones de las Américas: Artistic and Cultural Identity in the Western Hemisphere*. New York: Allworth Press, 1994.

Trouillot, Michel-Rolph. *Silencing the Past: Power and the Production of History*. Boston: Beacon Press, 1995.

Trujillo, Charley. *Soldados*. San Jose: Chusma House, 1990.

---. *Dogs from Illusion*. San Jose: Chusma House, 1994.

Usner, Daniel. "American Indians in Colonial New Orleans." In *Powhatan's Mantle: Indians in the Colonial Southeast*. Edited by Peter Wood, Gregory Waselkov, and M. Thomas Hatley. 24-41. Lincoln, NB: University of Nebraska Press, 1989.

---. American Indians in the Lower Mississippi Valley: Social and Economic Histories. Lincoln: University of Nebraska Press, 1998.

Vanderwerth, W.C. *Indian Oratory: Famous Speeches by Noted Indian Chieftains*. Norman: University of Oklahoma Press, 1971.

Viola, Herman. *After Columbus: The Smithsonian Chronicles of North American Indians*. New York: Orion Books, 1990.

Vogel, Susan, ed. *ART/artifact: African Art in Anthropology*. New York: Center for African Art, 1988a.

---. *The Art of Collecting African Art*. New York: Center for African Art, 1988b.

Wade, Mason. "French-Indian Policies." In *Handbook of North American Indians: Vol. IV. The History of Indian-White Relations*. Edited by Wilcomb Washburn. 1-4. Washington, DC: The Smithsonian Institution Press, 1988.

Walker, Nicola. "Letter from Perth." *Times Literary Supplement* Feb. 22, 2002:15.

Wallis, B. "A Forum, Not a Temple: Notes on the Return of Iconography to the Museum." *American Literary History* 9 (1997):617ff.

Washburn, Wilcomb, ed. *Handbook of North American Indians: Vol. IV. The History of Indian-White Relations.* Washington, DC: The Smithsonian Institution Press, 1988.

Webb, Walter Prescott. *The Texas Rangers: A Century of Frontier Defense.* Austin: University of Texas Press, 1965 [orig. 1935].

Wilentz, Sean. "Bombs Bursting In Air, Still." *The New York Times Magazine* June 25, 1995:40-1.

Williams, Eric. *Capitalism and Slavery.* Chapel Hill: University of North Carolina Press, 1994 [orig. 1944].

Winthrop, John. *The Journal of John Winthrop, 1630-1649.* Edited by Richard S. Dunn, James, Savage, and Laetitia Yeandle. (Cambridge, Mass: The Belknap Press of Harvard University Press, 1996.

Wood, Gordon. "Review: In the Name of War." *New York Review of Books* April 9, 1998:43.

Wood, Peter. *Black Majority: Negroes in Colonial South Carolina from 1670 Through the Stono Rebellion.* New York: Alfred A. Knopf, 1974.